TEXAS Coach®

TEKS Edition

Mathematics

GRADE **4**

D1292468

Texas Coach, TEKS Edition, Mathematics, Grade 4   594TXSE   ISBN-13: 978-1-62928-846-8
Cover Image: © Thinkstock; © Royalty-Free/Corbis

Triumph Learning® 136 Madison Avenue, 7th Floor, New York, NY 10016

CONTENTS

DEAR STUDENT

Welcome to *Texas Coach*!

We made this book to help you strengthen your mathematics skills. These skills are important to have for every subject you study this year, not just Mathematics.

Each lesson in this book has three parts:

GETTING THE IDEA ❶

Review some of the basic concepts and skills you've already learned.

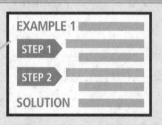

❷ COACHED EXAMPLE

Solve a problem. There are several questions that will help you along the way!

LESSON PRACTICE ❸

Now you're on your own! This part contains more problems to solve.

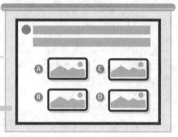

There are different types of test items in *Texas Coach*. For some, you will have to choose one answer from several possible choices. For others, you will grid in the numbers for your answer. Be sure to read the directions carefully so you know how to answer each item.

HAVE A GREAT YEAR!

Sincerely,
TRIUMPH LEARNING

CHAPTER

1

Numerical Representations and Relationships

Reading and Writing Whole Numbers

1 GETTING THE IDEA

Place value is the value of a digit based on its position in a number. A **whole number** can be written in different ways.

Standard form	36,215
Word form	thirty-six thousand, two hundred fifteen
Expanded form	30,000 + 6,000 + 200 + 10 + 5

Expanded form shows a number as a sum of the values of its digits.

A digit's place determines its value. The value of a digit in one place represents 10 times as much as what it represents in the place to its right and $\frac{1}{10}$ of what it represents in the place to its left. A place-value chart can help you understand the value of each digit in a number.

Place	Hundred Thousands	Ten Thousands	Thousands	Hundreds	Tens	Ones
Value	100,000	10,000	1,000	100	10	1

$\times 10$ $\times \frac{1}{10}$ $\times 10$ $\times \frac{1}{10}$ $\times 10$ $\times \frac{1}{10}$ $\times 10$ $\times \frac{1}{10}$ $\times 10$ $\times \frac{1}{10}$

Example 1

48,710 cars crossed Big River Bridge. Write the word form of the number.

Strategy   Use a place-value chart.

Step 1   Write the number in the place-value chart.

Thousands Period				Ones Period		
Hundreds	**Tens**	**Ones**	**,**	**Hundreds**	**Tens**	**Ones**
	4	8	,	7	1	0

Step 2   Write the word form for the number in the thousands period.

forty-eight

Step 3   Write the period name, *thousand*, and a comma.

forty-eight **thousand,**

Step 4   Write the word form for the number in the ones period.

forty-eight thousand, **seven hundred ten**

Solution   The word form for the number of cars is forty-eight thousand, seven hundred ten.

Example 2

23,694 hot dogs were sold at a major league baseball game. What is the value of the 3 in 23,694?

Strategy   Use a place-value chart.

Step 1   Write the number 23,694 in a place-value chart.

Thousands Period				Ones Period		
Hundreds	**Tens**	**Ones**	**,**	**Hundreds**	**Tens**	**Ones**
	2	3	,	6	9	4
	↓	↓		↓	↓	↓
	20,000	**3,000**	**,**	**600**	**90**	**4**

Step 2   Find 3 and identify its place.

3 is in the one thousands place.

Step 3   Multiply 3 by 1,000.

$3 \times 1{,}000 = 3{,}000$

Solution   The value of the 3 in 23,694 is 3,000.

Example 3

A machine puts caps on 206,389 bottles every hour. Write the number in expanded form.

Strategy   Use a place-value chart.

Step 1   Write the number in a place-value chart. Write the value of each digit in the chart.

Thousands Period				Ones Period		
Hundreds	**Tens**	**Ones**	**,**	**Hundreds**	**Tens**	**Ones**
2	0	6	,	3	8	9
						9
					8	0
				3	0	0
		6	,	0	0	0
	0	0	,	0	0	0
2	0	0	,	0	0	0

Step 2   Write the number as a sum.

$$206,389 = 200,000 + 6,000 + 300 + 80 + 9$$

The digit in the ten thousands place is a 0. You do not need to include that digit in the sum.

Solution   **The expanded form of 206,389 is 200,000 + 6,000 + 300 + 80 + 9.**

Example 4

There are 539,668 people living in Forestville. How many times greater is the value of the 6 in the hundreds place than the value of the 6 in the tens place?

Strategy   Use place value.

Step 1   Find the value of the 6 in the hundreds place.

600

Step 2   Find the value of the 6 in the tens place.

60

Step 3   Divide.

$600 \div 60 = 10$

Solution   The 6 in the hundreds place is 10 times greater than the 6 in the tens place.

Example 5

Over a period of 10 years, a factory produced two hundred thirty-nine million, seven thousand, nine hundred twenty-two marbles. Write this number in standard form.

Strategy   Use a place-value chart.

Step 1   Identify each period in the number.

two hundred thirty-nine million,	seven thousand,	nine hundred twenty-two
Millions Period	**Thousands Period**	**Ones Period**

Step 2   Write the value of each period in the place-value chart.

two hundred thirty-nine million,   seven thousand,   nine hundred twenty-two

Millions Period				Thousands Period				Ones Period		
Hundreds	Tens	Ones	,	Hundreds	Tens	Ones	,	Hundreds	Tens	Ones
2	3	9	,	0	0	7	,	9	2	2

When there is no value for a place-value position, a zero is placed in the chart.

Solution   The standard form of two hundred thirty-nine million, seven thousand, nine hundred twenty-two is 239,007,922.

642,075 copies of a magazine were sold in one month. Write the word form and the expanded form for the number.

First, write the word form for 642,075.

The word form for the number in the _thousand_ period is _six hundred forty two thousand_ .

Write the period name, _thousand_ , and a _comma_ .

The word form for the number in the _ones_ period is _seventy five_ .

So, the word form for 642,075 is _six hundred forty two thousand, seventy five_ .

Next, write the expanded form of 642,075. You can use a place-value chart or multiply each digit in 642,075 by its place value.

$6 \times 100,000 =$ _600,000_

$4 \times 10,000 =$ _40000_

$2 \times$ _1000_ $=$ _2_

$0 \times$ _100_ $=$ _0_

$7 \times$ _10_ $=$ _70_

$5 \times$ _1_ $=$ _5_

So, the expanded form for 642,075 is _____.

The word form for 642,075 is _____.

The expanded form for 642,075 is _____.

1 An airplane full of passengers and luggage weighed three hundred eighty thousand, nine hundred fifty-five pounds. What is this number in standard form?

A. 38,955

B. 308,955

C. 380,955

D. 3,800,955

2 Which of the following shows another way to write 81,027?

A. Eight hundred ten thousand, two hundred seven

B. Eighty-one thousand, twenty-seven

C. 800,000 + 10,000 + 200 + 70

D. 8,000 + 100 + 20 + 7

3 Write the standard form of nine hundred fifty-eight.

Record your answer and fill in the bubbles. Be sure to use the correct place value.

9	5	8	.	0	0
⓪	⓪	⓪		⓪	⓪
①	①	①		①	①
②	②	②		②	②
③	③	③		③	③
④	④	④		④	④
⑤	⑤	⑤		⑤	⑤
⑥	⑥	⑥		⑥	⑥
⑦	⑦	⑦		⑦	⑦
⑧	⑧	⑧		⑧	⑧
⑨	⑨	⑨		⑨	⑨

4 Doug is playing a game. In order to win a point, he must write a number that follows these rules.

- 4 in the hundred thousands place
- 7 in the hundreds place
- 5 in the tens place

Which number could Doug write to win a point?

A. 407,253

B. 142,751

C. 423,751

D. 4,237,510

5 What is the expanded form of 25,691?

A. 20,000 + 5,000 + 600 + 90 + 1

B. 200,000 + 5,000 + 600 + 91

C. 20,000 + 5,000 + 690 + 1

D. 2,000 + 500 + 60 + 91

6 Which number is the same as 100,000 + 40,000 + 400 + 80 + 1

A. 14,481

B. 140,481

C. 144,081

D. 1,044,081

7 The number of miles Ms. Ruiz has driven her car is shown below.

Write the word form of this number.

A. Six thousand, three hundred sixteen

B. Sixty-eight thousand, three hundred six

C. Six hundred eight thousand, three hundred sixteen

D. Sixty-eight thousand, three hundred sixteen

8 Angela wrote the number 17,902. Then she switched the 1 and 7 digits. What is the value of the 7 digit in Angela's new number?

A. 70,000

B. 7,000

C. 700

D. 70

9 Which number is the same as 50,709?

A. Five hundred thousand, seven hundred nine

B. Fifty thousand, seven hundred nine

C. Five thousand, seven hundred nine

D. Five hundred seventy-nine

10 Last year, a company earned a total of eight hundred ninety-five thousand, eight hundred sixty-four dollars. What is this number in standard form?

A. $864,890

B. $890,564

C. $890,864

D. $895,864

11 Write the value of the digit 3 in the number seven hundred thirty-one.

Record your answer and fill in the bubbles. Be sure to use the correct place value.

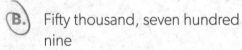

12 What is the expanded form of 704,130?

A. 700,000 + 4,000 + 100 + 30

B. 700,000 + 40,000 + 100 + 30

C. 700,000 + 4,000 + 100 + 3

D. 700,000 + 40,000 + 10 + 3

13 A football game drew 103,250 fans. What is another way to write this number?

A. One hundred thousand, three hundred twenty-five

B. 100,000 + 3,000 + 200 + 50

C. Thirteen thousand, two hundred fifty

D. 100,000 + 30,000 + 200 + 50

14 Mr. Lee asked four students to each write a 6-digit number. The number that each student wrote is shown below.

Student	Number
Martin	809,422
Ellie	877,561
Federico	238,110
Zoe	443,896

Which student's number has a digit in the hundreds place that is ten times the value of the digit on its right?

A. Martin

B. Ellie

C. Federico

D. Zoe

15 Taylor's home street address number has five digits. Two digits have values of 60,000 and 300. The last digit is 9. The value of each of the other digits is ten times the value of the digit on its right. What is Taylor's home street address number?

A. 63339

B. 63399

C. 66339

D. 69399

16 What is the standard form of 300 + 70 + 7?

Record your answer and fill in the bubbles. Be sure to use the correct place value.

3	7	7	.	0	0
⓪	⓪	⓪		⓪	⓪
①	①	①		①	①
②	②	②		②	②
③	③	③		③	③
④	④	④		④	④
⑤	⑤	⑤		⑤	⑤
⑥	⑥	⑥		⑥	⑥
⑦	⑦	⑦		⑦	⑦
⑧	⑧	⑧		⑧	⑧
⑨	⑨	⑨		⑨	⑨

LESSON 2

Reading and Writing Decimals

① GETTING THE IDEA

Decimals can be written in different ways, just like whole numbers.

Standard form	25.34
Word form	twenty-five and thirty-four hundredths
Expanded form	$2 \times 10 + 5 \times 1 + 3 \times \frac{1}{10} + 4 \times \frac{1}{100}$

Remember that expanded form is a way of writing a number as a sum of the values of its digits.

You can use place value to help you write a decimal in different ways.

Example 1

The Seikan Tunnel in Japan is the longest underwater tunnel in the world. It is approximately 53.11 kilometers long. Write the word form for 53.11 kilometers.

Strategy   Use a place-value chart.

Step 1   Write the number in a place-value chart.

Hundreds	Tens	Ones		Tenths	Hundredths
	5	3	·	1	1

Step 2   Write the word form for the whole-number part. Write *and* for the decimal point.

fifty-three and

Step 3   Write the word form for the decimal part. Use the name of the last decimal place to name the decimal.

fifty-three and eleven hundredths

Solution   The word form for 53.11 kilometers is **fifty-three and eleven hundredths** kilometers.

Example 2

Write the standard form and expanded form of two hundred forty-five and five hundredths.

Strategy   Use a place-value chart.

Step 1   Write the decimal in a place-value chart.

The word *hundredths* tells you that the last digit is in the hundredths place.

Use a zero as a placeholder for tenths. Use a decimal point for the word *and*.

Hundreds	Tens	Ones		Tenths	Hundredths
2	4	5	.	0	5

Step 2   Write the value of each digit in the place-value chart.

Hundreds	Tens	Ones		Tenths	Hundredths
2	4	5	.	0	5
2×100	4×10	5×1		$0 \times \frac{1}{10}$	$5 \times \frac{1}{100}$

Step 3   Write the decimal in expanded form as the sum of the values of the digits.

$$2 \times 100 + 4 \times 10 + 5 \times 1 + 5 \times \frac{1}{100}$$

It is not necessary to write the value of a zero in a number.

Solution   **In standard form, the decimal is 245.05. In expanded form, it is**

$$2 \times 100 + 4 \times 10 + 5 \times 1 + 5 \times \frac{1}{100}.$$

Example 3

A number written in expanded form is $3 \times 10 + 8 \times 1 + 2 \times \frac{1}{100}$. Which of the following shows the standard form of this number?

38.2   3.82   38.02   3,802

Strategy   Interpret the expanded form.

Step 1   Determine the value of each addend in the expanded form.

$$3 \times 10 + 8 \times 1 + 2 \times \frac{1}{100}$$

$\uparrow$ $\uparrow$ $\uparrow$

3 tens   8 ones   2 hundredths

Step 2	Check if there are any missing place values.

No tenths are shown between ones and hundredths.
So, there are 0 tenths.

Step 3	Write the number that has the digits with the same values.

The number 38.02 has 3 tens, 8 ones, 0 tenths, and 2 hundredths.

Solution The standard form of $3 \times 10 + 8 \times 1 + 2 \times \frac{1}{100}$ is 38.02.

② COACHED EXAMPLE

A bakery produced 163.58 kilograms of bread on Monday. Write the word form and expanded form for this number.

First, write the word form for 163.58.

The word form for the whole-number part is _____.

Write the word _____ for the decimal point.

The last digit in 163.58 is in the _____ place.

So, the word form for the decimal part is _____.

Next, write the expanded form of 163.58.

Complete the place-value chart.

Hundreds	Tens	Ones		Tenths	Hundredths
☐ × 100	☐ × 10	☐ × 1		☐ × $\frac{1}{10}$	☐ × $\frac{1}{100}$

The word form for 163.58 is _____

_____.

The expanded form for 163.58 is _____

_____.

1 Which shows the value of a digit in the number six hundred three and fifty-eight hundredths?

A. $3 \times \frac{1}{100}$

B. $5 \times \frac{1}{10}$

C. 6×1

D. 8×10

2 The longest snake in captivity has a weight of about three hundred fifty and nine hundredths pounds. What is this number written in standard form?

A. 350.90

B. 350.09

C. 305.90

D. 305.09

3 Karen finished a race in 30.43 seconds. Which number shows another way to write 30.43?

A. Thirty-four and three tenths

B. Thirty and forty-three tenths

C. Thirty-four and three hundredths

D. Thirty and forty-three hundredths

4 Which number in expanded form represents the number 37.19?

A. $3 \times 100 + 7 \times 10 + 1 \times \frac{1}{10} + 9 \times \frac{1}{100}$

B. $3 \times 100 + 7 \times 1 + 1 \times \frac{1}{10} + 9 \times \frac{1}{100}$

C. $3 \times 10 + 7 \times 1 + 1 \times \frac{1}{10} + 9 \times \frac{1}{100}$

D. $3 \times 10 + 1 \times \frac{1}{10}$

5 A zookeeper recorded the weight of 4 different bird eggs. The weights are shown below.

Type of Bird Egg	Weight (in ounces)
Ostrich	32.05
Emu	25.30
Bald eagle	4.53
Blue heron	2.45

Which bird egg's weight has a digit with a value equal to $4 \times \frac{1}{10}$?

A. Ostrich

B. Emu

C. Bald eagle

D. Blue heron

6 Which number in word form represents the number 180.32?

- **A.** One hundred eighty and thirty-two hundredths
- **B.** One hundred eighty-three and two tenths
- **C.** One hundred eight and two tenths
- **D.** One thousand eight hundred and thirty-two hundredths

7 Juanita wrote the number shown below.

three hundred twenty-four and eight hundredths

What is the standard form of the number Juanita wrote?

Record your answer and fill in the bubbles. Be sure to use the correct place value.

8 Which is the expanded form for 596.14?

- **A.** $5 \times 100 + 9 \times 10 + 6 \times 1 + 1 \times \frac{1}{10} + 4 \times \frac{1}{100}$
- **B.** $5 \times 1,000 + 9 \times 10 + 6 \times 1 + 1 \times \frac{1}{10} + 4 \times \frac{1}{100}$
- **C.** $5 \times 100 + 9 \times 10 + 6 \times 1 + 4 \times \frac{1}{100}$
- **D.** $5 + 9 + 6 + 1 + 4$

9 Which number is the same as $2 \times 100 + 7 \times 10 + 5 \times 1 + 3 \times \frac{1}{100}$?

- **A.** Two hundred seven and fifty-three hundredths
- **B.** 275.30
- **C.** Two hundred seventy and fifty-three hundredths
- **D.** 275.03

10 Nine hundred twenty and forty-seven hundredths is the word form of what number?

- **A.** 924.70
- **B.** 924.07
- **C.** 920.47
- **D.** 920.07

11. The Akashi-Kaikyo Bridge in Japan is one of the longest suspension bridges in the world. Its center span is approximately 1.24 miles long. What is the word form of 1.24?

A. Twelve and four tenths

B. One hundred twenty-four

C. One and twenty-four tenths

D. One and twenty-four hundredths

12. Raquel wrote the number shown below.

Tens	Ones	.	Tenths	Hundredths
8	0	.	7	1

Which is the expanded form for this number?

A. $80 \times 10 + 7 \times \frac{1}{10} + 1 \times \frac{1}{100}$

B. $8 \times 10 + 7 \times \frac{1}{10} + 1 \times \frac{1}{100}$

C. $8 \times 1 + 7 \times \frac{1}{10} + 1 \times \frac{1}{100}$

D. $8 \times 10 + 7 \times 1 + 1 \times \frac{1}{100}$

13. What is the standard form of six hundred twelve and seventy-four hundredths?

A. 6,127.4

B. 612.07

C. 612.74

D. 600.12

14. A restaurant sold 37.46 gallons of orange juice in 1 day. What is this number in word form?

A. Three hundred seventy-four and six hundredths

B. Thirty-seven and forty-six hundredths

C. Three hundred seventy-four and six tenths

D. Thirty-seven and forty-six tenths

15. What is the standard form of

$8 \times 100 + 1 \times 10 + 3 \times 1 +$

$1 \times \frac{1}{10} + 4 \times \frac{1}{100}$?

Record your answer and fill in the bubbles. Be sure to use the correct place value.

			.		
⓪	⓪	⓪		⓪	⓪
①	①	①		①	①
②	②	②		②	②
③	③	③		③	③
④	④	④		④	④
⑤	⑤	⑤		⑤	⑤
⑥	⑥	⑥		⑥	⑥
⑦	⑦	⑦		⑦	⑦
⑧	⑧	⑧		⑧	⑧
⑨	⑨	⑨		⑨	⑨

Comparing and Ordering Whole Numbers

1 GETTING THE IDEA

You can use place value to compare two whole numbers. First, start with the greatest place value. Then compare the values of the digits in the same place-value position.

The symbols $<$, $>$, and $=$ can be used to write whole-number comparisons.

$246 < 469$ 246 is **less than** 469

$734 > 354$ 734 is **greater than** 354

$573 = 573$ 573 is **equal to** 573

Example 1

Prime Pickles made 350,819 jars of pickles in August. The same month, Briney Pickles made 48,372 jars of pickles. Which business made more jars of pickles in August?

Strategy   Use a place-value chart.

Step 1   Write the two numbers in a place-value chart.

Thousands Period				Ones Period		
Hundreds	Tens	Ones	,	Hundreds	Tens	Ones
3	5	0	,	8	1	9
	4	8	,	3	7	2

Step 2   Compare the values of the digits in the greatest place value.

The greatest place value is the hundred thousands place.

In 350,819, the digit 3 has a value of 3 hundred thousand, or 300,000.

In 48,372, there is no digit in the hundred thousands place. Use the digit 0 to show no value.

300,000 is greater than 0.

Step 3   Compare the numbers. Use <, >, or =.

             300,000 is greater than 0. So 350,819 is greater than 48,372.

             350,819 > 48,372

Step 4   Decide which business made more jars of pickles.

             Prime Pickles made 350,819 jars.

             Briney Pickles made 48,372 jars.

Solution   **Prime Pickles made more jars of pickles in August than Briney Pickles.**

Example 2

The Web site for Caroline's Crafts received 274,366 hits its first year. Its second year, it received 278,902 hits. Compare the hits for the two years.

Strategy   **Line up the numbers by place value.**

Step 1   Write the numbers in a column. Line up the commas to help you line up the digits.

             274,366

             278,902

Step 2   Start at the left and compare the digits in each place value. Find the first place value that has different digits.

             274,366   Both numbers have **2** in the hundred thousands place.

             278,902

             2**7**4,366   Both numbers have **7** in the ten thousands place.

             2**7**8,902

             27**4**,366   The digits in the thousands place are different.

             27**8**,902

Step 3   Compare the values of the digits.

             The digit 4 has a value of 4,000.

             The digit 8 has a value of 8,000.

             4,000 is less than 8,000.

Step 4   Compare the numbers. Use <, >, or =.

             4,000 < 8,000

             So, 274,366 < 278,902.

Solution   **The Web site for Caroline's Crafts received more hits in its second year because 274,366 < 278,902.**

Example 3

Mia and her friends are playing a computer game. The table shows their scores.

Name	Score
Luke	800,036,832
Mia	886,011,308
Lily	898,093,016
Hunter	966,475,560
Camille	886,011,308

Which friends have higher scores than Mia?

Strategy   **Compare numbers using place value.**

Step 1   Compare Luke's score to Mia's score. Compare digits in the greatest place value. If the digits are the same, continue moving to the next greatest place value until the digits are different.

Luke's score: 8**0**0,036,832   The digits in the ten millions place are different.

Mia's score: 8**8**6,011,308

Compare the values of the digits.

0 < 80,000,000, so 800,036,832 < 886,011,308.

Luke's score is less than Mia's score.

Step 2   Compare Lily's score to Mia's score.

Lily's score: 8**9**8,093,016   The digits in the ten millions place are different.

Mia's score: 8**8**6,011,308

Compare the values of the digits.

90,000,000 > 80,000,000, so 898,093,016 > 886,011,308.

Lily's score is greater than Mia's score.

Step 3	Compare Hunter's score to Mia's score.	

Hunter's score: **9**66,475,560   The digits in the hundred millions place are different.

Mia's score: **8**86,011,308

Compare the values of the digits.

900,000,000 > 800,000,000, so 966,475,560 > 886,011,308.

Hunter's score is greater than Mia's score.

Step 4	Compare Camille's score to Mia's score.	

Camille's score: 886,011,308   The digits are the same in all nine place values.

Mia's score: 886,011,308

So, 886,011,308 = 886,011,308.

Camille's score is equal to Mia's score.

Solution   **Lily and Hunter have higher scores than Mia.**

② COACHED EXAMPLE

Sophia's car has been driven 103,764 miles. Liam's car has been driven 109,056 miles. Whose car has been driven a greater number of miles?

First, line up the digits by place value.

Sophia's car: ___ ___ ___,___ ___ ___

Liam's car: ___ ___ ___,___ ___ ___

Then compare the digits in the _____ place value.

The first place value with digits that are different is the _____ place.

Compare the values of the digits. Use <, >, or =.

_____ ◯ _____

Compare the numbers.

103,764 ◯ 109,056

Decide whose car has been driven the greater number of miles.

_____'s car has been driven a greater number of miles.

1 A humpback whale weighs 78,380 pounds. A blue whale weighs 108,392 pounds. Which statement is true?

   A. 78,380 < 108,392

   B. 78,380 > 108,392

   C. 108,392 < 78,380

   D. 108,392 = 78,380

2 Which number is less than 972,308?

   A. 973,569

   B. 992,300

   C. 995,607

   D. 970,710

3 Carlos is playing a card game.

   8 1 7 6 2 3

   To win the game, Carlos must use the cards to make a 6-digit number that is less than 123,786. What number can Carlos make that is less than 123,786?

   A. 123,678

   B. 213,786

   C. 123,876

   D. 213,867

4 The table shows the number of cars that entered Willow Park each month.

Month	Number of Cars
May	10,954
June	13,692
July	13,740
August	12,388

In which month did the greatest number of cars enter the park?

   A. May

   B. June

   C. July

   D. August

5 What whole number has a 1 in the ones place and is greater than 768, but less than 781?

Record your answer and fill in the bubbles. Be sure to use the correct place value.

6 The table shows the results of the election for the Mayor of Westville.

Name	Number of Votes
Lenka Taylor	271,482
Maria Diaz	271,348
Nancy Smith	275,921
Orline Carp	274,783

Which candidate had the least votes?

A. Lenka Taylor

B. Maria Diaz

C. Nancy Smith

D. Orline Carp

7 Which number is less than 99,000?

A. 207,100

B. 33,209

C. 99,000

D. 673,416

8 Which number is always greater than a 5-digit number?

A. A 3-digit number

B. A 4-digit number

C. A 5-digit number

D. A 6-digit number

9 The population of Emily's town can be written using the digits 1, 4, 7, 3, and 6. What is the least possible population of Emily's town?

A. 14,367

B. 14,736

C. 13,467

D. 13,764

10 Which statement is **not** true?

A. $688,856 > 645,576$

B. $27,827 = 28,727$

C. $515,719 < 543,591$

D. $68,453 = 68,453$

11 Frank earned $973 last month. This month, he earned $992. Which value, in dollars, is greater?

Record your answer and fill in the bubbles. Be sure to use the correct place value.

			.		
⓪	⓪	⓪		⓪	⓪
①	①	①		①	①
②	②	②		②	②
③	③	③		③	③
④	④	④		④	④
⑤	⑤	⑤		⑤	⑤
⑥	⑥	⑥		⑥	⑥
⑦	⑦	⑦		⑦	⑦
⑧	⑧	⑧		⑧	⑧
⑨	⑨	⑨		⑨	⑨

12 The table shows the areas of the Great Lakes.

Lake	Area (in square kilometers)
Erie	25,657
Huron	59,500
Michigan	57,750
Ontario	18,960
Superior	82,100

Which statement is true?

A. Lake Michigan has a lesser area than Lake Superior.

B. Lake Huron has a lesser area than Lake Ontario.

C. Lake Ontario has a greater area than Lake Erie.

D. Lake Erie has a greater area than Lake Michigan.

13 For a certain game, players have to score more than 7,500 points to advance to the next round. Which score would **not** advance?

A. 7,505

B. 7,742

C. 7,915

D. 7,493

14 Emerich Park received the following number of visitors each of the past 4 years.

96,559   73,033   85,900   93,699

Which was the least number of visitors?

A. 96,559

B. 73,033

C. 85,900

D. 93,699

15 One adult bottlenose dolphin has a mass of 199 kilograms. A second adult bottlenose dolphin has a mass of 187 kilograms. Which is the greater mass, in kilograms?

Record your answer and fill in the bubbles. Be sure to use the correct place value.

Rounding Whole Numbers

① GETTING THE IDEA

To **round** means to adjust a number upward or downward to a given place value. You can use rounding to make estimates.

A bus is carrying 28 passengers.

28 rounded to the nearest ten is 30.

The bus is carrying *about* 30 passengers.

Example 1

Brian has 287 rocks in his collection. What is 287 rounded to the nearest ten?

Strategy   **Use a number line.**

Step 1   Identify the digit in the tens place.

2**8**7   287 is between 280 and 290.

Step 2   Locate 280 and 290 on a number line.

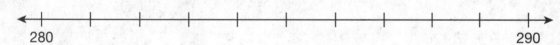

280   290

Step 3   Locate the number halfway between 280 and 290.

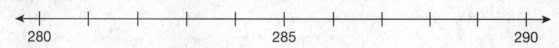

280   285   290

285 is halfway between 280 and 290.

Step 4   Locate 287 on the number line. Use the halfway number to help you decide if 287 is closer to 280 or 290.

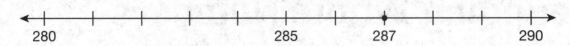

287 is more than 285. It is closer to 290 than to 280.

Solution   **287 rounded to the nearest ten is 290.**

Example 2

Last month, Tom's T-Shirt Factory made 52,316 T-shirts. About how many T-shirts were made last month? Round your answer to the nearest thousand.

Strategy   **Use a number line.**

Step 1   Identify the digit in the thousands place.

52,316   52,316 is between 52,000 and 53,000.

Step 2   Locate 52,000 and 53,000 on a number line.

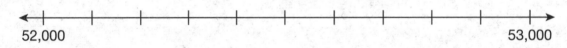

Step 3   Locate the number halfway between 52,000 and 53,000.

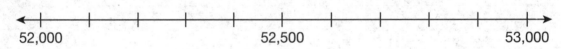

Step 4   Locate 52,316 on the number line. Use the halfway number to help you decide if 52,316 is closer to 52,000 or 53,000.

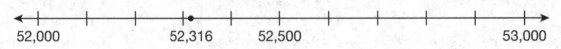

52,316 is less than 52,500. It is closer to 52,000 than to 53,000.

Solution   **Tom's T-shirt Factory made about 52,000 T-shirts last month.**

Example 3

An adult hippopotamus has a mass of 3,629,000 grams. What is this mass rounded to the nearest hundred thousand grams?

Strategy   Use a number line.

Step 1   Identify the digit in the hundred thousands place.

3,**6**29,000   3,629,000 is between 3,600,000 and 3,700,000.

Step 2   Locate 3,600,000 and 3,700,000 on a number line.

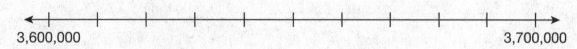

Step 3   Locate the number halfway between 3,600,000 and 3,700,000.

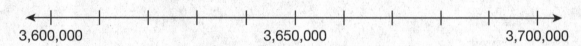

Step 4   Locate 3,629,000 on the number line. Use the halfway number to help you decide if 3,629,000 is closer to 3,600,000 or 3,700,000.

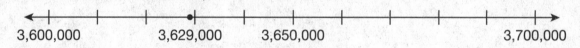

3,629,000 is less than 3,650,000.

It is closer to 3,600,000 than to 3,700,000.

Solution   3,629,000 grams rounded to the nearest hundred thousand is 3,600,000 grams.

You can also round a whole number by finding the digit in the rounding place. Then look at the digit to the right of the rounding place. Underline that digit.

- If that digit is less than 5, then the digit in the rounding place stays the same. Change the digits to the right to 0s.

- If that digit is 5 or greater, then the digit in the rounding place is increased by 1. Change the digits to the right to 0s.

Hundreds	Tens	Ones
	2	<u>8</u>

To round 28 to the nearest ten, look at the digit to the right of the tens place, 8.

Since 8 is greater than 5, the digit in the tens place increases by 1. The digits to the right change to 0.

So, 28 rounded to the nearest ten is 30.

Example 4

Round 329,755 to the nearest ten thousand and the nearest thousand.

Strategy   **Use place value to round.**

Step 1   Round 329,755 to the nearest ten thousand.

Identify the digit in the ten thousands place. Underline the digit to its right.

32**9**,755   Since 9 > 5, the digit 2 in the ten thousands place increases by 1.
↓   Change the digits to the right to 0s.
330,000

Step 2   Round 329,755 to the nearest thousand.

Identify the digit in the thousands place. Underline the digit to its right.

32**9**,<u>7</u>55   Since 7 > 5, the digit 9 in the thousands place increases by 1.
↓   This will make 10 thousands, or 1 ten thousand. So the 2 in the
330,000   ten thousands place becomes a 3.
Change the digits to the right to 0s.

Solution   **329,755 rounded to the nearest ten thousand is 330,000.**
329,755 rounded to the nearest thousand is 330,000.

A total of 16,272 tickets were sold for a concert. About how many tickets were sold? Round your answer to the nearest thousand.

Identify the digit in the _____ place. Underline the digit to its right.

16,272

The digit to the right of the place you are rounding to is ☐ .

    If the digit is less than _____, the digit in the rounding place _____.

    If the digit is _____ or greater, the digit in the rounding place _____.

    Change the digits to the right of the thousands place to _____.

Since _____ ◯ _____, the digit _____ in the rounding place

_____.

    16,272 rounds to _____.

About _____ **concert tickets were sold.**

1 Hannah flew 16,734 miles last summer. Which statement shows this number rounded correctly?

   A. To the nearest ten thousand, she flew about 10,000 miles.

   B. To the nearest thousand, she flew about 17,000 miles.

   C. To the nearest hundred, she flew about 16,800 miles.

   D. To the nearest ten, she flew about 16,740 miles.

2 The table shows 4 numbers.

Number	Rounded to the Nearest …	Rounded Number
808	ten	800
1,252	hundred	1,300
53,062	thousand	54,000
602,188	ten thousand	610,000

Which number is rounded correctly?

   A. 808

   B. 1,252

   C. 53,062

   D. 602,188

3 Gloria correctly rounded 85,736 to the nearest ten thousand. What was Gloria's answer?

   A. 86,736

   B. 95,736

   C. 80,000

   D. 90,000

4 When rounded to the nearest thousand, which number rounds to 27,000?

   A. 26,055

   B. 26,499

   C. 27,442

   D. 27,580

5 What is 425 rounded to the nearest hundred?

Record your answer and fill in the bubbles. Be sure to use the correct place value.

6 What is 57,860 rounded to the nearest hundred?

   A. 58,900

   B. 58,000

   C. 57,900

   D. 57,800

7 The scale shows the mass of a rock in grams.

What is the mass of the rock rounded to the nearest hundred?

   A. 1,460 grams

   B. 1,400 grams

   C. 1,560 grams

   D. 1,500 grams

8 When the number below is rounded to the nearest ten thousand, it is 390,000.

   38 ☐ ,854

Which digit could be the missing digit?

   A. 8

   B. 4

   C. 2

   D. 1

9 A number rounded to the nearest hundred thousand is 6,700,000. What could the number be?

   A. 6,690,045

   B. 6,784,382

   C. 6,618,746

   D. 6,780,243

10 What is 527 rounded to the nearest ten?

Record your answer and fill in the bubbles. Be sure to use the correct place value.

			.		
⓪	⓪	⓪		⓪	⓪
①	①	①		①	①
②	②	②		②	②
③	③	③		③	③
④	④	④		④	④
⑤	⑤	⑤		⑤	⑤
⑥	⑥	⑥		⑥	⑥
⑦	⑦	⑦		⑦	⑦
⑧	⑧	⑧		⑧	⑧
⑨	⑨	⑨		⑨	⑨

11 The minimum distance from Earth to Mars is approximately 33,926,867 miles. What is this distance rounded to the nearest ten thousand?

A. 33,920,000 miles

B. 33,930,000 miles

C. 33,900,000 miles

D. 33,927,000 miles

12 The thermometer shows the highest temperature ever recorded in the United States.

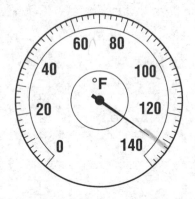

What is the temperature rounded to the nearest ten?

A. 130 °F

B. 140 °F

C. 200 °F

D. 240 °F

13 What is 618,082 rounded to the nearest thousand?

A. 619,000

B. 620,000

C. 618,000

D. 618,080

14 A factory made about 75,000 robots last year. The number of robots was rounded to the nearest thousand. Which number could be the actual number of robots the factory made?

A. 75,499

B. 75,500

C. 74,499

D. 74,300

15 What is 915 rounded to the nearest ten?

Record your answer and fill in the bubbles. Be sure to use the correct place value.

			.		
⓪	⓪	⓪		⓪	⓪
①	①	①		①	①
②	②	②		②	②
③	③	③		③	③
④	④	④		④	④
⑤	⑤	⑤		⑤	⑤
⑥	⑥	⑥		⑥	⑥
⑦	⑦	⑦		⑦	⑦
⑧	⑧	⑧		⑧	⑧
⑨	⑨	⑨		⑨	⑨

LESSON 5

Understanding Decimals

4.2(E), 4.2(H)

1 GETTING THE IDEA

A **decimal** is a number with one or more digits to the right of a decimal point. A **decimal point** is a symbol that separates the ones from the tenths in a decimal.

The value of each digit in a decimal is based on its position. Whole-number place values are to the left of the decimal point and decimal place values are to the right.

Ones	Decimal Point	Tenths	Hundredths
1	.	5	9

The models shown below each represent one whole. The part that is shaded can be written as a decimal.

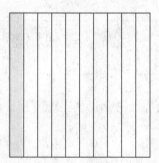

This model shows 10 tenths.
One tenth is shaded.
0.1
↑
decimal point

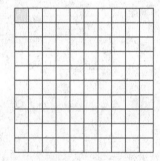

This model shows 100 hundredths.
One hundredth is shaded.
0.01
↑
decimal point

Example 1

What decimal describes the part of the model that is shaded?

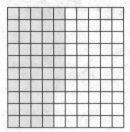

Strategy   Use a place-value chart.

Step 1   Count the number of hundredths that are shaded.

There are 100 squares. So each square is one hundredth.

47 hundredths are shaded.

Step 2   Write the decimal in a place-value chart.

There are no ones, so write 0 in the ones place.

There are 47 hundredths, so write the last digit in the hundredths place.

Ones	Decimal Point	Tenths	Hundredths
0	.	4	7

Solution   The decimal 0.47 describes the part of the model that is shaded.

Decimals are also used to represent amounts of money. The decimal point separates the dollars from the cents.

Example 2

Write the amount of money shown as a decimal.

Strategy   **Find the value of the bills and coins.**

Step 1   Count the number of dollars.

10, 15, 16, 17

There are 17 dollars.

Step 2   Count the number of cents.

25, 50, 60, 61, 62, 63

There are 63 cents.

Step 3   Write the decimal.

Write the dollar amount to the left of the decimal point.

Write the cents to the right of the decimal point.

$17.63

Solution   **The money shows $17.63.**

Example 3

What number is represented by point *D* on the number line?

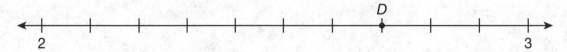

Strategy   Find the decimal represented by each part of the number line.

Step 1   Find the number of equal parts between 2 and 3.

There are 10 equal parts between 2 and 3.

So each part represents one tenth.

Step 2   Count the number of parts to find the decimal for the point.

The point is 7 parts to the right of 2, or 7 tenths.

Step 3   Write the decimal.

2 and 7 tenths is 2.7.

Solution   Point *D* represents the decimal 2.7.

---

② COACHED EXAMPLE

Mario spent the money shown below at the grocery store. How much did Mario spend?

Find the value of the bills and coins.

How many dollars did Mario spend? _____

How many cents did Mario spend? _____

Write the decimal.

Write the dollar amount to the _____ of the decimal point.

Write the cents to the _____ of the decimal point.

$_____._____

Mario spent _____ at the grocery store.

1 Melissa counted the money in her piggy bank.

How much money is in Melissa's piggy bank?

A. $7.84   C. $84.24

B. $24.12   D. $24.84

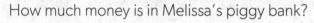

2 What part of the model is shaded?

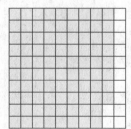

A. 0.12   C. 8.80

B. 0.88   D. 12.0

3 What is 21 hundredths written as a decimal?

A. 2.1   C. 0.21

B. 21   D. 210

4 Yolanda has 24 dollars and 79 cents in her pocket. Write this amount of money as a decimal.

Record your answer and fill in the bubbles. Be sure to use the correct place value.

			.		
0	0	0		0	0
1	1	1		1	1
2	2	2		2	2
3	3	3		3	3
4	4	4		4	4
5	5	5		5	5
6	6	6		6	6
7	7	7		7	7
8	8	8		8	8
9	9	9		9	9

5 What number is represented by point *N* on the number line?

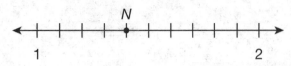

1   2

A. 1.4

B. 0.14

C. 14

D. 140

6 Andrea shaded some parts of a model showing hundredths. Then she wrote the decimal that represents the parts she shaded. How many digits did Andrea write to the right of the decimal point?

A. 3

B. 2

C. 1

D. 0

7 What part of the model is shaded?

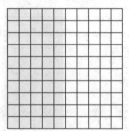

A. 50   C. 0.50

B. 5   D. 0.05

8 Mateo has 4 dollars, 2 quarters, 1 dime, 1 nickel, and 2 pennies. How much money does Mateo have?

A. $4.67

B. $4.62

C. $46.70

D. $46.20

9 What number is represented by point *A* on the number line?

7   8

Record your answer and fill in the bubbles. Be sure to use the correct place value.

			.		
⓪	⓪	⓪		⓪	⓪
①	①	①		①	①
②	②	②		②	②
③	③	③		③	③
④	④	④		④	④
⑤	⑤	⑤		⑤	⑤
⑥	⑥	⑥		⑥	⑥
⑦	⑦	⑦		⑦	⑦
⑧	⑧	⑧		⑧	⑧
⑨	⑨	⑨		⑨	⑨

10 What is 9 tenths written as a decimal?

A. 0.99

B. 0.09

C. 9.0

D. 0.9

11 There are 10 equal parts between the numbers 5 and 6 on a number line. What number could represent a point on this number line?

A. 0.5

B. 0.6

C. 5.6

D. 6.5

12 What part of the model is shaded?

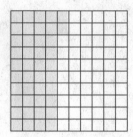

A. 0.58

B. 0.42

C. 42

D. 5.8

13 A number line starts with 8 and ends with 9. There are 100 equal parts between the two whole numbers. What decimal is a distance of 23 parts to the right of 8?

A. 8.23

B. 823

C. 0.23

D. 9.23

14 What number is represented by point X on the number line?

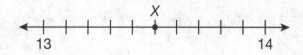

A. 14.5

B. 13.5

C. 5.13

D. 13.14

15 Mr. Armstrong has the following bills and coins in his wallet.

one $20 bill, three $10 bills, two $5 bills, 1 quarter, 1 dime, 4 pennies

Write the amount of money in Mr. Armstrong's wallet as a decimal.

Record your answer and fill in the bubbles. Be sure to use the correct place value.

			.		
⓪	⓪	⓪		⓪	⓪
①	①	①		①	①
②	②	②		②	②
③	③	③		③	③
④	④	④		④	④
⑤	⑤	⑤		⑤	⑤
⑥	⑥	⑥		⑥	⑥
⑦	⑦	⑦		⑦	⑦
⑧	⑧	⑧		⑧	⑧
⑨	⑨	⑨		⑨	⑨

4.2(F)

Comparing and Ordering Decimals

1 GETTING THE IDEA

You can use models or place value to compare decimals.

When you compare two decimals, the wholes that the decimals refer to must be the same size.

The models below show 0.4.

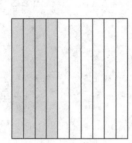 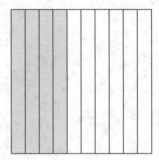

The wholes these decimals refer to are **not** the same size.

You cannot compare these decimals.

These models also show 0.4.

These wholes are the same size.

You can compare these decimals.

The shaded areas are the same, so 0.4 = 0.4.

Example 1

Use <, >, or = to compare 0.3 and 0.6.

Strategy   **Use models.**

Step 1   Use place-value blocks to model 1 whole.

The model shows 10 tenths, or 1 whole.

Step 2   Shade same-size models to show 0.3 and 0.6.

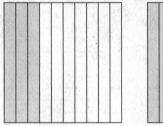 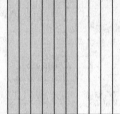

3 tenths   6 tenths

0.3   0.6

Step 3   Compare the decimals.

The area that represents 0.3 is less than the area that represents 0.6.

Solution   0.3 < 0.6

Example 2

Use <, >, or = to compare 0.24 and 0.08.

Strategy   Use models.

Step 1   Use 10 by 10 grids to model 1 whole.

The model shows 100 hundredths, or 1 whole.

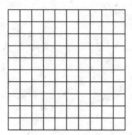

Step 2   Shade same-size models to show 0.24 and 0.08.

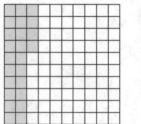 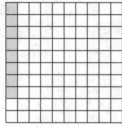

24 hundredths   8 hundredths

0.24   0.08

Step 3   Compare the decimals.

The area that represents 0.24 is greater than the area that represents 0.08.

Solution   **0.24 > 0.08**

To order a group of decimals, you can compare digits in the same place-value positions. Start with the greatest place value, and then work from left to right.

For the decimals below, the ones digits are the same. So, compare the tenths digits to order the decimals.

0.9 ← greatest

0.2 ← least

0.5 ← less than 0.6

0.6

The decimals ordered from least to greatest are 0.2, 0.5, 0.6, and 0.9.

Example 3

Order 0.35, 0.45, 0.42, and 0.38 from least to greatest.

Strategy Use a place-value chart.

Step 1 Write each decimal in a place-value chart and compare values from left to right.

Ones	.	Tenths	Hundredths
0	.	3	5
0	.	4	5
0	.	4	2
0	.	3	8

Step 2 Start with the greatest place value. Compare the ones.

All decimals have 0 ones.

Step 3 Compare the tenths.

3 tenths < 4 tenths

0.35 and 0.38 are less than 0.45 and 0.42.

Step 4 Compare the hundredths of 0.35 and 0.38 to find which is least.

5 hundredths < 8 hundredths

So, 0.35 < 0.38.

So, the least decimal is 0.35. It should be first in the ordered list.
0.38 should be listed next.

Step 5 Compare the hundredths of 0.45 and 0.42.

2 hundredths < 5 hundredths

So, 0.42 < 0.45.

List 0.42 after 0.38. Since 0.45 is the greatest decimal, it should be last in the ordered list.

Solution 0.35, 0.38, 0.42, 0.45

Order 0.27, 0.35, 0.3 and 0.25 from greatest to least.

Draw models to represent each decimal.

Use _____ same-size 10 by 10 grid models, each representing _____ whole.

Each whole model has _____ equal parts.

Shade the models.

For 0.27, _____ parts are shaded.

For 0.35, _____ parts are shaded.

For 0.3, _____ parts are shaded.

For 0.25, _____ parts are shaded.

Label each model to identify the decimal.

_____   _____   _____   _____

Compare the areas of the models.

The model for the decimal _____ has the greatest shaded area.

The model for the decimal _____ has the second greatest shaded area.

The model for the decimal _____ has the third greatest shaded area.

The model for the decimal _____ has the least shaded area.

Order the decimals from greatest to least.

_____, _____, _____, _____

1 Each model below shows a decimal number.

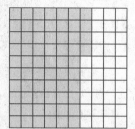 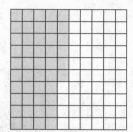

Which statement correctly compares these decimals?

A. 0.46 > 0.64   **C.** 0.46 > 0.54

B. 0.36 > 0.54   **D.** 0.46 < 0.64

2 Hugo caught a mayfly that is 0.63 centimeter long. Which length is longer than 0.63 centimeter?

A. 0.6 centimeter

B. 0.08 centimeter

C. 0.71 centimeter

D. 0.59 centimeter

3 Which list correctly shows 0.45, 0.09, 0.6, and 0.54 ordered from least to greatest?

A. 0.6, 0.54, 0.45, 0.09

B. 0.54, 0.45, 0.6, 0.09

C. 0.6, 0.09, 0.45, 0.54

D. 0.09, 0.45, 0.54, 0.6

4 Conrad ran 0.72 mile, Leon ran 0.59 mile, and Tricia ran 0.68 mile. Which number, in miles, is the shortest distance?

Record your answer and fill in the bubbles. Be sure to use the correct place value.

⓪	⓪	⓪	·	⓪	⓪
①	①	①		①	①
②	②	②		②	②
③	③	③		③	③
④	④	④		④	④
⑤	⑤	⑤		⑤	⑤
⑥	⑥	⑥		⑥	⑥
⑦	⑦	⑦		⑦	⑦
⑧	⑧	⑧		⑧	⑧
⑨	⑨	⑨		⑨	⑨

5 Use the 10 by 10 grid to help answer the question.

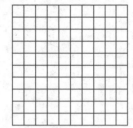

Which statement is true?

A. 0.45 < 0.36

B. 0.47 > 0.09

C. 0.08 > 0.72

D. 0.5 < 0.28

6 Elena bought 0.74 pound of ham and 0.68 pound of turkey. Which amount is between the weights of the turkey and ham?

A. 0.5 pound

B. 0.6 pound

C. 0.7 pound

D. 0.8 pound

7 Which decimal makes the statement true?

0.27 > ☐

A. 0.41

B. 0.32

C. 0.70

D. 0.19

Use the table for questions 8 and 9.

The table shows the heights of four tomato plants in Kyle's garden.

Tomato	Height (in meters)
Beefsteak	0.9
Eva purple	0.68
Green zebra	0.59
Black krim	0.77

8 Which tomato plant is taller than 0.6 meter and shorter than 0.7 meter?

A. Beefsteak

B. Eva purple

C. Green zebra

D. Black krim

9 Which of the following lists the tomato plants from shortest to tallest?

A. Green zebra, Eva purple, black krim, beefsteak

B. Beefsteak, green zebra, Eva purple, black krim

C. Green zebra, black krim, Eva purple, beefsteak

D. Beefsteak, black krim, Eva purple, green zebra

10 Use the place-value chart to help answer the question.

Ones	.	Tenths	Hundredths
	.		
	.		
	.		
	.		

Antoine has four model cars. They weigh 0.35 pound, 0.28 pound, 0.33 pound, and 0.24 pound. Which of the following lists the weights from least to greatest?

A. 0.35, 0.28, 0.33, 0.24

B. 0.24, 0.28, 0.33, 0.35

C. 0.33, 0.24, 0.35, 0.28

D. 0.33, 0.35, 0.24, 0.28

11 Denise buys 0.4 kilogram of granola, 0.62 kilogram of banana chips, 0.07 kilogram of dried peas, and 0.36 kilogram of cashews. Which statement is true?

A. Denise buys more granola than cashews.

B. Denise buys more cashews than banana chips.

C. Denise buys more dried peas than granola.

D. Denise buys more dried peas than cashews.

12 The table shows the distances from Lin's house to her friends' houses in the neighborhood.

Friend	Distance (in miles)
Javier	0.63
Janine	0.7
Kylie	0.29
Monica	0.4

Which friend lives closest to Lin?

A. Javier

B. Janine

C. Kylie

D. Monica

13 Which number in the list is the greatest?

0.07, 0.6, 0.32, 0.55

Record your answer and fill in the bubbles. Be sure to use the correct place value.

			.		
⓪	⓪	⓪		⓪	⓪
①	①	①		①	①
②	②	②		②	②
③	③	③		③	③
④	④	④		④	④
⑤	⑤	⑤		⑤	⑤
⑥	⑥	⑥		⑥	⑥
⑦	⑦	⑦		⑦	⑦
⑧	⑧	⑧		⑧	⑧
⑨	⑨	⑨		⑨	⑨

Relating Decimals to Fractions

1 GETTING THE IDEA

A **decimal** is another way to write a **fraction**. A decimal point separates the whole number part from the fractional part in a decimal. A fraction and a decimal that represent the same number are **equivalent**. An equivalent fraction and decimal can be represented using the same model. They can also be represented by the same distance from zero on a number line.

word form: six tenths

fraction: $\frac{6}{10}$

decimal: 0.6

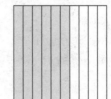

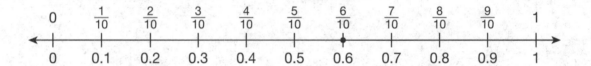

word form: forty-five hundredths

fraction: $\frac{45}{100}$

decimal: 0.45

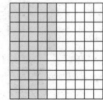

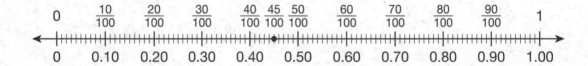

Example 1

Write $\frac{8}{10}$ as a decimal.

Strategy   Use models and a place-value chart.

   Step 1   Model $\frac{8}{10}$.

          8 out of 10 parts are shaded.

          8 tenths are shaded.

   Step 2   Write the decimal in a place-value chart.

          To write 8 tenths, write an 8 in the tenths place.

Ones	Decimal Point	Tenths	Hundredths
0	.	8	

Solution $\frac{8}{10}$ written as a decimal is 0.8.

Example 2

Write $\frac{34}{100}$ as a decimal.

Strategy   Use models and a place-value chart.

   Step 1   Model $\frac{34}{100}$.

          There are 100 squares in the grid. Each square represents $\frac{1}{100}$.

          Shade 34 squares.

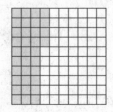

Step 2   Write the decimal in a place-value chart.

To write 34 hundredths, write the last digit of 34 in the hundredths place.

Ones	Decimal Point	Tenths	Hundredths
0	.	3	4

Solution $\frac{34}{100}$ written as a decimal is 0.34.

Example 3

Write $\frac{2}{10}$ as a decimal. Show the decimal on a number line.

Strategy   Show tenths on a number line.

Step 1   Read the fraction to identify the decimal.

$\frac{2}{10}$ is 2 tenths.

2 tenths written as a decimal has a 2 in the tenths place.

2 tenths = 0.2

Step 2   Draw a number line that represents tenths.

Divide one whole into 10 equal parts. Label each tenth on the number line.

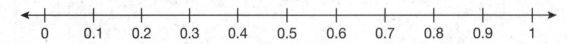

Step 3   Locate 0.2 on the number line.

Start at 0. Count 2 tick marks to the right. Since each mark represents 1 tenth, the second mark represents 2 tenths, or 0.2.

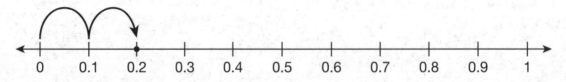

Solution $\frac{2}{10}$ written as a decimal is 0.2. The number line in Step 3 shows 0.2.

Write $\frac{68}{100}$ as a decimal. Show the decimal on a number line.

Read the fraction.

$\frac{68}{100}$ is [ ] hundredths.

Written as a decimal, sixty-eight hundredths should have a(n) [ ] in the tenths place and

a(n) [ ] in the hundredths place.

Write $\frac{68}{100}$ in the place-value chart.

Ones	Decimal Point	Tenths	Hundredths
	.		

This number line shows hundredths. There are _____ hundredths between each tenth.

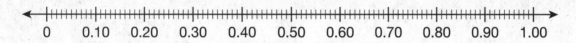

Plot a point at 0.68 on the number line.

Start at 0.60. Since each mark represents 1 _____, count _____ tick marks to the right.

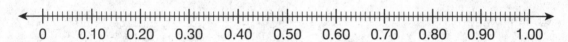

$\frac{68}{100}$ written as a decimal is _____. The decimal is shown on the number line.

1 Which fraction is represented by the point on the number line?

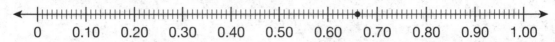

0   0.10   0.20   0.30   0.40   0.50   0.60   0.70   0.80   0.90   1.00

A. $\frac{66}{10}$

B. $\frac{60}{100}$

C. $\frac{6.6}{100}$

D. $\frac{66}{100}$

2 What is $\frac{4}{10}$ written as a decimal?

A. 0.4

B. 0.04

C. 4.10

D. 0.410

3 Which fraction is equivalent to 0.34?

A. $\frac{3.4}{10}$

B. $\frac{34}{10}$

C. $\frac{30}{400}$

D. $\frac{34}{100}$

4 For which model does the shaded part represent $\frac{25}{100}$?

A.

B.

C.

D.

5 Which number is represented by the point on the number line?

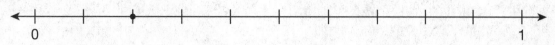

0   1

A. $\frac{2}{1}$

B. $\frac{20}{10}$

C. 0.2

D. 0.02

---

6 Which place-value chart shows an equivalent decimal for $\frac{57}{100}$?

A.

Ones	Decimal Point	Tenths	Hundredths
0	.	5	7

B.

Ones	Decimal Point	Tenths	Hundredths
0	.	7	5

C.

Ones	Decimal Point	Tenths	Hundredths
5	.	0	7

D.

Ones	Decimal Point	Tenths	Hundredths
5	.	7	0

7 Lee counted the dimes in his pocket. He said that the value of the dimes were $\frac{9}{10}$ of a dollar. Write $\frac{9}{10}$ as an equivalent decimal.

Record your answer and fill in the bubbles. Be sure to use the correct place value.

			.		
⓪	⓪	⓪		⓪	⓪
①	①	①		①	①
②	②	②		②	②
③	③	③		③	③
④	④	④		④	④
⑤	⑤	⑤		⑤	⑤
⑥	⑥	⑥		⑥	⑥
⑦	⑦	⑦		⑦	⑦
⑧	⑧	⑧		⑧	⑧
⑨	⑨	⑨		⑨	⑨

8   Cambria hiked a 1-mile trail. She used points on a number line to mark animals she saw along the trail. Which of the following is **not** an equivalent decimal for one of the fractions that mark the sightings?

Distances (in miles)

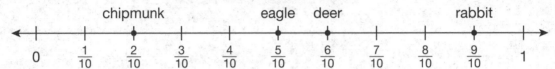

A.   Rabbit, 0.9 mile

B.   Chipmunk, 0.02 mile

C.   Eagle, 0.5 mile

D.   Deer, 0.6 mile

---

9   Julio lives 0.84 mile from the library. What is the distance written as a fraction?

A. $\frac{8}{4}$ miles

B. $\frac{84}{10}$ miles

C. $\frac{8.4}{100}$ mile

D. $\frac{84}{100}$ mile

10   Saki walks seventy-two hundredths mile to school. What is this distance written as a decimal?

A.   0.27 mile

B.   0.72 mile

C.   7.2 miles

D.   7,200 miles

11   A farmer divides a field into 100 same-sized plots. The farmer plants forty-five hundredths of the field with soy beans. Write the amount of the field planted with soy beans as a decimal.

Record your answer and fill in the bubbles. Be sure to use the correct place value.

			.		
⓪	⓪	⓪		⓪	⓪
①	①	①		①	①
②	②	②		②	②
③	③	③		③	③
④	④	④		④	④
⑤	⑤	⑤		⑤	⑤
⑥	⑥	⑥		⑥	⑥
⑦	⑦	⑦		⑦	⑦
⑧	⑧	⑧		⑧	⑧
⑨	⑨	⑨		⑨	⑨

Decomposing Fractions

A fraction is made up of two parts, the numerator and the denominator.

| $\frac{1}{10}$ | $\frac{1}{10}$ | $\frac{1}{10}$ | $\frac{1}{10}$ | $\frac{1}{10}$ | $\frac{1}{10}$ | $\frac{1}{10}$ | $\frac{1}{10}$ | $\frac{1}{10}$ | $\frac{1}{10}$ |

$\dfrac{6}{10}$ ← The **numerator** is the number of shaded equal parts of the whole.
← The **denominator** is the number of equal parts in the whole.

Fractions can be decomposed.

To **decompose** a fraction is to break the fraction into smaller parts.

A **unit fraction** is a fraction with 1 as the numerator.

$\dfrac{1}{4}$ ← numerator of 1

All fractions with a numerator greater than 1 can be decomposed into a sum of unit fractions.

The fraction $\frac{3}{4}$ can be decomposed into the sum $\frac{1}{4} + \frac{1}{4} + \frac{1}{4}$.

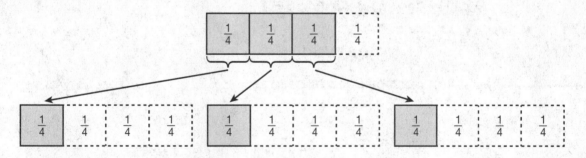

Fractions can usually be decomposed in more than one way.

$\frac{3}{4}$ can also be decomposed into the sum $\frac{2}{4} + \frac{1}{4}$.

Example 1

Decompose the fraction $\frac{4}{6}$ in two ways.

Strategy   Use fraction strips.

Step 1   Model the fraction with a fraction strip.

| $\frac{1}{6}$ | $\frac{1}{6}$ | $\frac{1}{6}$ | $\frac{1}{6}$ | $\frac{1}{6}$ | $\frac{1}{6}$ |

Step 2   Decompose $\frac{4}{6}$ into unit fractions.

There are four $\frac{1}{6}$ pieces.

$$\frac{4}{6} = \frac{1}{6} + \frac{1}{6} + \frac{1}{6} + \frac{1}{6}$$

Step 3   Separate $\frac{4}{6}$ into two parts. Make one part a unit fraction.

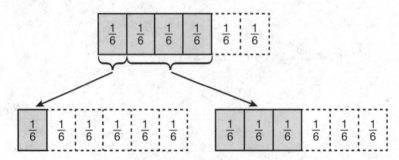

$\frac{4}{6}$ can be separated into $\frac{1}{6}$ and $\frac{3}{6}$.

$$\frac{4}{6} = \frac{1}{6} + \frac{3}{6}$$

Solution   The fraction $\frac{4}{6}$ can be decomposed as $\frac{1}{6} + \frac{1}{6} + \frac{1}{6} + \frac{1}{6}$ and as $\frac{1}{6} + \frac{3}{6}$.

Example 2

Decompose the fraction $\frac{5}{7}$ in two ways.

Strategy   **Use models.**

Step 1   Model the fraction.

$$\boxed{\frac{1}{7}}\boxed{\frac{1}{7}}\boxed{\frac{1}{7}}\boxed{\frac{1}{7}}\boxed{\frac{1}{7}}\ \vdots\frac{1}{7}\vdots\ \vdots\frac{1}{7}\vdots$$

Step 2   Decompose $\frac{5}{7}$ into unit fractions.

There are five $\frac{1}{7}$ parts.

$$\frac{5}{7} = \frac{1}{7} + \frac{1}{7} + \frac{1}{7} + \frac{1}{7} + \frac{1}{7}$$

Step 3   Separate $\frac{5}{7}$ into two parts without using unit fractions.

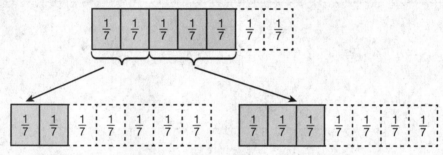

$\frac{5}{7}$ can be separated into $\frac{2}{7}$ and $\frac{3}{7}$.

$$\frac{5}{7} = \frac{2}{7} + \frac{3}{7}$$

Solution   **The fraction $\frac{5}{7}$ can be decomposed as $\frac{1}{7} + \frac{1}{7} + \frac{1}{7} + \frac{1}{7} + \frac{1}{7}$ and as $\frac{2}{7} + \frac{3}{7}$.**

Example 3

Decompose the fraction $\frac{3}{2}$ in two ways.

Strategy   Use models.

Step 1   Model the fraction.

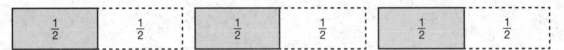

Because the numerator is greater than the denominator, more than one whole is needed. A model with two one-half parts shaded represents one whole.

Step 2   Decompose $\frac{3}{2}$ into unit fractions.

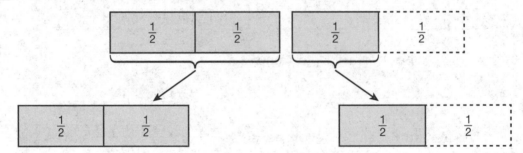

There are three one-half parts.

$$\frac{3}{2} = \frac{1}{2} + \frac{1}{2} + \frac{1}{2}$$

Step 3   Decompose $\frac{3}{2}$ into two parts. Make one part a whole.

$\frac{3}{2}$ can be decomposed into $\frac{2}{2}$ and $\frac{1}{2}$.

$$\frac{3}{2} = \frac{2}{2} + \frac{1}{2}$$

Solution   The fraction $\frac{3}{2}$ can be decomposed as the sums $\frac{1}{2} + \frac{1}{2} + \frac{1}{2}$ and as $\frac{2}{2} + \frac{1}{2}$.

Decompose the fraction $\frac{7}{4}$ in two ways.

Draw a model of the fraction using fraction strips.

The numerator is greater than the denominator so draw _____ wholes. Each whole

has four $\frac{\square}{\square}$ pieces.

One whole has _____ pieces shaded. The other whole has _____ pieces shaded.

Decompose $\frac{7}{4}$ into unit fractions.

There are seven $\frac{\square}{\square}$ pieces. Write the sum.

$\frac{7}{4} = \frac{\square}{4} + \frac{\square}{4} + \frac{\square}{4} + \frac{\square}{4} + \frac{\square}{4} + \frac{\square}{4} + \frac{\square}{4}$

Decompose the fraction into two parts. Make one part a whole.

$\square$ pieces shaded models one whole.

$\frac{7}{4}$ can be decomposed into $\frac{\square}{4}$ and $\frac{3}{4}$.

Write the sum.

$\frac{7}{4} = \frac{\square}{4} + \frac{\square}{4}$

The fraction $\frac{7}{4}$ can be decomposed as the sums

$\frac{\square}{\square} + \frac{\square}{\square} + \frac{\square}{\square} + \frac{\square}{\square} + \frac{\square}{\square} + \frac{\square}{\square} + \frac{\square}{\square}$ **and as** $\frac{\square}{\square} + \frac{\square}{\square}$.

1 Which is a model of a unit fraction?

A.
| $\frac{1}{10}$ | $\frac{1}{10}$ | $\frac{1}{10}$ | $\frac{1}{10}$ | $\frac{1}{10}$ | $\frac{1}{10}$ | $\frac{1}{10}$ | $\frac{1}{10}$ | $\frac{1}{10}$ | $\frac{1}{10}$ |

B.
| $\frac{1}{6}$ | $\frac{1}{6}$ | $\frac{1}{6}$ | $\frac{1}{6}$ | $\frac{1}{6}$ | $\frac{1}{6}$ |

C.
| $\frac{1}{2}$ | $\frac{1}{2}$ |

D.
| $\frac{1}{3}$ | $\frac{1}{3}$ | $\frac{1}{3}$ |

2 Which of the following shows one way to decompose $\frac{4}{3}$?

| $\frac{1}{3}$ | $\frac{1}{3}$ | $\frac{1}{3}$ |

| $\frac{1}{3}$ | $\frac{1}{3}$ | $\frac{1}{3}$ |

A. $\frac{1}{3} + \frac{1}{3} + \frac{1}{3}$

B. $\frac{1}{4} + \frac{1}{4} + \frac{1}{4}$

C. $\frac{3}{3} + \frac{1}{3}$

D. $\frac{3}{4} + \frac{3}{4}$

3 Four students were asked to decompose the fraction $\frac{6}{4}$. Their work is shown in the table.

Student	Student's Work
Madeline	$\frac{6}{4} = \frac{4}{4} + \frac{2}{4}$
Rosie	$\frac{6}{4} = \frac{4}{4} + \frac{1}{4} + \frac{1}{4}$
Bert	$\frac{6}{4} = \frac{1}{4} + \frac{1}{4} + \frac{1}{4} + \frac{1}{4} + \frac{1}{4}$
Tia	$\frac{6}{4} = \frac{1}{4} + \frac{1}{4} + \frac{1}{4} + \frac{1}{4} + \frac{2}{4}$

Which student did **not** correctly decompose $\frac{6}{4}$?

A. Madeline

B. Rosie

C. Bert

D. Tia

4 A fraction can be decomposed as $\frac{5}{10} + \frac{2}{10}$. What fraction does this sum represent?

A. $\frac{2}{10}$

B. $\frac{5}{10}$

C. $\frac{12}{10}$

D. $\frac{7}{10}$

5 Which sum makes the statement true?

$\frac{9}{12}$ can be decomposed as the

sum _____.

A. $\frac{3}{12} + \frac{6}{12}$

B. $\frac{1}{12} + \frac{9}{12}$

C. $\frac{11}{12} + \frac{1}{12}$

D. $\frac{4}{12} + \frac{7}{12}$

6 Jenna decomposed a fraction as shown below.

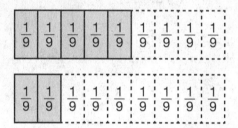

What fraction did she decompose?

A. $\frac{3}{9}$

B. $\frac{6}{9}$

C. $\frac{11}{9}$

D. $\frac{7}{9}$

7 Which model shows a fraction decomposed into unit fractions?

A.

| $\frac{1}{8}$ | $\frac{1}{8}$ | $\frac{1}{8}$ | $\frac{1}{8}$ | $\frac{1}{8}$ | $\frac{1}{8}$ | $\frac{1}{8}$ | $\frac{1}{8}$ |

B.

| $\frac{1}{3}$ | $\frac{1}{3}$ | $\frac{1}{3}$ |

| $\frac{1}{3}$ | $\frac{1}{3}$ | $\frac{1}{3}$ |

| $\frac{1}{3}$ | $\frac{1}{3}$ | $\frac{1}{3}$ |

C.

| $\frac{1}{6}$ | $\frac{1}{6}$ | $\frac{1}{6}$ | $\frac{1}{6}$ | $\frac{1}{6}$ | $\frac{1}{6}$ |

| $\frac{1}{6}$ | $\frac{1}{6}$ | $\frac{1}{6}$ | $\frac{1}{6}$ | $\frac{1}{6}$ | $\frac{1}{6}$ |

D.

| $\frac{1}{10}$ | $\frac{1}{10}$ | $\frac{1}{10}$ | $\frac{1}{10}$ | $\frac{1}{10}$ | $\frac{1}{10}$ | $\frac{1}{10}$ | $\frac{1}{10}$ | $\frac{1}{10}$ | $\frac{1}{10}$ |

| $\frac{1}{10}$ | $\frac{1}{10}$ | $\frac{1}{10}$ | $\frac{1}{10}$ | $\frac{1}{10}$ | $\frac{1}{10}$ | $\frac{1}{10}$ | $\frac{1}{10}$ | $\frac{1}{10}$ | $\frac{1}{10}$ |

8 Which statement is true?

A. $\frac{7}{5} = \frac{3}{5} + \frac{2}{5}$

B. $\frac{6}{7} = \frac{7}{7} + \frac{1}{7}$

C. $\frac{9}{8} = \frac{8}{8} + \frac{1}{8}$

D. $\frac{9}{10} = \frac{8}{10} + \frac{2}{10}$

9 Franklin drew this model of a decomposed fraction. Which statement describes the sum shown?

| $\frac{1}{3}$ | $\frac{1}{3}$ | $\frac{1}{3}$ |

| $\frac{1}{3}$ | $\frac{1}{3}$ | $\frac{1}{3}$ |

| $\frac{1}{3}$ | $\frac{1}{3}$ | $\frac{1}{3}$ |

| $\frac{1}{3}$ | $\frac{1}{3}$ | $\frac{1}{3}$ |

| $\frac{1}{3}$ | $\frac{1}{3}$ | $\frac{1}{3}$ |

A. The numerator is greater than the denominator.

B. The denominator is greater than the numerator.

C. The sum is less than one whole.

D. The sum is not a fraction.

10 Which of the following shows $\frac{7}{8}$ decomposed as a sum of unit fractions?

A. $\frac{1}{8} + \frac{1}{8} + \frac{1}{8} + \frac{1}{8} + \frac{1}{8} + \frac{1}{8} + \frac{1}{8} + \frac{1}{8}$

B. $\frac{8}{8} + \frac{1}{8}$

C. $\frac{1}{8} + \frac{1}{8} + \frac{1}{8} + \frac{1}{8} + \frac{1}{8} + \frac{1}{8} + \frac{1}{8}$

D. $\frac{6}{8} + \frac{1}{8}$

11 Omar correctly decomposed $\frac{6}{5}$ in two ways. Which sums could Omar have written?

A. $\frac{5}{5} + \frac{1}{5}$ and $\frac{6}{5} + \frac{1}{5}$

B. $\frac{1}{5} + \frac{1}{5} + \frac{1}{5} + \frac{1}{5} + \frac{1}{5} + \frac{1}{5}$ and $\frac{5}{5} + \frac{1}{5}$

C. $\frac{3}{5} + \frac{3}{5}$ and $\frac{6}{5} + \frac{1}{5}$

D. $\frac{1}{5} + \frac{1}{5} + \frac{1}{5} + \frac{1}{5} + \frac{1}{5}$ and $\frac{1}{5} + \frac{6}{5}$

12 What number makes this sum correct?

$$\frac{9}{10} = \frac{\boxed{}}{10} + \frac{2}{10}$$

Record your answer and fill in the bubbles. Be sure to use the correct place value.

			.		
⓪	⓪	⓪		⓪	⓪
①	①	①		①	①
②	②	②		②	②
③	③	③		③	③
④	④	④		④	④
⑤	⑤	⑤		⑤	⑤
⑥	⑥	⑥		⑥	⑥
⑦	⑦	⑦		⑦	⑦
⑧	⑧	⑧		⑧	⑧
⑨	⑨	⑨		⑨	⑨

Equivalent Fractions

A fraction names a part of a whole. **Equivalent fractions** name the same amount of their wholes using different numerators and denominators.

You can use fraction models to show that fractions are equivalent. Notice that the number of equal parts increases when the size of the parts decreases.

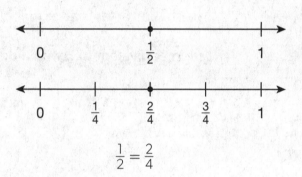

$$\frac{2}{3} = \frac{8}{12}$$

$$\frac{1}{2} = \frac{2}{4}$$

If you multiply both the numerator and the denominator of $\frac{2}{3}$ by 4, the result is $\frac{8}{12}$.

If you multiply both the numerator and the denominator of $\frac{1}{2}$ by 2, the result is $\frac{2}{4}$.

$$\frac{2}{3} = \frac{2 \times 4}{3 \times 4}$$

$$= \frac{8}{12}$$

$$\frac{1}{2} = \frac{1 \times 2}{2 \times 2}$$

$$= \frac{2}{4}$$

Example 1

Find a fraction equivalent to $\frac{1}{3}$ with a denominator of 12.

Strategy   **Multiply the numerator and denominator by the same number.**

Step 1   Find the factor to make a product of 12.

The denominator of $\frac{1}{3}$ is 3.

$3 \times \mathbf{4} = 12$

You can multiply the denominator by 4 to make a denominator of 12.

So, multiply the numerator by 4, too.

Step 2   Multiply to find the equivalent fraction.

Multiply the numerator and denominator by 4.

$$\frac{1}{3} = \frac{1 \times 4}{3 \times 4}$$

$$= \frac{4}{12}$$

Step 3   Use models to show the fractions are equivalent.

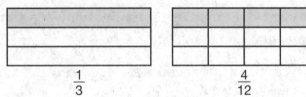

The shaded areas in each model are the same size, so they are equivalent.

Solution   A fraction equivalent to $\frac{1}{3}$ with a denominator of 12 is $\frac{4}{12}$.

Example 2

Find two fractions equivalent to $\frac{3}{5}$.

Strategy   **Use multiplication.**

Step 1   Multiply the numerator and denominator of $\frac{3}{5}$ by any number greater than 1.

Choose 2 as the first number. It is easy to multiply.

Multiply the numerator and denominator by 2.

$$\frac{3}{5} = \frac{3 \times 2}{5 \times 2}$$

$$= \frac{6}{10}$$

Step 2   Choose another number to multiply the numerator and denominator by.

Choose 10 as another number. It is also easy to multiply.

$$\frac{3}{5} = \frac{3 \times 10}{5 \times 10}$$

$$= \frac{30}{50}$$

Solution   Two fractions equivalent to $\frac{3}{5}$ are $\frac{6}{10}$ and $\frac{30}{50}$.

Example 3

Select the fractions that are equivalent to $\frac{1}{4}$.

$\frac{2}{5}, \frac{3}{6}, \frac{2}{8}, \frac{4}{10}, \frac{3}{12}$

Strategy Use multiplication to find the equivalent fractions.

Step 1 Multiply the numerator and denominator of $\frac{1}{4}$ by 2.

$$\frac{1}{4} = \frac{1 \times 2}{4 \times 2}$$

$$= \frac{2}{8}$$

$\frac{2}{8}$ is equivalent to $\frac{1}{4}$.

Step 2 Multiply the numerator and denominator of $\frac{1}{4}$ by 3.

$$\frac{1}{4} = \frac{1 \times 3}{4 \times 3}$$

$$= \frac{3}{12}$$

$\frac{3}{12}$ is equivalent to $\frac{1}{4}$.

Step 3 Model the equivalent fractions.

$\frac{1}{4}$ **1 of 4 equal parts shaded**	$\frac{2}{8}$ **2 of 8 equal parts shaded**	$\frac{3}{12}$ **3 of 12 equal parts shaded**

Step 4 Look back at the list to identify the equivalent fractions.

You have found fractions equivalent to $\frac{1}{4}$ with denominators of 8 and 12.

There are no whole numbers that you can multiply by 4 to get denominators of 5, 6, or 10.

$\frac{2}{5}, \frac{3}{6}$, and $\frac{4}{10}$ are not equivalent to $\frac{1}{4}$.

Solution The fractions in the list equivalent to $\frac{1}{4}$ are $\frac{2}{8}$ and $\frac{3}{12}$.

A fraction is in **lowest terms** when the only number that will divide evenly into both the numerator and denominator is 1. You can write a fraction in lowest terms by dividing both the numerator and denominator by the same number greater than 1.

Example 4

Determine if $\frac{8}{10}$ and $\frac{20}{25}$ are equivalent fractions.

Strategy   Use division to write the fractions in lowest terms.

Step 1   Divide the numerator and denominator of $\frac{8}{10}$ by a number greater than 1.

Choose 2. It will divide into 8 and into 10.

Divide the numerator and the denominator by 2.

$$\frac{8}{10} = \frac{8 \div 2}{10 \div 2}$$

$$= \frac{4}{5}$$

$\frac{4}{5}$ is in lowest terms because 1 is the only number that divides evenly into 4 and 5.

Step 2   Divide the numerator and denominator of $\frac{20}{25}$ by a number greater than 1.

Choose 5. It will divide into 20 and into 25.

Divide the numerator and the denominator by 5.

$$\frac{20}{25} = \frac{20 \div 5}{25 \div 5}$$

$$= \frac{4}{5}$$

Step 3   Compare the lowest terms of the fractions.

The fraction $\frac{8}{10}$ in lowest terms is $\frac{4}{5}$.

The fraction $\frac{20}{25}$ in lowest terms is $\frac{4}{5}$.

Step 4   Use models to show the fractions are equivalent.

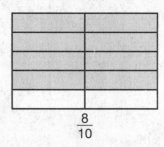

$$\frac{4}{5}$$ $$\frac{8}{10}$$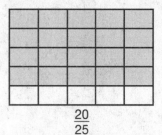

$$\frac{20}{25}$$

The shaded areas in each model are the same size, so the fractions are equivalent.

Solution   The fractions $\frac{8}{10}$ and $\frac{20}{25}$ are equivalent fractions.

Find two fractions equivalent to $\frac{2}{3}$.

Multiply the ___*numarator*___ and ___*denominater*___ of $\frac{2}{3}$ by 2 to find one equivalent fraction.

$$\frac{2}{3} = \frac{2 \times \boxed{4}}{3 \times \boxed{4}}$$

$$= \frac{\boxed{8}}{\boxed{12}}$$

Multiply the _____ and _____ of $\frac{2}{3}$ by 3 to find another equivalent fraction.

$$\frac{2}{3} = \frac{2 \times \boxed{}}{3 \times \boxed{}}$$

$$= \frac{\boxed{}}{\boxed{}}$$

Two fractions equivalent to $\frac{2}{3}$ are $\frac{\boxed{}}{\boxed{}}$ and $\frac{\boxed{}}{\boxed{}}$.

1 Look at the model below.

Which fraction is equivalent to the shaded part of the model?

A. $\frac{1}{4}$

B. $\frac{1}{3}$

C. $\frac{1}{2}$

D. $\frac{3}{4}$

2 Which fraction is equivalent to $\frac{2}{4}$?

A. $\frac{2}{3}$

B. $\frac{1}{2}$

C. $\frac{4}{10}$

D. $\frac{20}{100}$

3 Which number makes the statement true?

$$\frac{3}{8} = \frac{6}{\square}$$

A. 8

B. 11

C. 16

D. 24

4 Look at the fraction model below.

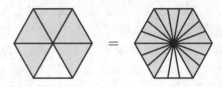

Which equivalent fractions are represented by the model?

A. $\frac{5}{6} = \frac{15}{18}$

B. $\frac{5}{15} = \frac{6}{18}$

C. $\frac{1}{3} = \frac{5}{15}$

D. $\frac{1}{5} = \frac{3}{15}$

5 Baxter wrote an equivalent fraction for $\frac{8}{9}$. The equivalent fraction had a denominator of 72. What number is in the numerator of Baxter's equivalent fraction?

Record your answer and fill in the bubbles. Be sure to use the correct place value.

6 Meredith has two identical pieces of felt. She cut one into thirds. She used two of these pieces to cover a small notebook. She then cut the second piece of felt into sixths.

How many of these pieces would she need to cover a second notebook of the same size?

Record your answer and fill in the bubbles. Be sure to use the correct place value.

0	0	4	.	0	0
⓪	⓪	⓪		⓪	⓪
①	①	①		①	①
②	②	②		②	②
③	③	③		③	③
④	④	④		④	④
⑤	⑤	⑤		⑤	⑤
⑥	⑥	⑥		⑥	⑥
⑦	⑦	⑦		⑦	⑦
⑧	⑧	⑧		⑧	⑧
⑨	⑨	⑨		⑨	⑨

7 Which number makes the statement true?

$$\frac{2}{5} = \frac{\square}{10}$$

A. 2

B. 4

C. 6

D. 8

8 Which fraction is **not** equivalent to $\frac{2}{6}$?

A. $\frac{1}{3}$

B. $\frac{2}{12}$

C. $\frac{4}{12}$

D. $\frac{8}{24}$

9 The model below is shaded to represent a fraction.

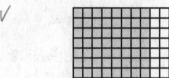

Which fraction is equivalent to the fraction shown?

A. $\frac{8}{100}$

B. $\frac{1}{8}$

C. $\frac{8}{10}$

D. $\frac{80}{20}$

10 Look at the fractions listed below.

$\frac{2}{10}$	$\frac{4}{10}$	$\frac{8}{12}$	$\frac{20}{10}$	$\frac{20}{100}$	$\frac{40}{100}$

Which statement is **not** true?

A. $\frac{8}{12}$ and $\frac{20}{10}$ are equivalent to $\frac{2}{3}$.

B. $\frac{4}{10}$ and $\frac{40}{100}$ are equivalent fractions.

C. $\frac{4}{10}$ and $\frac{40}{100}$ are equivalent to $\frac{2}{5}$.

D. $\frac{2}{10}$ and $\frac{20}{100}$ are equivalent fractions.

Use the information for questions 11–13.

Jeff ordered a small cheese pizza cut into 4 equal slices. His dad ordered a large cheese pizza cut into 8 equal slices.

11 Jeff ate one slice of the small pizza. What fraction represents the part of the small pizza Jeff ate?

A. $\frac{1}{4}$

B. $\frac{3}{4}$

C. $\frac{1}{8}$

D. $\frac{4}{8}$

12 Jeff's dad ate two slices of the large pizza. What fraction represents the part of the large pizza Jeff's dad ate?

A. $\frac{1}{2}$

B. $\frac{3}{4}$

C. $\frac{1}{4}$

D. $\frac{1}{6}$

13 Did Jeff and his dad eat the same amount of pizza?

A. Yes, because they each ate $\frac{1}{4}$ of their pizza.

B. Yes, because 1 slice of a small pizza is the same size as 2 slices of a large pizza.

C. No, because Jeff's dad has more slices of pizza left over.

D. No, because $\frac{1}{4}$ of a small pizza is not the same as $\frac{1}{4}$ of a large pizza.

14 Which fraction is **not** equivalent to $\frac{6}{10}$?

A. $\frac{12}{20}$

B. $\frac{11}{16}$

C. $\frac{9}{15}$

D. $\frac{3}{5}$

4.3(D)

Comparing Fractions

There are many ways you can compare two fractions to find which one is greater. When you compare two fractions, they must be fractions of wholes that are the same size.

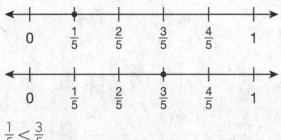

$\frac{1}{5} < \frac{3}{5}$

When the denominators are the same, compare the numerators. The fraction with the greater numerator is the greater fraction.

$\frac{2}{3} > \frac{2}{6}$

When the numerators are the same, compare the denominators. The fraction with the lesser denominator is the greater fraction.

You can compare two fractions when the numerators and denominators are not the same. Find a common numerator or common denominator, then write equivalent fractions and compare. A **common numerator** is a shared multiple of the numerators of two or more fractions. A **common denominator** is a shared multiple of the denominators of two or more fractions. A **multiple** of a given number is the product of that number and any whole number.

To find a common denominator of $\frac{3}{4}$ and $\frac{5}{6}$, look for a common multiple of both denominators.

List the multiples of 4 and 6.

Multiples of 4: 4, 8, 12, 16, …

Multiples of 6: 6, 12, 18, 24, …

A common denominator is 12.

To find a common numerator, look for a common multiple of both numerators.

Example 1

Compare $\frac{1}{2}$ and $\frac{2}{3}$. Use $<$, $>$, or $=$.

Strategy   **Write the fractions with common denominators.**

Step 1   Find a common denominator.

Look at the greater denominator. 3 is not a multiple of 2, so 3 cannot be used as a common denominator.

Find multiples of 3.

Multiples of 3: 3, 6, 9, …

Are any of the multiples of 3 also a multiple of 2?

6 is a multiple of 2 because $2 \times 3 = 6$.

Use 6 as the common denominator.

Step 2   Write equivalent fractions with a denominator of 6.

$2 \times 3 = 6$, so multiply the numerator and denominator of $\frac{1}{2}$ by 3.

$$\frac{1}{2} = \frac{1 \times 3}{2 \times 3}$$
$$= \frac{3}{6}$$

$3 \times 2 = 6$, so multiply the numerator and denominator of $\frac{2}{3}$ by 2.

$$\frac{2}{3} = \frac{2 \times 2}{3 \times 2}$$
$$= \frac{4}{6}$$

Step 3   Compare the fractions.

$$\frac{1}{2} \qquad\qquad \frac{2}{3}$$
$$\downarrow \qquad\qquad\quad \downarrow$$
$$\frac{3}{6} \qquad\qquad\quad \frac{4}{6}$$

The denominators are the same.

Compare the numerators: $3 < 4$.

$$\frac{3}{6} < \frac{4}{6}$$

$$\frac{1}{2} < \frac{2}{3}$$

Step 4   Use models to check.

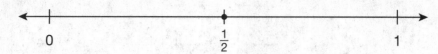

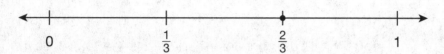

The number lines are the same length.

$\frac{1}{2}$ is closer to zero, farther to the left on the number line,

than $\frac{2}{3}$, so $\frac{1}{2} < \frac{2}{3}$.

Solution $\frac{1}{2} < \frac{2}{3}$

Example 2

Compare $\frac{4}{5}$ and $\frac{6}{10}$. Use $<$, $>$, or $=$.

Strategy   **Write the fractions with common denominators.**

Step 1   Find a common denominator.

Look at the greater denominator. 10 is a multiple of 5. 10 can be used as the common denominator.

Step 2   Multiply to find the equivalent fraction.

$5 \times 2 = 10$, so multiply the numerator and denominator of $\frac{4}{5}$ by 2.

$$\frac{4}{5} = \frac{4 \times 2}{5 \times 2}$$

$$= \frac{8}{10}$$

Step 3   Compare the fractions.

$$\frac{4}{5} \qquad\qquad \frac{6}{10}$$

$$\downarrow \qquad\qquad\quad \downarrow$$

$$\frac{8}{10} \qquad\qquad \frac{6}{10}$$

The denominators, 10, are the same.

Compare the numerators: $8 > 6$.

$$\frac{8}{10} > \frac{6}{10}$$

$$\frac{4}{5} > \frac{6}{10}$$

Step 4   Use models to check.

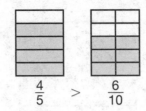

$$\frac{4}{5} \quad > \quad \frac{6}{10}$$

The model for $\frac{4}{5}$ has more area shaded than the same-size model for $\frac{6}{10}$.

Solution $\frac{4}{5} > \frac{6}{10}$

Example 3

Compare $\frac{5}{6}$ and $\frac{3}{4}$. Use $<$, $>$, or $=$.

Strategy   **Write the fractions with common numerators.**

Step 1   Find a common numerator.

Look at the greater numerator. 5 is not a multiple of 3, so 5 cannot be used as a common numerator.

Find multiples of 5.

Multiples of 5: 5, 10, 15, …

Are any of the multiples of 5 also a multiple of 3?

15 is a multiple of 3 because $3 \times 5 = 15$.

Use 15 as the common numerator.

Step 2   Write equivalent fractions with a numerator of 15.

$5 \times 3 = 15$, so multiply the numerator and denominator of $\frac{5}{6}$ by 3.

$$\frac{5}{6} = \frac{5 \times 3}{6 \times 3}$$

$$= \frac{15}{18}$$

$3 \times 5 = 15$, so multiply the numerator and denominator of $\frac{3}{4}$ by 5.

$$\frac{3}{4} = \frac{3 \times 5}{4 \times 5}$$

$$= \frac{15}{20}$$

Step 3 Compare the fractions.

$$\frac{5}{6} \qquad\qquad \frac{3}{4}$$

$$\downarrow \qquad\qquad \downarrow$$

$$\frac{15}{18} \qquad\qquad \frac{15}{20}$$

The numerators are the same.

Compare the denominators: $18 < 20$.

$$\frac{15}{18} > \frac{15}{20}$$

$$\frac{5}{6} > \frac{3}{4}$$

Solution $\frac{5}{6} > \frac{3}{4}$

② COACHED EXAMPLE

Compare $\frac{3}{8}$ and $\frac{7}{12}$. Use <, >, or +.

Find a common denominator.

Multiples of 8: _____, _____, _____, _____, ...

Multiples of 12: _____, _____, _____, _____, ...

A common denominator is _____.

$8 \times$ _____ = _____, so multiply the numerator and denominator of $\frac{3}{8}$ by _____.

$$\frac{3}{8} = \frac{3 \times \boxed{}}{8 \times \boxed{}} = \frac{\boxed{}}{\boxed{}}$$

$12 \times$ _____ = _____, so multiply the numerator and denominator of $\frac{7}{12}$ by _____.

$$\frac{7}{12} = \frac{7 \times \boxed{}}{12 \times \boxed{}} = \frac{\boxed{}}{\boxed{}}$$

The denominators are the same. Compare the numerators: _____ ◯ _____.

Compare the fractions: $\dfrac{\boxed{}}{\boxed{}}$ ◯ $\dfrac{\boxed{}}{\boxed{}}$

$\dfrac{3}{8}$ ◯ $\dfrac{7}{12}$

1 Which number makes the statement true?

$$\frac{\square}{8} > \frac{6}{8}$$

A. 5

B. 7

C. 4

D. 6

2 The models below are shaded to represent two different fractions.

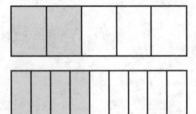

Which statement correctly compares the fractions?

A. $\frac{3}{5} < \frac{5}{9}$

B. $\frac{2}{3} > \frac{4}{5}$

C. $\frac{2}{5} < \frac{4}{9}$

D. $\frac{3}{5} < \frac{2}{5}$

3 Michaela walked $\frac{5}{12}$ mile to her friend's house. Which distance is shorter than $\frac{5}{12}$ mile?

A. $\frac{10}{24}$ mi

B. $\frac{5}{11}$ mi

C. $\frac{3}{8}$ mi

D. $\frac{4}{9}$ mi

4 Which fraction makes both statements true?

$$\square < \frac{4}{11}$$
$$\square > \frac{2}{9}$$

A. $\frac{2}{10}$

B. $\frac{3}{11}$

C. $\frac{4}{10}$

D. $\frac{4}{9}$

5 Benito wrote a true statement shown below. The denominator of one fraction was erased.

$$\frac{3}{5} < \frac{3}{\boxed{}}$$

Which number could Benito have written?

A. 5

B. 7

C. 4

D. 6

6 The table shows the amount of blueberries each child picked.

Child	Amount (in pounds)
Austin	$\frac{2}{5}$
Iona	$\frac{3}{10}$
Laine	$\frac{7}{15}$
Morgan	$\frac{7}{20}$
Raj	$\frac{4}{25}$

Who picked more blueberries than Austin?

A. Iona

B. Laine

C. Morgan

D. Raj

7 Angela has 3 feet each of blue ribbon and red ribbon. She uses $\frac{5}{8}$ of the blue ribbon and $\frac{2}{3}$ of the red ribbon.

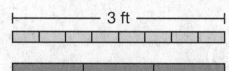

3 ft

Which statement correctly compares the amounts of blue and red ribbon?

A. $\frac{1}{3} > \frac{2}{3}$

B. $\frac{3}{8} < \frac{1}{3}$

C. $\frac{5}{8} < \frac{3}{8}$

D. $\frac{2}{3} > \frac{5}{8}$

8 Which statement is true?

A. $\frac{5}{12} > \frac{5}{11}$

B. $\frac{5}{12} < \frac{4}{12}$

C. $\frac{4}{11} < \frac{4}{12}$

D. $\frac{5}{11} > \frac{4}{11}$

9 Which fraction is less than $\frac{3}{12}$?

    A. $\frac{3}{15}$

    B. $\frac{3}{8}$

    C. $\frac{2}{6}$

    D. $\frac{1}{4}$

10 The table shows the distance from Erin's house to places in her neighborhood.

Place	Distance (in miles)
School	$\frac{7}{8}$
Park	$\frac{5}{6}$
Mall	$\frac{5}{7}$
Grocery store	$\frac{3}{4}$

Which place is farthest from Erin's house?

    A. School

    B. Park

    C. Mall

    D. Grocery store

11 Alfonso buys $\frac{1}{2}$ pound of raisins, $\frac{2}{5}$ pound of walnuts, $\frac{1}{3}$ pound of dried cranberries, and $\frac{4}{9}$ pound of almonds. Which statement is true?

    A. Alfonso buys more walnuts than raisins.

    B. Alfonso buys more dried cranberries than walnuts.

    C. Alfonso buys more almonds than raisins.

    D. Alfonso buys more almonds than walnuts.

12 What whole number makes both statements true?

$$\frac{\square}{8} < \frac{3}{4}$$

$$\frac{\square}{12} > \frac{3}{8}$$

Record your answer and fill in the bubbles. Be sure to use the correct place value.

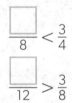

1 The population of a city is nine hundred eight thousand, seven hundred sixty-three. What is this number in standard form?

A 98,736

B 980,763

C 987,063

D 908,763

2 A mattress store had $236,547 in sales over the summer. What is 236,547 rounded to the nearest ten thousand?

F 230,000

G 236,000

H 237,000

J 240,000

3 Marlene walks 0.68 mile to get to her friend's house. Which fraction is equivalent to 0.68?

A $\dfrac{680}{100}$

B $\dfrac{68}{100}$

C $\dfrac{0.68}{100}$

D $\dfrac{68}{10}$

4 The place-value chart shows a decimal number.

Tens	Ones	.	Tenths	Hundredths
7	0	.	8	2

Which is the number in expanded form?

F $70 \times 10 + 8 \times \dfrac{1}{10} + 2 \times \dfrac{1}{100}$

G $7 \times 10 + 8 \times \dfrac{1}{10} + 2 \times \dfrac{1}{100}$

H $7 \times 1 + 8 \times \dfrac{1}{10} + 2 \times \dfrac{1}{100}$

J $7 \times 10 + 8 \times 1 + 2 \times \dfrac{1}{10}$

5 Each model below represents a decimal.

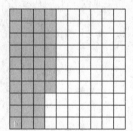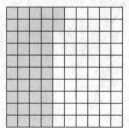

Which statement correctly compares the decimals shown?

A 0.33 > 0.48

B 0.37 > 0.42

C 0.73 < 0.56

D 0.37 < 0.42

6 Which is one way to decompose the fraction model shown below?

| $\frac{1}{6}$ | $\frac{1}{6}$ | $\frac{1}{6}$ | $\frac{1}{6}$ | $\frac{1}{6}$ | $\frac{1}{6}$ |

F $\frac{2}{3} + \frac{3}{3}$

G $\frac{1}{6} + \frac{3}{6}$

H $\frac{2}{6} + \frac{3}{6}$

J $\frac{2}{6} + \frac{4}{6}$

7 Which number makes the statement true?

$$\frac{3}{4} = \frac{6}{\square}$$

A 8

B 12

C 16

D 20

8 Which comparison statement is true?

F $8,343,356 < 8,235,798$

G $8,443,356 > 8,445,123$

H $8,441,356 > 8,439,769$

J $8,543,200 < 8,543,199$

9 For which number is the digit in the thousands place $\frac{1}{10}$ the value of the digit in the ten thousands place?

A 663,388

B 83,663

C 33,688

D 36,688

10 Write the amount of money shown as a decimal.

Record your answer and fill in the bubbles. Be sure to use the correct place value.

0	0	0		0	0
1	1	1		1	1
2	2	2		2	2
3	3	3		3	3
4	4	4		4	4
5	5	5		5	5
6	6	6		6	6
7	7	7		7	7
8	8	8		8	8
9	9	9		9	9

11 The attendance at a hockey game rounded to the nearest thousand is 22,000. Which number could be the actual attendance at the game?

Ⓐ 21,540

B 22,504

C 20,997

D 21,489

12 The models below are shaded to represent two different fractions.

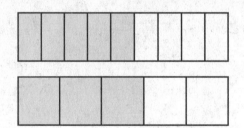

Which statement correctly compares the fractions?

Ⓕ $\frac{3}{5} > \frac{5}{9}$

G $\frac{2}{3} > \frac{4}{5}$

H $\frac{4}{9} < \frac{2}{5}$

J $\frac{5}{9} < \frac{4}{9}$

13 Tanner and his friends play in a pinball tournament. The table shows their final scores.

Player	Score
Alexa	25,643,895
Leo	24,133,395
Shannon	25,043,030
Tanner	25,023,144
Yuko	25,472,803

Which list shows all the friends who scored higher than Tanner?

A Alexa, Leo

B Alexa, Leo, Yuko

Ⓒ Alexa, Yuko

D Alexa, Shannon, Yuko

14 Ian weighs one hundred thirty-eight and eight hundredths pounds. Which shows his weight in standard form?

Ⓕ 138.08 pounds

G 138.8 pounds

H 130.38 pounds

J 130.08 pounds

15 Carla drew point *C* on the number line below.

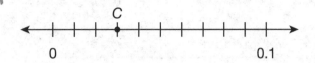

What number is represented by point *C*?

Record your answer and fill in the bubbles. Be sure to use the correct place value.

16 Which list correctly shows 0.57, 0.08, 0.5, and 0.43 ordered from least to greatest?

F   0.5, 0.08, 0.43, 0.47

G   0.43, 0.5, 0.57, 0.08

H   0.08, 0.43, 0.57, 0.5

J   0.08, 0.43, 0.5, 0.57

17 Use the model of $\frac{3}{8}$ to help answer the question.

Which of the following shows the fraction decomposed into unit fractions?

A $\frac{1}{8} + \frac{1}{8}$

B $\frac{1}{8} + \frac{1}{8} + \frac{1}{8}$

C $\frac{1}{8} + \frac{1}{8} + \frac{1}{8} + \frac{1}{8}$

D $\frac{1}{8} + \frac{1}{8} + \frac{1}{8} + \frac{1}{8} + \frac{1}{8}$

18 How is the value of 5 in 234,530 related to the value of 5 in 305,312?

F   The value of 5 in 234,530 is the same as the value of 5 in 305,312.

G   The value of 5 in 234,530 is 10 times the value of 5 in 305,312.

H   The value of 5 in 234,530 is $\frac{1}{10}$ the value of 5 in 305,312.

J   The value of 5 in 234,530 is 100 times the value of 5 in 305,312.

19 The weekend attendance of the county fair was 235,982. Which of the following has the same value as 235,982?

A 200,000 + 30,000 + 5,000 + 900 + 80

B 200,000 + 30,000 + 5,000 + 900 + 80 + 2

C 200,000 + 30,000 + 900 + 80 + 2

D 200,000 + 3,000 + 500 + 98 + 2

20 Use the place-value chart to help answer the question.

Ones	.	Tenths	Hundredths
	.		
	.		
	.		
	.		

The weights of four apples are 0.41 pound, 0.38 pound, 0.44 pound, and 0.33 pound. Which list shows the weights from greatest to least?

F 0.41, 0.44, 0.38, 0.33

G 0.44, 0.41, 0.38, 0.33

H 0.38, 0.33, 0.44, 0.41

J 0.38, 0.44, 0.33, 0.41

21 Kelsi draws the model to represent a decimal.

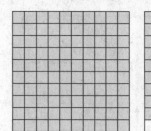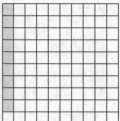

Which decimal does the model represent?

A 1.91

B 0.19

C 1.09

D 1.9

22 Warren ate $\frac{2}{6}$ of his hotdog. Which fraction is equivalent to $\frac{2}{6}$?

F $\frac{6}{10}$

G $\frac{4}{8}$

H $\frac{1}{3}$

J $\frac{3}{12}$

23 The table shows the weight of each child's race car.

Car	Weight (pounds)
Sonia's car	$\frac{1}{3}$
Regan's car	$\frac{3}{16}$
Quincy's car	$\frac{3}{12}$
Petra's car	$\frac{3}{8}$
Oliver's car	$\frac{1}{4}$

Which car weighed less than Oliver's car?

A Sonia's car

B Regan's car

C Quincy's car

D Petra's car

24 The population of Jacksonville is 836,507. What is the population rounded to the nearest hundred thousand?

F 900,000

G 850,000

H 840,000

J 800,000

25 What number is represented by point *P* on the number line?

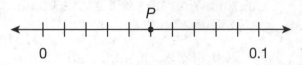

A $\frac{5}{10}$

B $\frac{55}{10}$

C $\frac{55}{100}$

D $\frac{5}{100}$

26 What decimal is equivalent to $\frac{67}{100}$?

Record your answer and fill in the bubbles. Be sure to use the correct place value.

CHAPTER 2

Computations and Algebraic Relationships

4.3(E), 4.3(F)

Adding and Subtracting Fractions

1 GETTING THE IDEA

Adding is joining parts.

To add $\frac{1}{3} + \frac{1}{3}$, join the two parts.

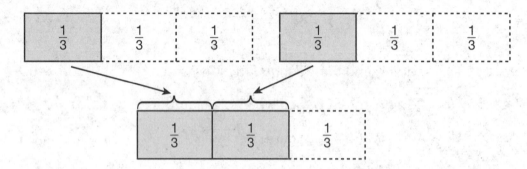

$\frac{1}{3} + \frac{1}{3} = \frac{2}{3}$

Subtracting is separating into parts.

To subtract $\frac{3}{4} - \frac{2}{4}$, separate $\frac{3}{4}$ into parts.

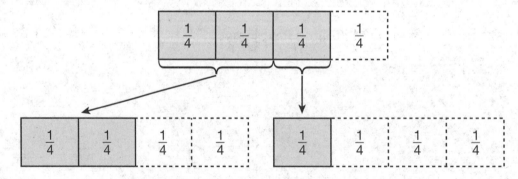

$\frac{3}{4} - \frac{2}{4} = \frac{1}{4}$

Example 1

Add $\frac{1}{5} + \frac{3}{5}$.

Strategy   Use fraction strips to model the sum.

Step 1   Model each fraction.

| $\frac{1}{5}$ | $\frac{1}{5}$ | $\frac{1}{5}$ | $\frac{1}{5}$ | $\frac{1}{5}$ |

| $\frac{1}{5}$ | $\frac{1}{5}$ | $\frac{1}{5}$ | $\frac{1}{5}$ | $\frac{1}{5}$ |

Step 2   Join the two groups to model the sum.

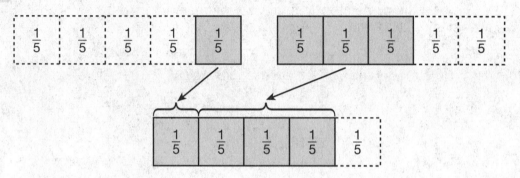

Step 3   Add the numerators to find the sum.

$$\frac{1}{5} + \frac{3}{5} = \frac{4}{5}$$

The model also shows $\frac{4}{5}$. The sum is $\frac{4}{5}$.

Solution $\frac{1}{5} + \frac{3}{5} = \frac{4}{5}$

Example 2

Subtract $\frac{5}{6} - \frac{1}{6}$.

Strategy   Use fraction strips.

Step 1   Model the first fraction.

| $\frac{1}{6}$ | $\frac{1}{6}$ | $\frac{1}{6}$ | $\frac{1}{6}$ | $\frac{1}{6}$ | $\frac{1}{6}$ |

Step 2   Separate into two groups.

Put $\frac{1}{6}$ in one group.

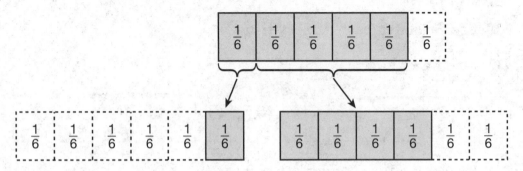

Step 3   Subtract the numerators to find the difference.

$$\frac{5}{6} - \frac{1}{6} = \frac{4}{6}$$

The model shows $\frac{4}{6}$ left after separating out $\frac{1}{6}$. The difference is $\frac{4}{6}$.

Solution $\frac{5}{6} - \frac{1}{6} = \frac{4}{6}$

Example 3

Add $\frac{3}{10} + \frac{2}{10}$.

Strategy   **Use a number line.**

Step 1   Draw and label a number line.

The denominator of the fractions is 10. Divide one whole into ten parts.

Label each part on the number line.

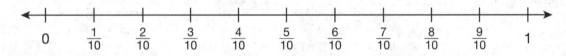

Step 2   Locate the first fraction on the number line.

Start at 0 and draw a line to $\frac{3}{10}$.

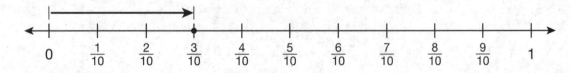

Step 3   Move the distance of the second fraction on the number line.

The second fraction is $\frac{2}{10}$, so move $\frac{2}{10}$ farther on the number line.

$\frac{3}{10} + \frac{2}{10}$

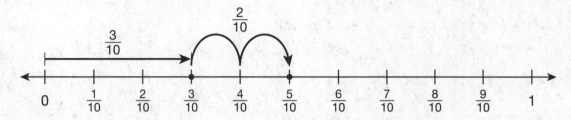

Step 4   Find the sum on the number line.

The sum is the endpoint. When you added $\frac{2}{10}$ more, you ended on $\frac{5}{10}$.

$\frac{3}{10} + \frac{2}{10} = \frac{5}{10}$

Solution $\frac{3}{10} + \frac{2}{10} = \frac{5}{10}$

A **benchmark fraction** is a common fraction that can be used to estimate. You can use benchmark fractions such as $\frac{1}{4}$, $\frac{1}{2}$, and $\frac{3}{4}$ to check the reasonableness of sums and differences.

Example 4

Margot writes $\frac{2}{9} + \frac{5}{9} = \frac{7}{18}$. Is her answer reasonable?

Strategy   Use benchmark fractions.

Step 1   Estimate the value of $\frac{2}{9}$ and $\frac{5}{9}$ using benchmark fractions.

Use number lines to compare $\frac{2}{9}$ and $\frac{5}{9}$ to benchmark fractions.

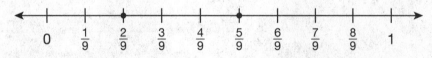

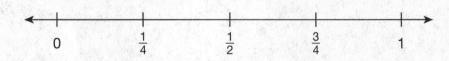

$\frac{2}{9}$ is close to $\frac{1}{4}$. $\frac{5}{9}$ is close to $\frac{1}{2}$.

Step 2 Compare the sum $\frac{7}{18}$ to the sum of the benchmark fractions.

$\frac{7}{18}$ is less than $\frac{1}{2}$ because 7 is less than half of 18.

$\frac{1}{4} + \frac{1}{2}$ must be greater than $\frac{1}{2}$ since one of the addends is $\frac{1}{2}$.

Solution Margot's answer is not reasonable.

Example 5

Uri writes $\frac{8}{14} - \frac{3}{20} = \frac{1}{2}$. Is his answer reasonable?

Strategy Use benchmark fractions.

Step 1 Find benchmark fractions that are close to Uri's fractions.

$\frac{8}{14}$ is about $\frac{1}{2}$ because 8 is a little more than half of 14.

$\frac{3}{20}$ is about $\frac{1}{4}$ because 3 is a little less than a quarter of 20.

Step 2 Compare Uri's difference to the difference of the benchmark fractions.

$$\frac{8}{14} \qquad - \qquad \frac{3}{20} \qquad = \qquad \frac{1}{2}$$

fraction about $\frac{1}{2}$ $\quad - \quad$ fraction about $\frac{1}{4}$ $\quad = \quad$ fraction less than $\frac{1}{2}$

Uri's answer is too great.

Solution Uri's answer is not reasonable.

Subtract $\frac{7}{8} - \frac{3}{8}$.

Draw a fraction strip model to show $\frac{7}{8}$.

To model $\frac{7}{8}$, I shade _____ parts out of _____.

$\frac{1}{8}$	$\frac{1}{8}$	$\frac{1}{8}$	$\frac{1}{8}$	$\frac{1}{8}$	$\frac{1}{8}$	$\frac{1}{8}$	$\frac{1}{8}$

Separate $\frac{7}{8}$ into _____ groups.

Draw two more models. To subtract $\frac{3}{8}$, shade _____ parts of the first model.

Shade the second model so that the two models combined have _____ parts shaded.

$\frac{1}{8}$	$\frac{1}{8}$	$\frac{1}{8}$	$\frac{1}{8}$	$\frac{1}{8}$	$\frac{1}{8}$	$\frac{1}{8}$	$\frac{1}{8}$

$\frac{1}{8}$	$\frac{1}{8}$	$\frac{1}{8}$	$\frac{1}{8}$	$\frac{1}{8}$	$\frac{1}{8}$	$\frac{1}{8}$	$\frac{1}{8}$

The model shows _____ left after separating out _____.

Record the difference. Subtract the _____ to find the difference.

$$\frac{7}{8} - \frac{3}{8} = \frac{\square}{\square}$$

1 Use the number line to answer the question.

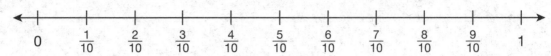

Jason walked $\frac{6}{10}$ mile from his house to the playground. He then walked $\frac{2}{10}$ mile from the playground to the library. How far did Jason walk?

A. $\frac{4}{10}$ mile

B. $\frac{6}{10}$ mile

C. $\frac{7}{10}$ mile

D. $\frac{8}{10}$ mile

2 Use the model to answer the question.

$\frac{1}{6}$	$\frac{1}{6}$	$\frac{1}{6}$	$\frac{1}{6}$	$\frac{1}{6}$	$\frac{1}{6}$

What is $\frac{4}{6} + \frac{1}{6}$?

A. $\frac{3}{6}$

B. $\frac{5}{6}$

C. $\frac{3}{12}$

D. $\frac{5}{12}$

3 Anya models the sum $\frac{3}{8} + \frac{2}{8}$ with fraction strips. Which model shows the sum?

A.
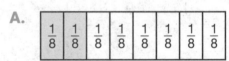

$\frac{1}{8}$	$\frac{1}{8}$	$\frac{1}{8}$	$\frac{1}{8}$	$\frac{1}{8}$	$\frac{1}{8}$	$\frac{1}{8}$	$\frac{1}{8}$

B.

$\frac{1}{8}$	$\frac{1}{8}$	$\frac{1}{8}$	$\frac{1}{8}$	$\frac{1}{8}$	$\frac{1}{8}$	$\frac{1}{8}$	$\frac{1}{8}$

C.

$\frac{1}{8}$	$\frac{1}{8}$	$\frac{1}{8}$	$\frac{1}{8}$	$\frac{1}{8}$	$\frac{1}{8}$	$\frac{1}{8}$	$\frac{1}{8}$

D.

$\frac{1}{8}$	$\frac{1}{8}$	$\frac{1}{8}$	$\frac{1}{8}$	$\frac{1}{8}$	$\frac{1}{8}$	$\frac{1}{8}$	$\frac{1}{8}$

4 Use the number line to answer the question.

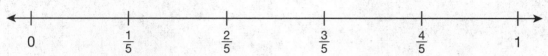

Which expression is equal to $\frac{3}{5}$?

A. $\frac{4}{5} - \frac{1}{5}$

B. $\frac{4}{5} + \frac{1}{5}$

C. $\frac{3}{5} + \frac{1}{5}$

D. $\frac{3}{5} - \frac{1}{5}$

---

5 Use the model to answer the question.

$\frac{1}{8}$	$\frac{1}{8}$	$\frac{1}{8}$	$\frac{1}{8}$	$\frac{1}{8}$	$\frac{1}{8}$	$\frac{1}{8}$	$\frac{1}{8}$

Tanika has $\frac{5}{8}$ cup of flour. She uses $\frac{2}{8}$ cup of flour to make pancakes. How much flour does she have left?

A. $\frac{7}{8}$ cup

B. $\frac{5}{8}$ cup

C. $\frac{3}{8}$ cup

D. $\frac{2}{8}$ cup

6 Which statement best describes $\frac{6}{12} + \frac{5}{12}$?

A. The sum is about $\frac{1}{4}$.

B. The sum is about $\frac{1}{2}$.

C. The sum is about $\frac{3}{4}$.

D. The sum is about 1.

7 Use the number lines to help answer the question.

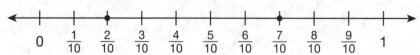

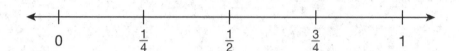

Which statement is correct?

A. $\frac{7}{10} - \frac{2}{10}$ is close to 0.

B. $\frac{7}{10} - \frac{2}{10}$ is close to $\frac{1}{4}$.

C. $\frac{7}{10} - \frac{2}{10}$ is close to $\frac{1}{2}$.

D. $\frac{7}{10} - \frac{2}{10}$ is close to $\frac{3}{4}$.

---

8 Harvey buys $\frac{1}{8}$ pound of walnuts and $\frac{5}{8}$ pound of almonds. How many total pounds of nuts did he buy?

A. $\frac{6}{8}$ pound

B. $\frac{5}{8}$ pound

C. $\frac{4}{8}$ pound

D. $\frac{3}{8}$ pound

9 What number makes the equation true?

$$\frac{6}{12} - \frac{4}{12} = \frac{\square}{12}$$

Record your answer and fill in the bubbles. Be sure to use the correct place value.

			.		
⓪	⓪	⓪		⓪	⓪
①	①	①		①	①
②	②	②		②	②
③	③	③		③	③
④	④	④		④	④
⑤	⑤	⑤		⑤	⑤
⑥	⑥	⑥		⑥	⑥
⑦	⑦	⑦		⑦	⑦
⑧	⑧	⑧		⑧	⑧
⑨	⑨	⑨		⑨	⑨

Adding and Subtracting Whole Numbers

1 GETTING THE IDEA

Use place value to line up numbers when you add or subtract. Then add or subtract each place from right to left.

The numbers you add are **addends**. The total number is called the **sum**.

$$
\begin{array}{r}
17{,}643 \\
+\ 2{,}155 \\
\hline
19{,}798
\end{array}
\quad
\begin{array}{l}
\text{addend} \\
\text{addend} \\
\text{sum}
\end{array}
$$

Example 1

Mr. Washington's fourth-grade class recycled 3,622 bottles in March and 4,185 bottles in April. How many bottles did they recycle in March and April?

Strategy   Add using place value.

Step 1   Write the numbers in a column. Line up the digits by place value.

$$
\begin{array}{r}
3{,}622 \\
+\ 4{,}185
\end{array}
$$

Step 2   Add the digits in the ones place.

$$
\begin{array}{r}
3{,}622 \\
+\ 4{,}185 \\
\hline
7
\end{array}
$$
   $2 + 5 = 7$
   Write the 7 in the sum below the ones place.

Step 3 Add the digits in the tens place.

$$
\begin{array}{r}
1 \\
3{,}622 \\
+\ 4{,}185 \\
\hline
\mathbf{0}7
\end{array}
$$

2 tens + 8 tens = 10 tens. 10 tens = 100, so regroup 10 tens as 1 hundred.

Write 0 tens in the sum. Write 1 hundred above the digits in the hundreds place.

Step 4 Add the digits in the hundreds place.

$$
\begin{array}{r}
1 \\
3{,}622 \\
+\ 4{,}185 \\
\hline
\mathbf{8}07
\end{array}
$$

1 hundred + 6 hundreds + 1 hundred = 8 hundreds

Write 8 hundreds in the sum.

Step 5 Add the digits in the thousands place.

$$
\begin{array}{r}
1 \\
3{,}622 \\
+\ 4{,}185 \\
\hline
\mathbf{7}{,}807
\end{array}
$$

3 thousands + 4 thousands = 7 thousands

Write 7 in the thousands place.

Write a comma between the thousands and hundreds places.

Solution Mr. Washington's class recycled 7,807 bottles in March and April.

Example 2

A conductor on a train traveled 12,384 miles on one trip. On her next trip, she traveled 9,472 miles. How far did she travel on the two trips?

Strategy Add using place value.

Step 1 Line up the digits by place value.

$$12{,}384$$
$$+\ 9{,}472$$

Step 2 Add the numbers in each place. Start with the ones place. Regroup if needed.

Add ones.	Add tens. Regroup.	Add hundreds.	Add thousands. Regroup.	Add ten thousands.
12,384	¹ 12,384	¹ 12,384	¹ ¹ 12,384	¹ ¹ 12,384
+ 9,472	+ 9,472	+ 9,472	+ 9,472	+ 9,472
6	**5**6	**8**56	**1**,856	**2**1,856

Solution The conductor traveled 21,856 miles on the two trips.

To subtract, line up digits by place value. Then subtract from right to left.

The number you subtract from is called the **minuend**. The number you subtract is called the **subtrahend**. The result is called the **difference**.

57,206	minuend
− 8,715	subtrahend
48,491	difference

Example 3

There are 5,742 books in the town library. There are 2,475 children's books. How many books in the library are not children's books?

Strategy   Subtract using place value.

Step 1   Line up the digits by place value.

$$
\begin{array}{r}
5{,}742 \\
-\ 2{,}475 \\
\end{array}
$$

Step 2   Subtract the ones digits.

$$
\begin{array}{r}
^{3\ 12} \\
5{,}7\cancel{4}\cancel{2} \\
-\ 2{,}475 \\
\hline
7 \\
\end{array}
$$

You cannot subtract 5 ones from 2, so regroup 1 ten as 10 ones.
10 + 2 = 12 ones
12 − 5 = 7
Write 7 in the ones place in the difference.

Step 3   Subtract the tens.

$$
\begin{array}{r}
^{13} \\
^{6\ \cancel{3}\ 12} \\
5{,}\cancel{7}\ \cancel{4}\ \cancel{2} \\
-\ 2{,}475 \\
\hline
67 \\
\end{array}
$$

7 tens cannot be subtracted from 3 tens, so regroup 1 hundred as 10 tens.
13 tens − 7 tens = 6 tens
Write 6 in the tens place.

Step 4   Subtract hundreds. Then subtract thousands.

$$
\begin{array}{r}
^{13} \\
^{6\ \cancel{3}\ 12} \\
\mathbf{5{,}}\cancel{7}\ \cancel{4}\ \cancel{2} \\
-\ \mathbf{2{,}4}\,75 \\
\hline
\mathbf{3{,}2}\,67 \\
\end{array}
$$

6 hundreds − 4 hundreds = 2 hundreds. Write 2 in the hundreds place.
5 thousands − 2 thousands = 3 thousands. Write 3 in the thousands place.

Step 5   Use addition to check your answer.

Add the difference and the subtrahend. If the sum is the minuend, your answer is correct.

3,267	difference
+ 2,475	subtrahend
5,742	minuend The answer is correct.

Solution   **3,267 books in the library are not children's books.**

Pet Food Palace received a shipment of 18,260 cans of pet food. There are 7,335 cans of cat food. The rest is dog food. How many cans of dog food are there?

To find the number of cans of dog food, I will _____.

First, I will line up the two numbers by _____.

Then I will subtract starting with the _____ place.

I can _____ if the digit I need to subtract from is less than the digit I need to subtract.

To check my answer, I can find the sum of my answer and the _____.

There are _____ cans of dog food.

1 A flight attendant flew 12,895 miles one week. The next week, he flew 13,687 miles. How many miles did he fly during the two weeks?

    A. 25,572 miles

    B. 26,572 miles

    C. 26,482 miles

    D. 26,582 miles

2 A video game maker sold 24,567 copies of their first game, Final Shark. Their second game, Little Dragon, sold 32,856 copies. How many more copies of Little Dragon were sold than Final Shark?

    A. 12,311

    B. 8,289

    C. 8,291

    D. 7,281

3 Emerald Park is a rectangle that is 6,335 feet long. Its width is 1,423 feet less than its length. What is its width?

    A. 4,912 feet

    B. 5,912 feet

    C. 7,758 feet

    D. 5,112 feet

Use the information and table for questions 4 and 5.

Three bridges are being built in Benton. The table shows the number of bolts needed for each bridge.

Bridge	Number of Bolts
Deer Canyon Bridge	8,415
Badger Bridge	44,361
Lazy River Bridge	35,232

4 How many bolts are needed for all three bridges?

    A. 87,008

    B. 77,908

    C. 88,008

    D. 88,908

5 How many more bolts are needed for Badger Bridge than for Deer Canyon Bridge?

    A. 35,954

    B. 35,946

    C. 35,956

    D. 36,956

Use the information and table for questions 6–9.

The table shows the scores for the top four players in the Dodging Dragons Tournament.

Player	Game 1	Game 2
Chandra	8,915	12,023
Vivian	11,315	9,584
Molly	10,522	10,591
Paola	9,886	10,985

6 How many more points did Chandra score than Vivian in Game 2?

   A. 2,439

   B. 2,441

   C. 2,561

   D. 3,439

7 How many more points did Paola score in Game 2 than in Game 1?

   A. 199

   B. 1,199

   C. 1,101

   D. 1,099

8 The winner of the tournament is the person with the highest total score for the two games. Who won?

   A. Chandra

   B. Vivian

   C. Molly

   D. Paola

9 Which player's score in Game 2 increased the most from Game 1?

   A. Chandra

   B. Vivian

   C. Molly

   D. Paola

10 Kelly starts with 1,200 toothpicks. She used 485 to build a model of a train and 440 to build a model of an airplane. How many toothpicks does she have left over?

Record your answer and fill in the bubbles. Be sure to use the correct place value.

Use the information and table for questions 11–15.

The table shows the number of cans collected for recycling in April and May by three classes.

Class	April	May
Mr. Allen's class	3,822	5,223
Ms. Perez's class	4,513	4,522
Ms. Lee's class	5,190	3,905

11. How many cans were collected by Ms. Perez's class in April and May?

   A. 9,135
   B. 8,035
   C. 9,035
   D. 8,135

12. How many more cans did Mr. Allen's class collect in May than in April?

   A. 1,401
   B. 2,401
   C. 1,409
   D. 2,601

13. How many cans were collected in April altogether?

   A. 13,425
   B. 12,425
   C. 12,525
   D. 13,525

14. How many cans were collected in May altogether?

   A. 14,650
   B. 13,650
   C. 13,640
   D. 12,640

15. How many more cans were collected in May than in April?

   A. 235
   B. 215
   C. 125
   D. 115

16. Mr. Silver went on a three-day business trip. He traveled 235 miles the first day, 211 miles the second day, and 109 miles the third day. How many miles did he travel on his business trip?

   Record your answer and fill in the bubbles. Be sure to use the correct place value.

Adding and Subtracting Decimals

You can use place-value models to add and subtract decimals.

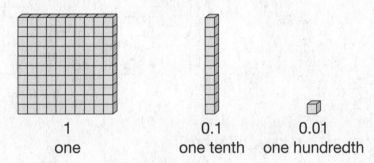

| 1 | 0.1 | 0.01 |
| one | one tenth | one hundredth |

You can combine ones, tenths, and hundredths to show addition. You can remove hundredths, tenths, and ones from a model to show subtraction.

Example 1

Elsa rode her bicycle 1.28 kilometers to the park. She rode 2.55 kilometers around the park. How many kilometers did Elsa ride her bicycle?

Strategy   **Use models to add.**

Step 1   Write a problem you can solve.

You want to know how many kilometers Elsa rode in all.
Add to find the total.

1.28 + 2.55

Step 2   Add the hundredths.

8 + 5 = 13 hundredths

Regroup 13 hundredths as
1 tenth 3 hundredths.

$$\begin{array}{r} \overset{1}{}1.2\mathbf{8} \\ +\ 2.5\mathbf{5} \\ \hline \mathbf{3} \end{array}$$

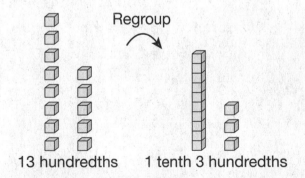

Regroup

13 hundredths   1 tenth 3 hundredths

Step 3	Add the tenths. Remember to add the regrouped tenth.

$$1 + 2 + 5 = 8 \text{ tenths}$$

Write the decimal point in the sum.

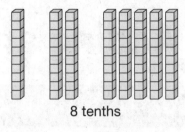
8 tenths

$$
\begin{array}{r}
\overset{1}{} \\
1.\mathbf{2}8 \\
+\ 2.\mathbf{5}5 \\
\hline
.\mathbf{8}3
\end{array}
$$

Step 4	Add the ones.

$$1 + 2 = 3 \text{ ones}$$

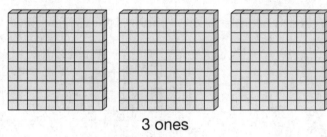
3 ones

$$
\begin{array}{r}
\overset{1}{} \\
\mathbf{1}.28 \\
+\ \mathbf{2}.55 \\
\hline
\mathbf{3}.83
\end{array}
$$

Solution   Elsa rode her bicycle 3.83 kilometers.

Example 2

Emilio bought cheddar cheese and Swiss cheese to make grilled cheese sandwiches. The cheddar weighed 4.56 pounds. The Swiss weighed 2.79 pounds. How many more pounds did the cheddar cheese weigh than the Swiss cheese?

Strategy   **Use models to subtract.**

Step 1	Write a problem you can solve.

You want to know how many more pounds the cheddar cheese weighed than the Swiss cheese. Subtract to find how much more.

$$4.56 - 2.79$$

Step 2	Subtract the hundredths.

There are not enough hundredths to subtract 9.
Regroup 1 tenth as 10 hundredths.

$$16 - 9 = 7 \text{ hundredths}$$

$$
\begin{array}{r}
4\,\mathbf{16} \\
4.5\mathbf{6} \\
-\ 2.7\mathbf{9} \\
\hline
\mathbf{7}
\end{array}
$$

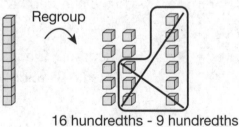
16 hundredths - 9 hundredths

Step 3   Subtract the tenths.

There are not enough tenths to subtract 7 tenths.
Regroup 1 whole as 10 tenths.

14 − 7 = 7 tenths

Write the decimal point in the difference.

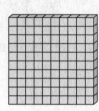

$$
\begin{array}{r}
\mathbf{3}\ \cancel{4}16 \\
\mathbf{4.5}\cancel{6} \\
-\ 2.\mathbf{7}9 \\
\hline
.\mathbf{7}7
\end{array}
$$

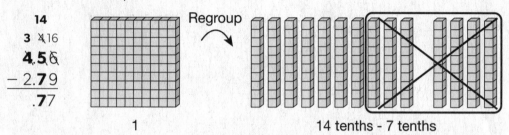

Regroup

1   14 tenths - 7 tenths

Step 4   Subtract the ones.

3 − 2 = 1 one

$$
\begin{array}{r}
1\ 4 \\
\mathbf{3}\ \cancel{4}\ 1\cancel{6} \\
4.5\cancel{6} \\
-\ \mathbf{2}.79 \\
\hline
\mathbf{1}.77
\end{array}
$$

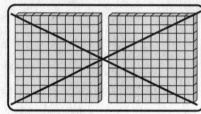

3 ones - 2 ones

Step 5   Check the answer using addition.

Add the difference to 2.79. The sum should be 4.56.

$$
\begin{array}{r}
1\ 1 \\
1.77 \\
+\ 2.79 \\
\hline
4.56
\end{array}
$$

The sum is 4.56. The answer is correct.

Solution   **The cheddar cheese weighed 1.77 pounds more than the Swiss cheese.**

Example 3

Subtract 40 − 15.47.

Strategy   **Use place value to subtract.**

Step 1   Write the problem in vertical form.

Write 40 as an equivalent decimal in hundredths.

40 = 40.00

Align the decimal points.

```
  40.00
− 15.47
```

Step 2   Subtract the hundredths.

You cannot subtract 7 hundredths from 0 hundredths.

Regroup 1 ten as 10 ones. Record 3 in the tens place.
Record 10 in the ones place.

Regroup 1 one as 10 tenths. Record 9 in the ones place.
Record 10 in the tenths place.

Regroup 1 tenth as 10 hundredths. Record 9 in the tenths place.
Record 10 in the hundredths place.

10 − 7 = 3 hundredths

```
    9 9
  3 10 10 10
  4 0.0 0
 − 1 5.4 7
       . 3
```

Step 3   Subtract the tenths.

9 − 4 = 5 tenths

```
    9 9
  3 10 10 10
  4 0.0 0
 − 1 5.4 7
      .5 3
```

Step 4   Subtract the ones.

$$9 - 5 = 4 \text{ ones}$$

```
      9 9
   3 10 10 10
   4 0 . 0 0
 -  1 5 . 4 7
        4 . 5 3
```

Step 5   Subtract the tens.

$$3 - 1 = 2 \text{ tens}$$

```
      9 9
   3 10 10 10
   4 0 . 0 0
 -  1 5 . 4 7
      2 4 . 5 3
```

Step 6   Check the answer using addition.

```
   1 1 1
   24.53
 + 15.47
   40.00
```

The sum is 40.00. The answer is correct.

Solution   **40 − 15.47 = 24.53**

Maya bought a scarf and hat. The scarf cost $32.18. The hat cost $19.86. How much did Maya pay in all for the scarf and hat?

Write a problem you can solve.

_____ + _____ = ☐

Write the problem in vertical form.

☐☐.☐☐
+ ☐☐.☐☐
‾‾‾‾‾‾‾‾‾‾
☐☐.☐☐

First, I add the _____.

_____ + _____ = _____

Regroup _____ as _____.

Second, I add the _____.

_____ + _____ + _____ = _____

Regroup _____ as _____.

Third, I add the _____.

_____ + _____ + _____ = _____

Regroup _____ as _____.

Fourth, I add the _____.

_____ + _____ + _____ = _____

Write _____ in the sum.

I can use _____ to check the answer.

☐☐.☐☐
− ☐☐.☐☐
‾‾‾‾‾‾‾‾‾‾
☐☐.☐☐

Maya paid _____ in all for the scarf and hat.

LESSON PRACTICE

1 Use the models to answer the question.

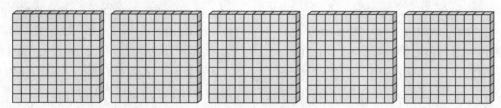

Paul ran 1.27 kilometers. He then ran 2.94 kilometers. How many kilometers did Paul run in all?

A. 3.11 kilometers

B. 3.21 kilometers

C. 4.11 kilometers

D. 4.21 kilometers

Use the information for questions 2 and 3.

Nami is wrapping packages with green and pink ribbon. She has 11.85 meters of green ribbon and 13.4 meters of pink ribbon.

2 How many meters of ribbon does Nami have in all?

A. 25.25 meters

B. 35.25 meters

C. 24.89 meters

D. 24.25 meters

3 How many more meters of pink ribbon does Nami have than green ribbon?

A. 2.45 meters

B. 1.55 meters

C. 1.65 meters

D. 1.19 meters

4 Marcus buys a CD that costs $14.28. He pays for the CD with a $20 bill. Write the amount of change Marcus receives as a decimal.

Record your answer and fill in the bubbles. Be sure to use the correct place value.

			.		
⓪	⓪	⓪		⓪	⓪
①	①	①		①	①
②	②	②		②	②
③	③	③		③	③
④	④	④		④	④
⑤	⑤	⑤		⑤	⑤
⑥	⑥	⑥		⑥	⑥
⑦	⑦	⑦		⑦	⑦
⑧	⑧	⑧		⑧	⑧
⑨	⑨	⑨		⑨	⑨

5 Emily has 4.28 pounds of hamburger in the refrigerator. She cooks 2.85 pounds of hamburger for her friends. How much hamburger does she have left?

   A. 1.47 pounds
   B. 1.43 pounds
   C. 2.63 pounds
   D. 2.43 pounds

Use the information for questions 6 and 7.

Jacques ran the 50-yard dash in 9.13 seconds and Dembe ran it in 8.93 seconds.

6 What was their combined running time?

   A. 17.06 seconds
   B. 18.16 seconds
   C. 17.16 seconds
   D. 18.06 seconds

7 How much faster did Dembe run than Jacques?

   A. 0.02 second
   B. 0.1 second
   C. 0.2 second
   D. 1.2 seconds

8 Hana is roller skating along an 8-mile trail. She stopped for water after roller skating 2.4 miles. After going another 3.1 miles, she stopped for lunch. How many more miles does she have to go to reach the end of the trail?

Record your answer and fill in the bubbles. Be sure to use the correct place value.

			.		
⓪	⓪	⓪		⓪	⓪
①	①	①		①	①
②	②	②		②	②
③	③	③		③	③
④	④	④		④	④
⑤	⑤	⑤		⑤	⑤
⑥	⑥	⑥		⑥	⑥
⑦	⑦	⑦		⑦	⑦
⑧	⑧	⑧		⑧	⑧
⑨	⑨	⑨		⑨	⑨

9 Which problem has an answer of 6.23?

   A. $5.18 + 2.5$
   B. $5.3 + 1.93$
   C. $9.8 - 3.57$
   D. $8.25 - 2.3$

Use the information and table for questions 10–13.

The table shows the price for items at a store.

Item	Cost
Binder	$12.76
Box of pencils	$8.24
Markers	$11.53
Padded envelopes	$15.97

10 How much does it cost for a box of pencils and padded envelopes?

A. $24.21   C. $23.21

B. $24.11   D. $23.11

11 The cashier receives $40 for a binder and markers. How much change does the cashier give back?

A. $17.71

B. $16.71

C. $15.71

D. $14.71

12 Samantha has $20 to spend at the store. Which two items can she purchase with $20?

A. Markers and padded envelopes

B. Padded envelopes and binder

C. Binder and box of pencils

D. Box of pencils and markers

13 What is the difference in price between the item that costs the most and the item that costs the least?

A. $7.73

B. $4.52

C. $4.44

D. $3.73

14 It takes Venus 0.62 year to orbit the Sun. It takes Saturn 29.46 years to orbit the Sun. How many more years does Saturn take to orbit the Sun than Venus?

Record your answer and fill in the bubbles. Be sure to use the correct place value.

			.		
⓪	⓪	⓪		⓪	⓪
①	①	①		①	①
②	②	②		②	②
③	③	③		③	③
④	④	④		④	④
⑤	⑤	⑤		⑤	⑤
⑥	⑥	⑥		⑥	⑥
⑦	⑦	⑦		⑦	⑦
⑧	⑧	⑧		⑧	⑧
⑨	⑨	⑨		⑨	⑨

Multiplying by 10 and 100

One way to multiply by 10 and 100 is to use place value.

When multiplying by 10, increase the place value of each digit in the other factor by moving each digit one place to the left.

$42 \times 10 = ?$

Thousands Period				Ones Period		
Hundreds	Tens	Ones	,	Hundreds	Tens	Ones
					4	2
				4	2	0

$\leftarrow 42 \times 10$

When multiplying by 100, increase the place value of each digit in the other factor by moving each digit two places to the left.

$42 \times 100 = ?$

Thousands Period				Ones Period		
Hundreds	Tens	Ones	,	Hundreds	Tens	Ones
					4	2
		4	,	2	0	0

$\leftarrow 42 \times 100$

Example 1

Multiply 324 × 10.

Strategy   Use place value.

Step 1   Write the number being multiplied by 10 in a place-value chart.

Thousands Period				Ones Period		
Hundreds	Tens	Ones	,	Hundreds	Tens	Ones
				3	2	4

Step 2   Increase the place value of each digit by moving each digit one place to the left.

Move the 4 to the tens place.

Move the 2 to the hundreds place.

Move the 3 to the thousands place.

Thousands Period				Ones Period		
Hundreds	Tens	Ones	,	Hundreds	Tens	Ones
				3	2	4
		3	,	2	4	0

Solution   324 × 10 = 3,240

Example 2

Multiply 563 × 100.

Strategy   Use place value.

Step 1   Write the number being multiplied by 100 in a place-value chart.

Thousands Period				Ones Period		
Hundreds	Tens	Ones	,	Hundreds	Tens	Ones
				5	6	3

Step 2   Increase the place value of each digit by moving each digit two places to the left.

Move the 3 to the hundreds place.

Move the 6 to the thousands place.

Move the 5 to the ten thousands place.

Thousands Period				Ones Period		
Hundreds	Tens	Ones	,	Hundreds	Tens	Ones
				5	6	3
	5	6	,	3	0	0

Solution   563 × 100 = 56,300

Multiply 912 × 10 and 912 × 100.

First, find the product of 912 and 10.

Move the 2 to the _____ place.

Move the 1 to the _____ place.

Move the 9 to the _____ place.

Write the product in the place-value chart.

Write a 0 in the _____ place.

Thousands Period				Ones Period		
Hundreds	Tens	Ones	,	Hundreds	Tens	Ones

Next, find the product of 912 and 100.

Move the 2 to the _____ place.

Move the 1 to the _____ place.

Move the 9 to the _____ place.

Write the product in the place-value chart.

Write a 0 in the _____ and _____ places.

Thousands Period				Ones Period		
Hundreds	Tens	Ones	,	Hundreds	Tens	Ones

912 × 10 = _____

912 × 100 = _____

1 Use the place-value chart to help answer the question.

Thousands Period				Ones Period		
Hundreds	Tens	Ones	,	Hundreds	Tens	Ones

A warehouse receives a shipment of 100 boxes of soup cans. Each box contains 128 cans. How many cans of soup does the warehouse receive?

A. 1,280

B. 128

C. 128,000

D. 12,800

2 What is the place of the digit 2 in the product of 423 and 100?

A. Hundreds

B. Thousands

C. Ten thousands

D. Hundred thousands

3 A zoo has 10 elephants. Each elephant weighs 7,500 pounds. What is the total weight of all the elephants?

A. 750,000 pounds

B. 75,000 pounds

C. 7,500,000 pounds

D. 7,500 pounds

4 Danielle has her collection of baseball cards in albums. Each page holds 10 cards. She has 82 full pages and one page with 8 cards. How many cards does she have in all?

Record your answer and fill in the bubbles. Be sure to use the correct place value.

5 Use the place-value chart to help answer the question.

Thousands Period				Ones Period		
Hundreds	Tens	Ones	,	Hundreds	Tens	Ones

Srini has 134 CDs in his collection. He paid $10 for each CD. How much did he spend on his CD collection?

A. $1,340

B. $134

C. $134,000

D. $13,400

---

6 Jocelyn practices the violin for 65 minutes each day for 100 days. How many minutes did she practice her violin in all?

A. 65,000 minutes

B. 6,500 minutes

C. 650,000 minutes

D. 650 minutes

7 What is the place of the digit 8 in the product of 83,564 and 10?

A. Hundreds

B. Thousands

C. Ten thousands

D. Hundred thousands

8 A grocery store receives 100 boxes of melons. Each box has 8 melons. How many melons did the grocery store receive in all?

Record your answer and fill in the bubbles. Be sure to use the correct place value.

9 Use the place-value chart to help answer the question.

Thousands Period				Ones Period		
Hundreds	Tens	Ones	,	Hundreds	Tens	Ones

Mr. Davis drove 100 miles each day for work. He worked 232 days last year. How many miles did Mr. Davis drive last year for work?

A. 2,320 miles

B. 232 miles

C. 232,000 miles

D. 23,200 miles

---

10 A car made at a manufacturing plant requires 2,356 pounds of steel. How many pounds of steel is needed for 100 cars?

A. 23,560 pounds

B. 2,356,000 pounds

C. 235,600 pounds

D. 23,560,000 pounds

11 What is the place of the digit 6 in the product of 23,645 and 100?

A. Hundreds

B. Thousands

C. Ten thousands

D. Hundred thousands

12 A decade is the same as 10 years. Grandpa Joe has lived for 6 decades and 8 years. How many years old is Grandpa Joe?

Record your answer and fill in the bubbles. Be sure to use the correct place value.

Multiplying Whole Numbers

1 ▶ GETTING THE IDEA

A **factor** is a number that is multiplied to get a product. A **product** is the result of multiplying two or more factors.

Use an array to multiply two whole numbers. Start with the ones digit of the first factor and multiply it by each digit of the second factor. Then multiply the tens digit of the first factor by each digit of the second factor.

$14 \times 13 = (1 \text{ ten} + 4 \text{ ones}) \times (1 \text{ ten} + 3 \text{ ones})$

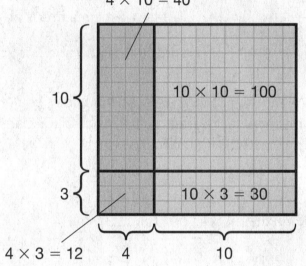

```
    13
×   14
    12   ←   4 × 3 = 12
    40   ←   4 × 10 = 40
    30   ←   10 × 3 = 30
+ 100   ←   10 × 10 = 100
   182
```

Example 1

Find the product of 253 and 3.

Strategy   Use an area model.

Step 1   Draw a diagram to represent the problem.

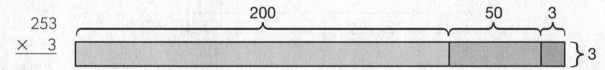

```
  253
×   3
```

Step 2   Multiply the ones digit.

```
  253
×   3
    9   ←   3 × 3 = 9
```

Write 9 in the ones place.

Step 3   Multiply the tens digit.

$$
\begin{array}{r}
1 \\
253 \\
\times \quad 3 \\
\hline
\mathbf{5}9
\end{array}
$$

$\leftarrow$ 3×5 tens $= 15$ tens

Write 5 in the tens place and regroup 1 hundred.

Step 4   Multiply the hundreds digit.

$$
\begin{array}{r}
1 \\
253 \\
\times \quad 3 \\
\hline
\mathbf{7}59
\end{array}
$$

$\leftarrow$ 3×2 hundreds $= 6$ hundreds; 6 hundreds $+$ 1 hundred
$= 7$ hundreds

Write 7 in the hundreds place.

Solution   **The product of 253 and 3 is 759.**

When multiplying by a greater number, sometimes it is helpful to break apart that number by place value. You can multiply each of the parts to find **partial products**, then add the partial products to find the final product.

Example 2

Find the product of 45 and 23.

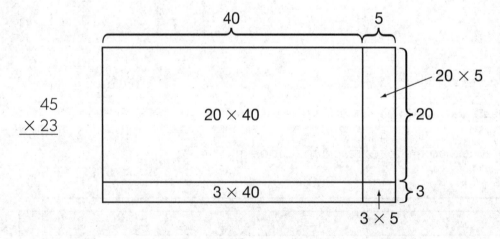

Strategy   **Connect the area model with each partial product.**

Step 1   Multiply the ones digits.

$$\begin{array}{r} 4\mathbf{5} \\ \times\ 2\mathbf{3} \\ \hline \mathbf{15} \end{array}\quad = 3 \times 5$$

Step 2   Multiply the ones digit by the tens digit.

$$\begin{array}{r} \mathbf{4}5 \\ \times\ 2\mathbf{3} \\ \hline 15 \\ \mathbf{120} \end{array}\quad = 3 \times 40$$

Step 3   Multiply the tens digit by the ones digit.

$$\begin{array}{r} 4\mathbf{5} \\ \times\ \mathbf{2}3 \\ \hline 15 \\ 120 \\ \mathbf{100} \end{array}\quad = 20 \times 5$$

Step 4   Multiply the tens digit times the tens digit.

$$\begin{array}{r} \mathbf{4}5 \\ \times\ \mathbf{2}3 \\ \hline 15 \\ 120 \\ 100 \\ \mathbf{800} \end{array}\quad = 20 \times 40$$

Step 5   Find the sum of all the partial products.

$$\begin{array}{r} 45 \\ \times\ 23 \\ \hline 15 \\ 120 \\ 100 \\ +\ 800 \\ \hline 1{,}035 \end{array}$$

Solution   The product of 23 and 45 is 1,035.

The distributive property allows you to break one factor in a multiplication problem into a sum. Multiply each addend by the other factor and then add the partial products. You can use this property to help you find the product of a 1-digit number and a greater number.

$$5 \times 136 = 5 \times (100 + 30 + 6)$$
$$= (5 \times 100) + (5 \times 30) + (5 \times 6)$$
$$= 500 + 150 + 30$$
$$= 680$$

Example 3

Find the product of 3,657 and 9.

Strategy   **Use the distributive property.**

Step 1   Write the greater factor in expanded form.
$$3,657 = 3,000 + 600 + 50 + 7$$

Step 2   Multiply each addend by the factor 9.
$$9 \times 3,657 = 9 \times (3,000 + 600 + 50 + 7)$$
$$= (9 \times 3,000) + (9 \times 600) + (9 \times 50) + (9 \times 7)$$
$$= \quad 27,000 \quad + \quad 5,400 \quad + \quad 450 \quad + \quad 63$$

Step 3   Find the sum of the partial products. Regroup when needed.

$$
\begin{array}{r}
{}^{1}\ \ {}^{1} \\
27{,}000 \\
5{,}400 \\
450 \\
+\quad 63 \\
\hline
32{,}913
\end{array}
$$

Solution   The product of 3,657 and 9 is 32,913.

Example 4

Find the product of 7,302 and 4.

Strategy   Multiply the one-digit factor by each digit of the four-digit factor.

Step 1   Write the multiplication vertically.

$$
\begin{array}{r}
7{,}302 \\
\times \quad\ 4 \\
\hline
\end{array}
$$

Step 2   Multiply the ones digits.

$$
\begin{array}{r}
7{,}30\mathbf{2} \\
\times \quad\ \mathbf{4} \\
\hline
\mathbf{8} \\
\end{array}
$$
    $\leftarrow$ 4 × 2 = 8

Write 8 in the ones place.

Step 3   Multiply the ones digit by the tens digit.

$$
\begin{array}{r}
7{,}3\mathbf{0}2 \\
\times \quad\ \mathbf{4} \\
\hline
\mathbf{0}8 \\
\end{array}
$$
    $\leftarrow$ 4 × 0 tens = 0 tens

Write 0 in the tens place.

Step 4   Multiply the ones digit by the hundreds digit.

$$
\begin{array}{r}
^{1} \quad\quad \\
7{,}\mathbf{3}02 \\
\times \quad\ \mathbf{4} \\
\hline
\mathbf{2}08 \\
\end{array}
$$
    $\leftarrow$ 4 × 3 hundreds = 12 hundreds

Write 2 in the hundreds place and regroup 1 thousand.

Step 5   Multiply the ones digit by the thousands digit.

$$
\begin{array}{r}
^{1} \quad\quad \\
\mathbf{7}{,}302 \\
\times \quad\ \mathbf{4} \\
\hline
\mathbf{29}{,}208 \\
\end{array}
$$
    $\leftarrow$ 4 × 7 thousands = 28 thousands

28 thousands + 1 thousand = 29 thousands

29 thousands = 2 ten thousands 9 thousands

Write 2 in the ten thousands place and 9 in the thousands place.

Solution   **The product of 7,302 and 4 is 29,208.**

Find the product of 42 and 38.

Complete the area model.

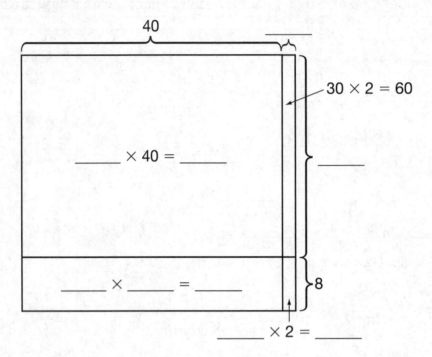

Write an equation for the sum of the partial products.

_____ + _____ + 60 + _____ = _____

The product of 42 and 38 is _____.

1 Use the model to help answer the question.

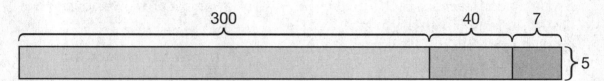

Which multiplication problem does the model represent?

A. 340×7

B. 345×5

C. 347×5

D. 435×7

2 Use the model to help answer the question.

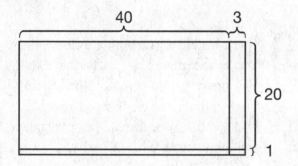

What is the product of 43 and 21?

A. 600

B. 800

C. 860

D. 903

3 What is the product of 382×5?

A. 1,500

B. 1,550

C. 1,900

D. 1,910

4 Mikayla works at a farm stand. One month, she sold 370 pounds of peaches. The peaches cost $2 per pound. How much did she make, in dollars, from peach sales that month?

Record your answer and fill in the bubbles. Be sure to use the correct place value.

			.		
⓪	⓪	⓪		⓪	⓪
①	①	①		①	①
②	②	②		②	②
③	③	③		③	③
④	④	④		④	④
⑤	⑤	⑤		⑤	⑤
⑥	⑥	⑥		⑥	⑥
⑦	⑦	⑦		⑦	⑦
⑧	⑧	⑧		⑧	⑧
⑨	⑨	⑨		⑨	⑨

5 Oakwood Elementary School has 5 fourth-grade teachers. Each teacher has 22 students. How many fourth-grade students attend Oakwood Elementary School?

A. 26

B. 27

C. 88

D. 110

6 Renny drew this area model to help her find the product of two numbers.

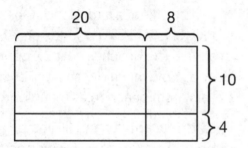

According to the model, which product is Renny trying to find?

A. 28 × 14

B. 28 × 10

C. 20 × 8

D. 10 × 4

7 Which multiplication problem does **not** have a product of 1,920?

A. 4 × 480

B. 9 × 240

C. 24 × 80

D. 32 × 60

8 The list below shows the number of lawns Joseph mowed during one week.

- He mowed 6 lawns on Monday.
- He mowed 9 lawns on Wednesday.
- He mowed 8 lawns on Friday.

Joseph charged $25 to mow each lawn. What was the total amount he earned mowing lawns during the week?

A. $350

B. $375

C. $425

D. $575

9 The bleachers in a gym are divided into 6 sections. Each section will seat 144 people. Which shows how the distributive property can be used to find the total number of people that the gym will seat?

A. 6 + 144

B. 6 × (100 + 40)

C. 6 × (100 + 40 + 4)

D. 6 × (1,000 + 400 + 4)

10 What is the product of 69 × 45?

A. 4,005

B. 3,105

C. 2,765

D. 2,511

11 Which area model should **not** be used to find the product of 26 and 57?

A.

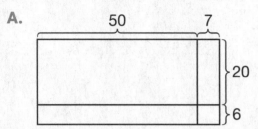

B.

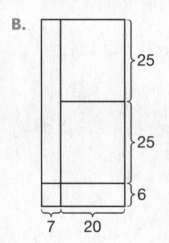

C.

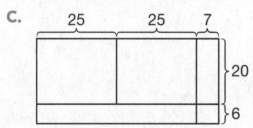

D.

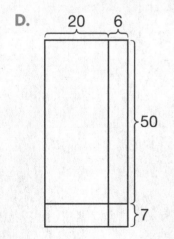

12 The school set aside space for a garden. The space is a rectangle that is 32 feet by 29 feet. What is the area of the garden, in square feet?

Record your answer and fill in the bubbles. Be sure to use the correct place value.

⓪①②③④⑤⑥⑦⑧⑨	⓪①②③④⑤⑥⑦⑧⑨	⓪①②③④⑤⑥⑦⑧⑨	.	⓪①②③④⑤⑥⑦⑧⑨	⓪①②③④⑤⑥⑦⑧⑨

13 Which multiplication problem has a product that is less than 500?

A. 173×3

B. 21×16

C. 32×31

D. 28×20

14 Which numbers could be used to complete the number sentence below?

$$7{,}032 = \boxed{} \times \bigcirc$$

A. 6 and 1,172

B. 6 and 1,170

C. 5 and 1,406

D. 4 and 1,759

Dividing Whole Numbers

1 GETTING THE IDEA

Use place value to divide whole numbers.

When you divide, you start with the greatest place, so you go from left to right.

The **dividend** is the number being divided.

The **divisor** is the number by which the dividend is divided.

The **quotient** is the result.

Division problems can be written two different ways, with a division house or as an equation.

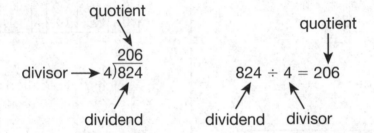

Example 1

Divide 312 ÷ 3.

Strategy   Use area models.

Step 1   Model the dividend using an area model.

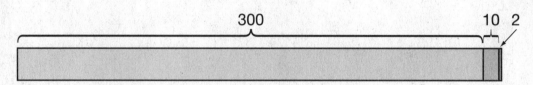

300   10 2

Step 2   Divide starting at the left with the greatest place value.

Divide 300 into 3 equal parts.

Each part is 100.

300

| 100 | 100 | 100 |

Write 1 in the hundreds place of the quotient.

$$
\begin{array}{r}
1 \\
3\overline{)312} \\
-3 \\
\hline
0
\end{array}
$$

← 1 hundred in each group

← 1 hundred × 3 = 3 hundreds used

← 0 hundreds left over

Step 3   There are no hundreds left over. So divide 10 into 3 equal parts.

10 cannot be divided into 3 equal parts, so write 0 in the tens place of the quotient.

$$
\begin{array}{r}
10 \\
3\overline{)312} \\
-3\downarrow \\
\hline
01 \\
-0 \\
\hline
1
\end{array}
$$

← 0 tens in each group

← 0 tens × 3 = 0 tens used

← 1 ten left over

Step 4 1 ten is left over. So combine the 10 and the 2. Then divide into 3 equal parts.

10 + 2 = 12

Divide 12 into 3 equal parts.

Each part is 4.

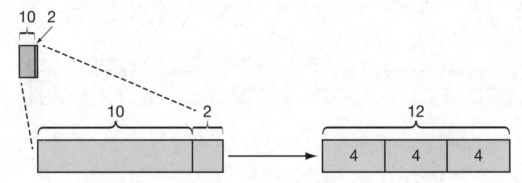

Write 4 in the ones place of the quotient.

```
      104   ←   4 ones in each group
  3)312
   − 3↓
     01
    − 0↓
     12
    − 12   ←   4 ones × 3 = 12 ones used
      0    ←   0 ones left over
```

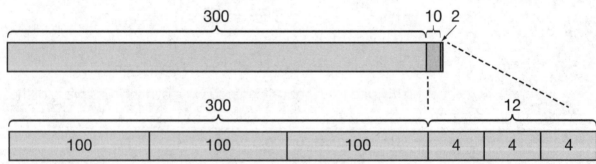

Step 5 Check the quotient using multiplication.

Multiply the quotient by the divisor. The product should equal the dividend.

```
    104   ←   quotient
  ×   3   ←   divisor
    312   ←   dividend
```

The quotient is correct.

Solution 312 ÷ 3 = 104

Some division problems have a remainder. A **remainder** is a number that is left over when a dividend cannot be divided evenly.

Example 2

Divide 229 ÷ 4.

Strategy   Use place value.

Step 1   Write the problem with a division house.

$$4\overline{)229}$$

Step 2   Divide starting at the left.

$$4\overline{)\mathbf{2}29}$$

There are not enough hundreds to divide by 4, so the first digit of the quotient is in the tens place. Divide 22 tens by 4.

$$
\begin{array}{r}
\mathbf{5} \\
4\overline{)229} \\
-\mathbf{20} \\
\hline
2
\end{array}
$$

← 22 tens ÷ 4 = ?

← 5 tens × 4 = 20 tens

← 2 tens left over

Step 3   Bring down the ones digit. Divide the ones.

$$
\begin{array}{r}
5\mathbf{7} \\
4\overline{)229} \\
-20\downarrow \\
\hline
29 \\
-28 \\
\hline
1
\end{array}
$$

← 29 ones ÷ 4 = ?

← 7 ones × 4 = 28 ones

← 1 one left over

1 < 4, so 1 one cannot be divided evenly by 4. The remainder is 1.

Step 4   Write the remainder in the quotient.

$$
\begin{array}{r}
57\ \mathbf{R1} \\
4\overline{)229} \\
-20 \\
\hline
29 \\
-28 \\
\hline
\mathbf{1}
\end{array}
$$

Step 5 Check the answer using multiplication and addition.

Multiply the quotient by the divisor. The product plus the remainder should equal the dividend.

$57 \times 4 = 228$

$228 + 1 = 229$

The answer is correct.

Solution $229 \div 4 = 57\,R1$

Example 3

A restaurant used 1,435 jumbo cans of tomato sauce in one year. A case of tomato sauce has 6 jumbo cans. How many cases of tomato sauce did the restaurant need for the year?

Strategy **Write an equation.**

Step 1 Write an equation to solve the problem. Let c be the unknown number of cases.

$1,435 \div 6 = c$

Step 2 Divide starting at the left.

$$6\overline{)1,435}$$

There are not enough thousands to divide by 6, so the first digit of the quotient is in the hundreds place. Divide 14 hundreds by 6.

$$\begin{array}{r} 2 \\ 6\overline{)1,435} \\ -\ 12 \\ \hline 2 \end{array}$$

← 14 hundreds $\div$ 6 = ?

← 2 hundreds $\times$ 6 = 12 hundreds

Step 3 Bring down the tens digit. Divide the tens.

$$\begin{array}{r} 23 \\ 6\overline{)1,435} \\ -\ 12\downarrow \\ \hline 23 \\ -\ 18 \\ \hline 5 \end{array}$$

← 20 tens + 3 tens = 23 tens

← 3 tens $\times$ 6 = 18 tens

← 5 tens left over

Step 4   Bring down the ones digit. Divide the ones.

$$
\begin{array}{r}
23\mathbf{9} \\
6\overline{)1,435} \\
-12 \\
\hline
23 \\
-18 \\
\hline
55 \\
-\;\mathbf{54} \\
\hline
1
\end{array}
$$

← 50 ones + 5 ones = 55 ones
← 9 ones × 6 = 54 ones
← 1 one left over

Step 5   Write the remainder in the quotient.

$$
\begin{array}{r}
239\;\mathbf{R1} \\
6\overline{)1,435} \\
-12 \\
\hline
23 \\
-18 \\
\hline
55 \\
-54 \\
\hline
\mathbf{1}
\end{array}
$$

Step 6   Check the answer using multiplication and addition.

Multiply the quotient by the divisor. The product plus the remainder should equal the dividend.

$$
\begin{array}{r}
239 \\
\times\quad 6 \\
\hline
1,434 \\
+\qquad 1 \\
\hline
1,435
\end{array}
$$

← quotient
← divisor

← remainder
← dividend

The answer is correct.

Step 7   Interpret the remainder.

The restaurant used 239 cases of tomato sauce plus 1 more can. So the restaurant needed 240 cases of tomato sauce.

Solution   **The restaurant needed 240 cases for the year.**

The Apple Barn packs 9 apples in each gift box. There are 1,348 apples. How many full gift boxes can they pack? How many apples will be left over?

Write an equation to solve the problem.

There are _____ apples.

    The Apple Barn packs _____ apples in each gift box.

    Let b represent _____.

    _____ ÷ _____ = b

Complete the division. Divide each place from left to right.

$9\overline{)1{,}348}$

The remainder is _____.

Check the division using multiplication and addition.

    Multiply the divisor by the quotient.

    _____ × _____ = _____

    Add the remainder.

    _____ + _____ = _____

Does your answer match the dividend? _____

The Apple Barn can pack _____ full gift boxes. There will be _____ apples left over.

1 Use the division model to help answer the question.

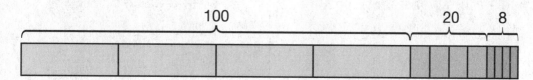

Which division problem does the model represent?

A. 128 ÷ 4

B. 32 ÷ 4

C. 108 ÷ 32

D. 128 ÷ 32

2 Use the division model to help answer the question.

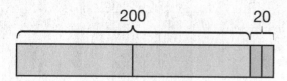

Which statement is true?

A. The divisor is 20.

B. The quotient is 220.

C. The dividend is 220.

D. The remainder is 10.

3 Which division problem does **not** have a quotient of 206?

A. 618 ÷ 3

B. 824 ÷ 4

C. 1,442 ÷ 7

D. 1,845 ÷ 9

4 What is the quotient of 4,781 ÷ 7?

A. 518

B. 608

C. 683

D. 740

5 Rebecca is using multiplication to check a division problem. She has almost finished her check.

$$48$$
$$\times\ 7$$
$$\overline{336}$$
$$+\ \ \ 5$$

Which equation represents the division problem Rebecca is checking?

A. 336 ÷ 7 = 48

B. 336 ÷ 7 = 48 R5

C. 341 ÷ 7 = 48

D. 341 ÷ 7 = 48 R5

6 Which pair of numbers can be used to complete the number sentence?

$$\square \div \bigcirc = 59$$

A. 187 and 3

B. 177 and 3

C. 177 and 4

D. 173 and 5

7 Jeremy completed the division problem shown below.

$$
\begin{array}{r}
83 \text{ R2} \\
6\overline{)498} \\
-48 \\
\hline
18 \\
-16 \\
\hline
2
\end{array}
$$

Which statement explains why Jeremy's work is incorrect?

A. The quotient should have a remainder of 6.

B. The remainder is less than the divisor.

C. $83 \times 6 = 496$ and $496 + 2 = 498$

D. $3 \times 6 = 18$, not 16

8 Which number could be a remainder when dividing by 7?

A. 6

B. 7

C. 8

D. 9

9 Mr. Wright bought 3 tickets for a musical. He spent a total of $141. What was the cost, in dollars, of each ticket?

Record your answer and fill in the bubbles. Be sure to use the correct place value.

10 Luke has 1,253 stickers. He divides the stickers equally among 8 of his friends and he keeps any left over stickers for himself. How many stickers will Luke get?

A. 8

B. 7

C. 6

D. 5

11 Which division problem has a quotient with no remainder?

A. 289 ÷ 3

B. 816 ÷ 6

C. 1,263 ÷ 2

D. 431 ÷ 5

12 Miguel made a batch of soup that contains 931 calories. He places the same amount of soup into each of 7 containers. How many calories are in each container of soup?

A. 13

B. 14

C. 133

D. 134

13 Sofia has 112 muffins to place into equal packages of 8. The packages will sell for $5 each. What is the total value of the complete packages of muffins?

A. $40

B. $50

C. $70

D. $560

14 There are 139 students and 10 adults on a field trip to a museum. The museum gives tours in groups no greater than 8. What is the least number of groups that will allow everyone to go on the tour?

A. 19

B. 18

C. 17

D. 14

15 The table shows the number of books that were returned to the library last week.

Day	Number of Books
Monday	30
Tuesday	39
Wednesday	15
Thursday	10
Friday	4

Mrs. Sloan collects all the books. Then she places the same number of books onto each of 7 shelves. How many books does Mrs. Sloan put on each shelf?

A. 686

B. 98

C. 14

D. 7

Estimating Solutions

 GETTING THE IDEA

When you do not need an exact answer, you can estimate. When you **estimate**, you find about how many or about how much.

One way to estimate is by rounding. When you **round**, you find the nearest multiple of 10, 100, or 1,000 that a given number is closest to. The examples below show how to round to the nearest ten, hundred, and thousand.

Rounding		
To the Nearest Ten	**To the Nearest Hundred**	**To the Nearest Thousand**
3<u>6</u> → 40	5<u>0</u>8 → 500	7,<u>8</u>74 → 8,000
Look at the digit to the right of the tens place.	Look at the digit to the right of the hundreds place.	Look at the digit to the right of the thousands place.
$6 \geq 5$, so increase the tens digit by 1 and write a 0 in the ones place.	$0 < 5$, so keep the hundreds digit the same and write 0s in the places to its right.	$8 \geq 5$, so increase the thousands digit by 1 and write 0s in the places to its right.

Example 1

The population of the town of Middleboro is 23,116. The population of the town of Springfield is 59,869. Estimate the combined population of the two towns.

Strategy   Round to the nearest ten thousand.

Step 1   Round the population of Middleboro to the nearest ten thousand.

Underline the digit to the right of the ten thousands place.   2<u>3</u>,116

$3 < 5$, so keep the ten thousands digit the same. Write 0s in the places to its right.

23,116 → 20,000

The population of Middleboro is about 20,000.

Step 2   Round the population of Springfield to the nearest ten thousand.

Underline the digit to the right of the ten thousands place.   5<u>9</u>,869

9 ≥ 5, so increase the ten thousands digit by 1. Write 0s in the places to its right.

59,869 → 60,000

The population of Springfield is about 60,000.

Step 3   Add the rounded numbers.

23,116	→	20,000
+ 59,869	→	+ 60,000
		80,000

Solution   **The combined population of the two towns is about 80,000.**

Example 2

Sasha is saving up for a new laptop computer. Right now, she has $105. The laptop computer costs $1,389. About how much more money does Sasha need to save to buy the laptop?

Strategy   **Round to the nearest hundred.**

Step 1   Round the cost of the laptop to the nearest hundred.

Underline the digit to the right of the hundreds place.   1,3<u>8</u>9

8 ≥ 5, so increase the hundreds digit by 1. Write 0s in the places to its right.

1,389 → 1,400

The laptop costs about $1,400.

Step 2   Round the amount Sasha has saved to the nearest hundred.

Underline the digit to the right of the hundreds place.   1<u>0</u>5

0 < 5, so keep the hundreds digit the same. Write 0s in the places to its right.

105 → 100

Sasha has saved about $100.

Step 3	Subtract the rounded numbers.

$$
\begin{array}{r}
1{,}389 \\
-\ \ \ 105 \\
\end{array}
\quad\rightarrow\quad
\begin{array}{r}
1{,}400 \\
-\ \ \ 100 \\
\hline
1{,}300
\end{array}
$$

Solution   Sasha needs to save about $1,300 more to buy the laptop.

Example 3

Mrs. Bailey and her students went on a field trip to pick apples. They filled 12 containers. Each container held 18 pounds of apples. About how many pounds of apples did Mrs. Bailey and her students pick?

Strategy   Round to the nearest ten.

Step 1   Round the number of containers to the nearest ten.

Underline the digit to the right of the tens place.   1<u>2</u>

2 < 5, so keep the tens digit the same. Write a 0 in the ones place.

12 → 10

About 10 containers were filled.

Step 2   Round the amount each container held to the nearest ten.

Underline the digit to the right of the tens place.   1<u>8</u>

8 ≥ 5, so increase the tens digit by 1. Write a 0 in the ones place.

18 → 20

Each container held about 20 pounds of apples.

Step 3   Multiply the rounded numbers.

$$
\begin{array}{r}
12 \\
\times\ 18 \\
\end{array}
\quad\rightarrow\quad
\begin{array}{r}
10 \\
\times\ 20 \\
\hline
200
\end{array}
$$

Solution   Mrs. Bailey and her students picked about 200 pounds of apples.

You can also use compatible numbers to estimate. **Compatible numbers** are numbers that are close to the value of the actual numbers and make mental math easy.

$47 \div 7$
↓
$49 \div 7$

You can use mental math to divide 49 by 7.
So, 49 and 7 are compatible numbers.

Example 4

Raul and his family went on vacation. In 4 days, they drove 355 miles. They drove the same number of miles each day. About how far did Raul and his family drive each day?

Strategy   Use compatible numbers.

Step 1   Write an expression that represents how far Raul and his family drove each day.

Divide the total number of miles driven by the total number of days.

$355 \div 4$

Step 2   Find a number that is close to 355 and compatible with 4.

360 is close to 355 and compatible with 4. So, change 355 to 360. The division fact $36 \div 4$ can be used to mentally divide $360 \div 4$.

$355 \div 4$
↓
$360 \div 4$

Step 3   Use mental math to divide.

$360 \div 4 = 90$

Solution   Raul and his family drove about 90 miles per day.

Vincent worked in his family's bakery a total of 11 days last month. Each day he worked, he baked 84 muffins. About how many muffins did Vincent bake last month?

Round the number of muffins Vincent baked each day to the nearest ten.

Write the number of muffins Vincent baked each day. ☐

Underline the digit to the right of the _____ place.

4 _____ 5, so keep the tens digit the _____. Write a 0 in the _____ place.

84 → _____

Vincent baked about _____ muffins each day.

Round the number of days Vincent worked last month to the nearest ten.

Write the number of days Vincent worked. ☐

Underline the digit to the right of the _____ place.

1 _____ 5, so keep the tens digit the _____. Write a 0 in the _____ place.

11 → _____

Vincent worked about _____ days last month.

Multiply the rounded numbers.

$$
\begin{array}{r}
84 \\
\times\ 11 \\
\end{array}
\quad \rightarrow \quad
\begin{array}{r}
\square \\
\times\ \square \\
\hline
\square \\
\end{array}
$$

So, Vincent baked about _____ muffins last month.

1 The enrollment at Jones Elementary School is 743. The enrollment at Nichols Middle School is 589. What is the best estimate for the combined enrollment at the two schools?

A. 1,200

B. 1,300

C. 1,400

D. 1,500

2 What is 529 rounded to the nearest ten?

Record your answer and fill in the bubbles. Be sure to use the correct place value.

3 Which is the best estimate for 3,584 − 898?

A. 1,500

B. 2,000

C. 2,700

D. 4,000

4 Liam is saving up for a new video game system. Right now, he has $73. The video game system costs $298. About how much more money does Liam need to save before he can buy the video game system?

A. $300

B. $200

C. $150

D. $100

5 Natalie is using compatible numbers to estimate the quotient shown below.

$$341 \div 7$$

$$\downarrow$$

$$\square \div 7$$

To find the best estimate, she will choose a number that is close to 341 and compatible with 7. Which number could she have chosen?

A. 350

B. 340

C. 300

D. 210

6 Which expression gives the best estimate for 253×8?

A. 300×10

B. 250×10

C. 200×6

D. 200×5

7 Lauren works at a flower shop. In one weekend, she assembled 38 flower arrangements. Each arrangement contained 19 flowers. About how many flowers did Lauren use to make the arrangements?

A. 300

B. 400

C. 600

D. 800

8 Finn uses compatible numbers to estimate the product shown below.

$$118 \times 6$$

Which expression would give Finn the best estimate?

A. 100×6

B. 110×5

C. 120×6

D. 150×10

9 Which statement is true?

A. If you round 45 to the nearest ten, the result is 40.

B. If you round 319 to the nearest ten, the result is 300.

C. If you round 2,478 to the nearest hundred, the result is 2,000.

D. If you round 9,021 to the nearest thousand, the result is 9,000.

10 The table shows how many people attended a concert each day over the weekend.

Day	Attendance
Friday	118
Saturday	237
Sunday	72

To the nearest hundred, about how many people attended the concert in all?

Record your answer and fill in the bubbles. Be sure to use the correct place value.

11 Which number, when rounded to the nearest hundred, rounds to 23,500?

A. 23,491

B. 23,584

C. 23,628

D. 24,000

Use the information for questions 12 and 13.

Timothy works in a deli. He sold a total of 74 sandwiches in 8 hours. He sold about the same number of sandwiches each hour.

12 To find about how many sandwiches Timothy sold each hour, you decide to use compatible numbers.

$$74 \div 8$$
↓
$$\square \div 8$$

What number is close to 74 and compatible with 8?

A. 56

B. 70

C. 72

D. 100

13 About how many sandwiches did Timothy sell each hour?

A. 12

B. 9

C. 7

D. 6

14 You are reading a book that has 294 pages. The first day, you read 19 pages. The second day, you read 32 pages. What is the best estimate of the number of pages you have left to read?

A. 300

B. 250

C. 160

D. 150

15 The cost of five train tickets is $44. Which expression would give the best estimate for the cost of one train ticket?

A. $45 \div 5$

B. $48 \div 4$

C. $40 \div 10$

D. $50 \div 10$

16 At the store, Mariel bought 2 DVD players. Each player cost $99. She also bought a speaker system for $115. About how much money did Mariel spend?

A. $100

B. $200

C. $300

D. $400

Solving One- and Two-Step Multiplication and Division Problems

 GETTING THE IDEA

One-step word problems can be solved using one operation. Two-step word problems can be solved using two operations. To solve, read through the problem. You can draw diagrams to help understand the problem and determine which operation to use. You can also write and solve one or more equations to solve the problem.

Example 1

A store sells monitors for $228. Today, the store sold six monitors. How much money did the store make?

Strategy   **Use a diagram to help write an equation.**

> **Step 1**   Draw a diagram to represent the problem.

$228	$228	$228	$228	$228	$228

> Use multiplication to find the total. Multiply 228 by 6.

> **Step 2**   Write the multiplication equation.
>
> $228 \times 6 = t$

> **Step 3**   Solve the equation for t.
>
> Multiply using the standard algorithm.
>
> $$\begin{array}{r} {\scriptstyle 1\,4} \\ 228 \\ \times \quad 6 \\ \hline 1{,}368 \end{array}$$
>
> $t = 1{,}368$

Solution   **The store made $1,368.**

Example 2

Antonia is reading a 284 page book. She reads 12 pages each hour. After reading for 4 hours, how many more pages does she have left to read?

Strategy   Use a diagram to help write an equation for each step.

Step 1   Draw a diagram to represent the problem.

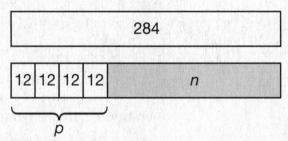

Step 2   Decide which operation to do first.

Antonia reads 12 pages each hour. She reads for 4 hours. Multiply 12 by 4.

Step 3   Write and solve the multiplication equation.

$$12 \times 4 = p$$
$$48 = p$$

Step 4   Decide which operation to do next.

The book has 284 pages. Antonia has read 48 pages. Subtract 48 from 284.

Step 5   Write and solve the subtraction equation.

$$284 - 48 = n$$
$$236 = n$$

$$\begin{array}{r} {\scriptstyle 7\,14} \\ 2\cancel{8}\cancel{4} \\ -\ \ 48 \\ \hline 236 \end{array}$$

Solution   **Antonia has 236 more pages to read.**

When a word problem involves division, you may need to interpret remainders. To do so, you need to know what the **quotient** and **remainder** mean in the problem. The answer depends on the question asked.

Problem	Division	Interpreting the Remainder
There are 14 students signed up for a relay race. A relay team has exactly 4 members. *How many teams will there be?*	$14 \div 4 = \mathbf{3}\,R2$	**Solution is the quotient.** Since there must be 4 people on a team, there will be only 3 teams. The solution is the quotient, **3**. There will be **3** teams.
There are 14 students signed up for a relay race. A relay team has exactly 4 members. *How many students will not be on a relay team?*	$14 \div 4 = 3\,\mathbf{R2}$	**Solution is the remainder.** Since there must be 4 people on a team, there will be 3 teams. The remainder represents 2 extra students who cannot be on a relay team. The solution is the remainder **2**. **2** students cannot run in the relay race.
There are 14 students who need rides to the park where the race will be held. Each car holds up to 4 students. *How many cars are needed to transport all the students?*	$14 \div 4 = 3\,\mathbf{R2}$	**Solution is the quotient increased by 1.** All 14 students need rides to the park. Three cars can hold 4 students each or 12 students. The remainder represents 2 students who still need a ride. One more car is needed, so increase the quotient by 1. **4** cars are needed.

Example 3

A baker produces 286 muffins. He packs 8 muffins per package. How many packages does he pack? How many muffins are left over?

Strategy Write and solve an equation.

Step 1 Write an equation to solve the problem.

p is the unknown number of packages.

$286 \div 8 = p$

Step 2	Solve the equation for p.

Divide using the standard algorithm.

$p = 35$ R6

$$\begin{array}{r} 35 \text{ R6} \\ 8\overline{)286} \\ -24 \\ \hline 46 \\ -40 \\ \hline 6 \end{array}$$

Step 3	Interpret the remainder.

The quotient 35 represents the number of packages the baker packed. The remainder 6 represents the number of muffins left over.

Solution   **The baker packed 35 packages and had 6 muffins left over.**

Example 4

On a field trip, there are 87 boys and 98 girls. A chaperone is needed for every group of 9 students. How many chaperones are needed for the field trip?

Strategy   **Write and solve an equation for each step.**

Step 1	Decide which operation to do first.

Find the total number of students. Add 87 and 98.

Step 2	Write and solve the addition equation.

$$87 + 98 = n$$
$$185 = n$$

$$\begin{array}{r} ^1 \\ 87 \\ +98 \\ \hline 185 \end{array}$$

Step 3	Decide which operation to do next.

Each group of 9 students needs a chaperone. Divide 185 by 9.

Step 4	Write and solve the equation.

$$185 \div 9 = n$$
$$20 \text{ R5} = n$$

$$\begin{array}{r} 20 \text{ R5} \\ 9\overline{)185} \\ -18 \\ \hline 5 \\ -0 \\ \hline 5 \end{array}$$

Step 5	Interpret the remainder.

The question asks for the number of chaperones needed for the field trip.

The quotient, 20, is the number of chaperones for 20 groups of 9.

The remainder represents 5 students who still need a chaperone. So one more chaperone is needed. Add 1 to the quotient, $20 + 1 = 21$.

Solution   **21 chaperones are needed.**

Jose wants to buy 4 sweatshirts for $35 each. He plans to save $8 each week. How many weeks will he need to save in order to buy the sweatshirts?

To find the total cost of the sweatshirts, _____ the number of sweatshirts,

_____, and the cost of each, $_____.

Write an equation for the total cost *t* of the sweatshirts.

_____ $\bigcirc$ _____ = t

Show your work to solve the equation.

So, *t* = _____.

To find the number of weeks Jose needs to save, _____ the total cost, $_____,

by the amount saved each week, $_____.

Write an equation to find the number of weeks *n*.

_____ $\bigcirc$ _____ = n

Show your work to solve the equation.

So, *n* = _____.

The quotient is _____. The remainder is _____.

The question asks how long, so the answer is a number of _____.

In _____ weeks, he will save $_____. That _____ enough money,

so add _____ to the quotient.

He will have enough money in _____ weeks.

Jose will need to save for _____ weeks.

1 Jerome draws the following diagram to represent a problem.

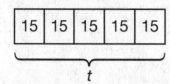

Which problem could the diagram represent?

A. Henry wants to buy a model car for $15. He saves money for 5 days. How much did he save each day?

B. Henry wants to buy a model car for $15 and accessories for $5. What is the total cost?

C. Henry wants to buy 5 model cars. Each car costs $15. How much does he need to save?

D. Henry wants to buy 3 model cars. Each car costs $5. How much does he need to save?

2 Ariel saved $330 each month for 6 months. How much did Ariel save in all?

A. $55

B. $336

C. $1,800

D. $1,980

3 Mrs. Reynolds makes gift boxes with oranges. She has 106 oranges. She places 8 oranges in each gift box. If she makes as many gift boxes as possible, how many oranges will she have left over?

A. 0

B. 2

C. 4

D. 6

4 Gabriel read 150 pages of a 236-page book. If he reads 9 pages each day, in how many days will he finish the book?

Record your answer and fill in the bubbles. Be sure to use the correct place value.

			.		
⓪	⓪	⓪		⓪	⓪
①	①	①		①	①
②	②	②		②	②
③	③	③		③	③
④	④	④		④	④
⑤	⑤	⑤		⑤	⑤
⑥	⑥	⑥		⑥	⑥
⑦	⑦	⑦		⑦	⑦
⑧	⑧	⑧		⑧	⑧
⑨	⑨	⑨		⑨	⑨

Use the information and diagram for questions 5–7.

Jasmine combines 37 ounces of grape juice and 13 ounces of apple juice to make punch. She will pour the punch into 6-ounce cups.

37	13

n

5   Which equation is represented by the diagram?

   A. $37 \div 13 = n$

   B. $37 - 13 = n$

   C. $37 \times 13 = n$

   D. $37 + 13 = n$

6   Which expression can be used to find how many cups of punch Jasmine can pour?

   A. $37 \div 6$

   B. $13 \div 6$

   C. $24 \div 6$

   D. $50 \div 6$

7   How many full cups of punch can Jasmine pour?

   A. 8

   B. 9

   C. 2

   D. 10

8   A rental company has 6 times as many cars as trucks. The company has 54 trucks. How many cars does the company have?

   A. 9

   B. 60

   C. 324

   D. 300

9   The Powell family is driving 829 miles in four days. In the first three days, they drive 230 miles each day. How many miles do they drive the fourth day?

   Record your answer and fill in the bubbles. Be sure to use the correct place value.

10   Monica is putting 342 photos in a photo album. Each page can hold 8 photos. How many full pages of photos will Monica have?

   A. 6

   B. 42

   C. 43

   D. 350

11 Six classes are going to a baseball game. Each class has 22 students. Vans will take them to the game. If each van can hold 8 students, how many vans are needed?

A. 17

B. 16

C. 8

D. 4

12 Use the following diagram to answer the question.

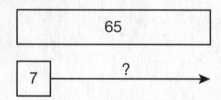

Elle has 65 baseball cards. She puts 7 cards on each page of her album. How many full pages does she have?

A. 9

B. 7

C. 2

D. 10

13 Nikolai sold 13 of his comic books for $15 each. How much money did Nikolai make?

A. $2

B. $28

C. $150

D. $195

14 Keli is putting together flower arrangements for a party. She has 18 vases. Each vase will have an assortment of 9 flowers. She also has a centerpiece with 24 flowers. How many flowers does she use in all?

A. 216

B. 162

C. 186

D. 234

15 Diego has 153 books. He gives away 48 books. He places the remaining books equally on 5 shelves. How many books does he put on each shelf?

Record your answer and fill in the bubbles. Be sure to use the correct place value.

			.		
⓪	⓪	⓪		⓪	⓪
①	①	①		①	①
②	②	②		②	②
③	③	③		③	③
④	④	④		④	④
⑤	⑤	⑤		⑤	⑤
⑥	⑥	⑥		⑥	⑥
⑦	⑦	⑦		⑦	⑦
⑧	⑧	⑧		⑧	⑧
⑨	⑨	⑨		⑨	⑨

Multi-Step Word Problems

A multi-step problem usually requires more than one operation to solve.

Look at the chart that lists colors of Mia's T-shirts and Steve's T-shirts.

T-shirts

	Color	Number
Mia	red	2
	pink	4
	purple	1
	blue	3
Steve	black	4
	blue	1

A problem that asks you to *find the number of T-shirts Mia has* requires just one step to solve. Add to find the total.

Equation	Solution
$2 + 4 + 1 + 3 = m$	$m = 10$

A problem that asks you to *find how many times as many T-shirts Mia has as Steve* requires more than one step.

Step	Equation	Solution
Add to find the number of T-shirts Mia has.	$2 + 4 + 1 + 3 = m$	$m = 10$
Add to find the number of T-shirts Steve has.	$4 + 1 = s$	$s = 5$
Write and solve a comparison equation.	$5 \times n = 10$	$n = 2$

So, Mia has 2 times as many T-shirts as Steve.

Example 1

Lucas has $33 in a savings account. He is saving to buy a new skateboard. The skateboard costs $78. If Lucas saves $5 each week, in how many weeks will he have enough saved to buy the skateboard?

Strategy   Use a diagram to help you write an equation for each step.

Step 1   Draw a diagram to represent the problem.

You know that the skateboard costs $78. Lucas has $33 in savings.

You do not know how much more money he needs. Also, you do not know how long it will take for him to save the remaining money.

78

33	n

Step 2   Decide which operation to do first.

Lucas needs $78. He has $33. Subtract to find the amount he needs.

Step 3   Write and solve the subtraction equation.

$78 - 33 = n$

$45 = n$

Lucas needs $45 more.

Step 4   Decide which operation to do next.

Lucas saves $5 each week. Divide to find the number of weeks it will take to reach $45.

Step 5   Write and solve the division equation.

$45 \div 5 = r$

$9 = r$

Solution   Lucas will have enough money to buy the skateboard in 9 weeks.

You can use rounding to check the reasonableness of your answer. When you round to check your answer, the rounded answer should be close to the actual answer. If you made a mistake, your answer is not likely to be close to the actual answer.

Example 2

A family is driving 885 miles to a family reunion. They drove 328 miles the first day and 285 miles the second day. How many miles should they drive the third day to reach their destination?

Strategy   **Write and solve an equation for each step.**

Step 1   Decide which operation to do first.

The family drove 328 miles and 285 miles. Add to find the total.

Step 2   Write and solve the addition equation.

$328 + 285 = d$

$613 = d$ ⟵ 613 miles driven so far

$$\begin{array}{r} {\scriptstyle 11} \\ 328 \\ + 285 \\ \hline 613 \end{array}$$

Step 3   Decide which operation to do next.

The distance to the reunion is 885 miles. Subtract the distance they have driven so far from the total distance.

Step 4   Write and solve the subtraction equation.

$885 - 613 = x$

$272 = x$ ⟵ miles left to drive

$$\begin{array}{r} 885 \\ - 613 \\ \hline 272 \end{array}$$

Step 5   Check the reasonableness of your answer.

The problem involves 3-digit numbers. Round to the nearest hundred to find an estimate.

328	rounds to	300
+ 285	rounds to	+ 300

about 600 miles driven so far

885	rounds to	900
		− 600

about 300 miles left to drive

The estimate, 300, is close to 272, so the answer is reasonable.

Solution   **The family should drive 272 miles.**

Example 3

Esther wants to buy a video game system that costs $432. She walks dogs to earn money and charges $8 per dog. Esther has walked 32 dogs so far. How many more dogs does she have to walk to earn enough money?

Strategy   Write and solve an equation for each step.

Step 1   Decide which operation to do first.

To find the total number of dogs she needs to walk, divide 432 by 8.

Step 2   Write and solve the division equation.

$432 \div 8 = d$

$54 = d$ ⟵ Esther needs to walk 54 dogs.

$$\begin{array}{r} 54 \\ 8\overline{)432} \\ -40 \\ \hline 32 \\ -32 \\ \hline 0 \end{array}$$

Step 3   Decide which operation to do next.

To find how many more dogs she has to walk, subtract the number of dogs she has already walked from 54.

Step 4   Write and solve the subtraction equation.

$54 - 32 = m$

$22 = m$ ⟵ Esther has to walk 22 more dogs.

$$\begin{array}{r} 54 \\ -32 \\ \hline 22 \end{array}$$

Step 5   Check the reasonableness of your answer.

The problem involves 1-digit, 2-digit, and 3-digit numbers. Use compatible numbers and rounding to find an estimate.

$432 \div 8$ is close to $400 \div 8$.

$400 \div 8 = 50$ ⟵ Esther needs to walk about 50 dogs in all.

32 rounds to 30.

$50 - 30 = 20$ ⟵ Esther needs to walk about more 20 dogs.

The estimate, 20, is close to 22, so the answer is reasonable.

Solution   **Esther has to walk 22 more dogs to earn enough money.**

There were 27 women and 22 men who stood in line to buy the first tickets for a new movie. By the end of the first hour, 4 times that number of tickets had been sold through the movie theater's Web site. How many tickets were sold in all?

Draw a diagram to represent the problem.

```
 _____   _____
|       |       |
| men   | women |
|_____|_____|
    _____/
        t
```

```
|_____|_____|_____|_____|
 _____/
              w
```

Web site sales   _____ times as many

To find the total number of tickets, t, sold to the people standing in line, _____

the number of _____ and the number of _____.

Write an equation using t for the unknown number of tickets sold to those who stood in line.

_____

Solve the equation to find that the value of t is _____.

At the end of the hour, _____ times as many tickets were sold through the Web site.

Write an equation using w for the unknown number of tickets sold through the Web site.

_____

Solve the equation to find that the value of w is _____.

What operation will you use to find the total number of tickets sold? _____

Write an equation using n for the unknown number of tickets sold in all.

_____

Solve the equation to find that the value of n is _____.

To see if the answer is reasonable, _____ to the nearest _____.

The estimate, _____, is close to my answer, _____, so the answer is reasonable.

_____ tickets in all were sold during the first hour.

1 Use the diagram to help solve the problem.

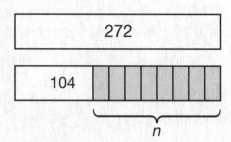

Ellie is reading a book that is 272 pages long. She read 104 pages so far. How many pages does she have to read each day to finish reading the book in 8 days?

A. 13

B. 21

C. 34

D. 47

2 The Garcia family spent 3 weeks at a campground. They made many stops on the way to the campground. The drive there took 4 days. The return trip took 1 day. Which is the first equation that can be solved to find how many days the Garcia family was away from home?

A. $3 \times 7 = n$

B. $4 + 3 = n$

C. $7 + 3 = n$

D. $4 - 1 = n$

3 Amil took 216 photos with his new digital camera. He deleted 28 of them. Then he arranged the rest in 4 folders on his computer. Each folder had the same number of photos. How many photos did he put into each folder?

A. 54

B. 26

C. 7

D. 47

4 A bakery had 14 bran muffins, 19 banana muffins, and 23 pumpkin muffins left at the end of the day. The left-over muffins were placed into boxes of assorted muffins. There were 8 muffins in each box. How many boxes of assorted muffins were there?

Record your answer and fill in the bubbles. Be sure to use the correct place value.

			.		
⓪	⓪	⓪		⓪	⓪
①	①	①		①	①
②	②	②		②	②
③	③	③		③	③
④	④	④		④	④
⑤	⑤	⑤		⑤	⑤
⑥	⑥	⑥		⑥	⑥
⑦	⑦	⑦		⑦	⑦
⑧	⑧	⑧		⑧	⑧
⑨	⑨	⑨		⑨	⑨

5 Lucia is a florist. She made 9 rose bouquets, 9 carnation bouquets, and 9 daisy bouquets.

Flower	Number in a Bouquet
Rose	18
Carnation	39
Daisy	42

How many flowers did she use for all of the bouquets?

A. 11

B. 99

C. 900

D. 891

6 Paul wants to buy a bike that costs $245 dollars. He mows lawns to earn the money and charges $25 for each lawn. Paul has mowed 5 lawns and earned $12 in tips. How much more money does he need to buy the bike?

A. $108

B. $120

C. $160

D. $137

7 Mrs. Yee spent $180 for 6 tickets to a play. She bought 2 adult tickets and 4 child tickets. Each adult ticket was $40. How much was each child ticket?

A. $30

B. $45

C. $40

D. $25

8 An office supply store receives 12 boxes of staplers. Each box has 24 staplers. The store already has 48 staplers in stock. How many staplers does the store have now?

Record your answer and fill in the bubbles. Be sure to use the correct place value.

			.		
⓪	⓪	⓪		⓪	⓪
①	①	①		①	①
②	②	②		②	②
③	③	③		③	③
④	④	④		④	④
⑤	⑤	⑤		⑤	⑤
⑥	⑥	⑥		⑥	⑥
⑦	⑦	⑦		⑦	⑦
⑧	⑧	⑧		⑧	⑧
⑨	⑨	⑨		⑨	⑨

9 Diana used this diagram to represent a multi-step problem.

117	25

n

x	59

Which problem could be illustrated by the diagram?

A. Bill had $117. He spent $59. Then he saved $59 more. How much did Bill have?

B. Don had $117. Bill had $25. Alexis had $59. How much money did they have altogether?

C. Bill had $117. He received $25 more as a gift. Then he spent $59. How much did Bill have left?

D. Bill had $25 more than Don. Don had $59. How much did they have altogether?

10 A jeweler has 4 packages of beads. Each package has 150 beads. He uses the beads to make 6 necklaces, each with 80 beads. How many beads does he have left over?

A. 1,080

B. 230

C. 120

D. 580

11 Nancy buys 6 dozen bagels for a party. 32 people attend the party. Each person takes 2 bagels. How many bagels are left over?
(1 dozen = 12 bagels)

A. 0

B. 8

C. 16

D. 40

12 The table lists the prices of some items at a bake fair.

Item	Price
Cookie	$1
Cupcake	$2
Slice of cake	$4

Mr. Sanchez buys 5 cookies, 5 cupcakes, and 4 slices of cake for his family. He pays the cashier $40 dollars. How many dollars does he get back in change?

Record your answer and fill in the bubbles. Be sure to use the correct place value.

⊙	⊙	⊙	.	⊙	⊙
⓪	⓪	⓪		⓪	⓪
①	①	①		①	①
②	②	②		②	②
③	③	③		③	③
④	④	④		④	④
⑤	⑤	⑤		⑤	⑤
⑥	⑥	⑥		⑥	⑥
⑦	⑦	⑦		⑦	⑦
⑧	⑧	⑧		⑧	⑧
⑨	⑨	⑨		⑨	⑨

Number Patterns

A **pattern** is an ordered set of numbers that follows a rule. A **rule** is a set of instructions.

Each number in the pattern is called a **term**. The terms can be numbered from left to right to show the position of each term.

Term ⟶	2	4	6	8	10	12	14
Position Numbers ⟶	1st	2nd	3rd	4th	5th	6th	7th

Number patterns can be repeating, increasing, or decreasing. In an increasing number pattern, the values of the numbers increase. In a decreasing number pattern, the values of the numbers decrease.

The rules for number patterns may use addition, subtraction, multiplication, or division. Here is an increasing number pattern that uses multiplication.

$$\overset{\times 2}{\curvearrowright} \quad \overset{\times 2}{\curvearrowright} \quad \overset{\times 2}{\curvearrowright} \quad \overset{\times 2}{\curvearrowright}$$
$$3 \quad 6 \quad 12 \quad 24 \quad 48$$

The starting number is 3 and the rule is *multiply by 2*. The starting number is the first term in the pattern. You can use commas to list the terms in this number pattern.

3, 6, 12, 24, 48

The rule for an increasing number pattern usually uses addition or multiplication. The rule for a decreasing number pattern usually uses subtraction or division.

Example 1

Create a pattern with 6 terms.

Starting number: 94

Rule: subtract 10

What do you notice about the terms in the pattern that is not described in the rule?

Strategy   **Use the starting number and the rule to write the pattern.**

Step 1   Write the first number in the pattern.

The starting number is 94. So, 94 is the first term.

Step 2   Use the rule *subtract 10* to find the second term.

$94 - 10 = 84$

Step 3   This pattern has 6 terms, so keep subtracting 10 until you have 6 terms.

$$-10 \quad -10 \quad -10 \quad -10 \quad -10$$

94   84   74   64   54   44

Step 4   Write the terms in a row with commas between them.

94, 84, 74, 64, 54, 44

Step 5   Describe the terms without using the rule.

The pattern is decreasing. Every term is an even number. Every term has 4 as the ones digit.

Solution   **The pattern is 94, 84, 74, 64, 54, 44. Every term is an even number and has 4 as the ones digit.**

Example 2

Write a rule for the pattern below. Use your rule to find the next term. What do you notice about the terms in the pattern that is not described in the rule?

92, 83, 74, 65, 56, 47

Strategy   **Determine if the rule uses adding, subtracting, multiplying, or dividing. Write the rule, find the next term, and describe the terms without using the rule.**

Step 1   Is the pattern repeating, increasing, or decreasing?

Each term in the pattern is less than the one before it.

The pattern is decreasing.

Step 2   Look for a number you can subtract from each term or divide each term by to get the next term.

First, try subtraction. What number can you subtract from the first term to get the second term?

$92 - 9 = 83$

What number can you subtract from the second term to get the third term?

$83 - 9 = 74$

Each term appears to be 9 less than the previous term.

It looks like the rule is *subtract 9*.

Step 3   Make sure the rule works for all of the terms.

$74 - 9 = 65, 65 - 9 = 56, 56 - 9 = 47$

The rule *subtract 9* works for all of the terms.

Step 4   Use the rule *subtract 9* to find the next term.

$47 - 9 = 38$

Step 5   Describe the terms without using the rule.

The pattern is decreasing. The terms alternate between even and odd. The sum of the digits is always 11.

Solution   **A rule for the pattern is *subtract 9*. The next term is 38. The terms alternate between even and odd, and the sum of the digits in each term is always 11.**

The rules for some patterns can use more than one operation.

Example 3

Find a rule for the pattern below. Then write the missing term. What do you notice about the terms in the pattern that is not described in the rule?

10, 19, 18, 27, 26, _____, 34, 43, 42, 51

Strategy   **Use the given terms to find a rule. Then use the rule to find the missing term.**

Step 1   Is the pattern repeating, increasing, or decreasing?

The pattern alternates between increasing and decreasing.

Step 2   Look for a rule that works for the terms before the missing term.

First, try addition, and then subtraction.

What number can you add to 10 to get 19?

$10 + 9 = 19$

What number can you subtract from 19 to get 18?

$19 - 1 = 18$

What number can you add to 18 to get 27?

$18 + 9 = 27$

What number can you subtract from 27 to get 26?

$27 - 1 = 26$

The terms appear to follow the rule *add 9, subtract 1*.

Step 3   Continue the rule to find the missing term.

$26 + 9 = 35$

Step 4   Make sure the rule works for the other given terms.

$35 - 1 = 34, 34 + 9 = 43, 43 - 1 = 42, 42 + 9 = 51$

Step 5   Describe the terms without using the rule.

The pattern alternates between increasing and decreasing. The terms alternate between even and odd.

Solution   **A rule for the pattern is *add 9, subtract 1*. The missing term is 35. The terms alternate between even and odd.**

Some patterns have two sets of numbers, inputs and outputs. You can show these patterns in a table. The rule for the pattern tells the relationship between each input number and its output number.

Example 4

Create a pattern with 6 terms using the rule *multiply by 10*. Complete the input-output table to write the pattern.

Input	Output
6	
8	
10	
12	
14	
16	

What do you notice about the pattern that is not described in the rule?

Strategy   Use the inputs and the rule.

Step 1   Use the rule *multiply by 10* to complete the table.

Input	Operation	Output
6	6 × 10	60
8	8 × 10	80
10	10 × 10	100
12	12 × 10	120
14	14 × 10	140
16	16 × 10	160

Step 2   Describe the terms without using the rule.

The pattern is increasing. Every output is a multiple of 10. Each output is 20 more than the output preceding it.

Solution   The pattern is shown in the input-output table in Step 1. The pattern is increasing. Every output is a multiple of 10. Each output is 20 more than the output preceding it.

Example 5

Find a rule for the pattern below. Then write the missing term. What do you notice about the pattern that is not described in the rule?

Input	Output
3	12
8	17
13	22
18	27
23	32
28	
33	42
38	47

Strategy   Use the given inputs and outputs to find a rule. Then use the rule to find the missing term.

Step 1   Determine if the difference between each input and its output is the same.

Input	Output	
3	12	$12 - 3 = \mathbf{9}$
8	17	$17 - 8 = \mathbf{9}$
13	22	$22 - 13 = \mathbf{9}$
18	27	$27 - 18 = \mathbf{9}$
23	32	$32 - 23 = \mathbf{9}$
28		
33	42	$42 - 33 = \mathbf{9}$
38	47	$47 - 38 = \mathbf{9}$

Each output is 9 more than its input.

Step 2   State the rule.

Since each output is 9 more than its input, the rule is *add 9*.

Step 3   Continue the rule to find the missing term.

$28 + \mathbf{9} = 37$

Step 4   Describe the terms without using the rule.

Each output is 5 more than the preceding output. The outputs alternate between even and odd, and the ones digit in each output alternates between 2 and 7.

Solution   The missing term is 37. Each output is 5 more than the preceding output. The outputs alternate between even and odd, and the ones digit in each output alternates between 2 and 7.

Find a rule for the pattern below. Then find the missing term. What do you notice about the terms in the pattern that is not described in the rule?

8, 5, 10, 7, 14, _____, 22, 19

The pattern alternates between _____ and _____.

Look for a rule that works for the terms before the missing term.

First, _____, and then multiply.

8 ◯ _____ = 5

5 × _____ = 10

10 ◯ _____ = 7

7 × _____ = 14

The terms appear to follow the rule _____, _____.

To find the missing term, _____ from 14 to get _____.

Make sure the rule works for the other given terms.

11 ◯ _____ = 22

22 ◯ _____ = _____

Describe the terms without using the rule.

[ ]

The rule is _____, _____.

The missing term is _____. The terms _____ between even and _____.

1 The rule for the pattern below is *add 10, multiply by 2*. What is the missing term in the pattern?

5, 15, 30, 40, _____, 90, 180

A. 50

B. 80

C. 10

D. 85

2 Which number pattern is created using only an addition or subtraction rule?

A. 2, 4, 6, 8, 10, 12, 14, 16

B. 160, 80, 40, 20, 10, 5

C. 3, 6, 12, 24, 48, 96

D. 6, 2, 8, 4, 16, 12, 48

3 What term completes the number pattern?

Input	Output
6	18
14	42
22	66
30	90
38	114
46	

A. 138

B. 122

C. 90

D. 58

4 Which statement describes the following number pattern?

64, 32, 16, 8, 4, 2

A. The 7th term is 4.

B. The rule is *divide by 2*.

C. An addition rule could be written for the pattern.

D. The terms alternate between even and odd.

5 What term is missing from the pattern below?

6; 30; 150; _____; 3,750

Record your answer and fill in the bubbles. Be sure to use the correct place value.

6 What is the rule for the pattern below?

1, 5, 3, 7, 5, 9, 7

A. Add 4

B. Subtract 2

C. Subtract 2, add 4

D. Add 4, subtract 2

7 What is the missing term in the number pattern below?

Input	Output
2	7
12	17
22	27
32	37
42	
52	57

A. 127

B. 67

C. 47

D. 107

8 Which number pattern follows the rule *add 7*?

A. 117; 649; 16,807; 2,401; 343; 49

B. 8; 56; 392; 2,744; 19,208

C. 58, 51, 44, 37, 30

D. 71, 78, 85, 92, 99

9 What is the rule for the pattern below?

1, 9, 3, 27, 9, 81, 27

A. Multiply by 3, divide by 9

B. Multiply by 9, divide by 3

C. Multiply by 9

D. Divide by 3

10 What is the starting term for the number pattern below?

_____, 14, 19, 24, 29, 34, 39

Record your answer and fill in the bubbles. Be sure to use the correct place value.

			.		
⓪	⓪	⓪		⓪	⓪
①	①	①		①	①
②	②	②		②	②
③	③	③		③	③
④	④	④		④	④
⑤	⑤	⑤		⑤	⑤
⑥	⑥	⑥		⑥	⑥
⑦	⑦	⑦		⑦	⑦
⑧	⑧	⑧		⑧	⑧
⑨	⑨	⑨		⑨	⑨

11 The starting term of a number pattern is 2. The rule for the pattern is *multiply by 4*. Which statement about the terms in the pattern is correct?

A. The terms alternate between even and odd.

B. The pattern is decreasing.

C. All of the terms are multiples of 2.

D. The ones digit for each term is 2.

12 Which statement is true about the number pattern below?

    5, 10, 20, 40, 80, 160

A. All of the terms are even.

B. All of the terms are multiples of 10.

C. The pattern is decreasing.

D. The pattern is increasing.

13 What is the rule for the input-output table shown below?

Input	Output
9	5
11	7
13	9
15	11
17	13
19	15

A. Add 4

B. Multiply by 4

C. Divide by 4

D. Subtract 4

14 What is the rule for the number pattern below?

    14, 6, 12, 4, 8

A. Subtract 8, multiply by 2

B. Multiply by 2, subtract 8

C. Multiply by 2

D. Subtract 8

15 What term is missing from the number pattern below?

   34, 29, 58, 53, 106, 101, _____

Record your answer and fill in the bubbles. Be sure to use the correct place value.

			.		
⓪	⓪	⓪		⓪	⓪
①	①	①		①	①
②	②	②		②	②
③	③	③		③	③
④	④	④		④	④
⑤	⑤	⑤		⑤	⑤
⑥	⑥	⑥		⑥	⑥
⑦	⑦	⑦		⑦	⑦
⑧	⑧	⑧		⑧	⑧
⑨	⑨	⑨		⑨	⑨

1 Use the number line to help answer the question.

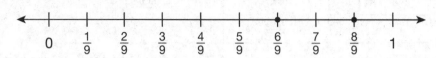

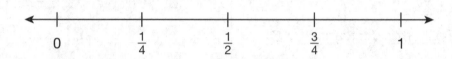

Which statement is correct?

A $\frac{8}{9} - \frac{6}{9}$ is close to 0.

C $\frac{8}{9} - \frac{6}{9}$ is close to $\frac{1}{2}$.

B $\frac{8}{9} - \frac{6}{9}$ is close to $\frac{1}{4}$.

D $\frac{8}{9} - \frac{6}{9}$ is close to $\frac{3}{4}$.

---

2 Lara buys a new shirt for $23.86. She gives the cashier $30. How much change does she get back?

F $7.14

G $7.24

H $6.14

J $6.24

3 Sasha bought 4 games and 2 lamps. The price of each game was $18 and the price of each lamp was $32. About how much did Sasha spend?

A $100

B $120

C $130

D $140

4 What is the missing term in the number pattern below?

Input	Output
1	125
3	375
5	625
7	875
9	

F 1,250

G 1,125

H 1,175

J 1,225

5 Use the place-value chart to help answer the question.

Thousands Period				Ones Period		
Hundreds	Tens	Ones	,	Hundreds	Tens	Ones

A factory produced 285 packages of coffee filters. Each package has 100 filters. How many filters did the factory produce?

A 285,000

B 28,500

C 2,850

D 285

---

6 Natalia draws the model to help her find the quotient of two numbers.

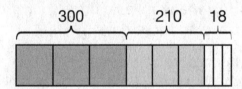

300   210   18

Which division problem does Natalia's model represent?

F 328 ÷ 3

G 510 ÷ 3

H 518 ÷ 3

J 528 ÷ 3

7 Mr. Jameson's backyard is a rectangle. The width is 26 feet and the length is 32 feet. What is the area of his backyard in square feet?

Record your answer and fill in the bubbles. Be sure to use the correct place value.

			.		
⓪	⓪	⓪		⓪	⓪
①	①	①		①	①
②	②	②		②	②
③	③	③		③	③
④	④	④		④	④
⑤	⑤	⑤		⑤	⑤
⑥	⑥	⑥		⑥	⑥
⑦	⑦	⑦		⑦	⑦
⑧	⑧	⑧		⑧	⑧
⑨	⑨	⑨		⑨	⑨

8 Use the number line to help answer the question.

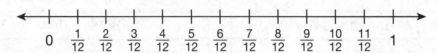

Kimmi buys $\frac{3}{12}$ pound of mixed nuts. She also buys $\frac{7}{12}$ pound of dried fruits. How many pounds does she buy in all?

F $\frac{4}{12}$ pound

H $\frac{4}{24}$ pound

G $\frac{10}{12}$ pound

J $\frac{10}{24}$ pound

---

9 Zoe has a 182-page book and a 210-page book to read over the summer. She reads 9 pages each day. How many days does it take Zoe to read her books?

A 40 days

B 43 days

C 44 days

D 50 days

10 Mr. Allen has three delivery vans. Each van weighs 3,758 pounds. What is the total weight of all three vans?

F 11,174 pounds

G 11,274 pounds

H 11,254 pounds

J 11,154 pounds

11 Ms. Aldridge was part of a tour group. The tour traveled 125 miles the first day, 323 miles the second day, and 88 miles the third day. How many miles did the tour group travel in three days?

Record your answer and fill in the bubbles. Be sure to use the correct place value.

			.		
⓪	⓪	⓪		⓪	⓪
①	①	①		①	①
②	②	②		②	②
③	③	③		③	③
④	④	④		④	④
⑤	⑤	⑤		⑤	⑤
⑥	⑥	⑥		⑥	⑥
⑦	⑦	⑦		⑦	⑦
⑧	⑧	⑧		⑧	⑧
⑨	⑨	⑨		⑨	⑨

12 Carlos draws the area model below to find the product of two numbers.

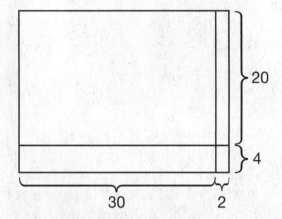

Which equation does his area model represent?

F 32 × 24 = 768

G 32 × 24 = 608

H 30 × 20 = 600

J 34 × 22 = 608

13 The fourth-grade class collected 4,820 pounds of newspaper for recycling. The fifth-grade class collected 3,582 pounds of newspaper. How much more newspaper did the fourth-grade class collect than the fifth-grade class?

A 1,362 pounds

B 1,348 pounds

C 1,242 pounds

D 1,238 pounds

14 Mario and his five friends had a yard sale. They made $768. They divided the money evenly. How much did each person get?

F $102

G $120

H $128

J $103

15 The table lists the prices of some items on sale at a store.

Item	Price
Shorts	$15
Pants	$24
Shirts	$12

Rasheed has $200. He buys 4 pairs of shorts, 2 pairs of pants, and 5 shirts. How many dollars does he have left over?

Record your answer and fill in the bubbles. Be sure to use the correct place value.

			.		
⓪	⓪	⓪		⓪	⓪
①	①	①		①	①
②	②	②		②	②
③	③	③		③	③
④	④	④		④	④
⑤	⑤	⑤		⑤	⑤
⑥	⑥	⑥		⑥	⑥
⑦	⑦	⑦		⑦	⑦
⑧	⑧	⑧		⑧	⑧
⑨	⑨	⑨		⑨	⑨

16 Fabio ran for 4.72 miles. Pierre ran for 2.89 miles. How much farther did Fabio run than Pierre?

F 2.17 miles

G 1.17 miles

H 1.93 miles

J 1.83 miles

17 A store had $2,383 in sales in 6 days. The store had about the same amount of sales each day. Which expression can be used to find the best estimate of the amount of sales each day?

A 3,000 ÷ 6

B 2,500 ÷ 6

C 2,400 ÷ 6

D 2,000 ÷ 6

18 Mrs. Ulrich baked 79 bagels. She froze them in packages of 8. How many packages did she freeze?

F 9

G 10

H 8

J 7

19 A decade is 10 years. A century is 100 years. The antique dresser Jane bought is 2 centuries, 6 decades, and 4 years old. How many years old is the dresser?

Record your answer and fill in the bubbles. Be sure to use the correct place value.

			.		
⓪	⓪	⓪		⓪	⓪
①	①	①		①	①
②	②	②		②	②
③	③	③		③	③
④	④	④		④	④
⑤	⑤	⑤		⑤	⑤
⑥	⑥	⑥		⑥	⑥
⑦	⑦	⑦		⑦	⑦
⑧	⑧	⑧		⑧	⑧
⑨	⑨	⑨		⑨	⑨

20 What is the missing term in the number pattern below?

Input	Output
8	144
16	288
24	432
32	
40	720

F 288

G 540

H 576

J 600

21 Use the diagram to help solve the problem.

180

72						

n

Nina and her friends bake 180 cookies. They save 72 cookies and divide the rest evenly in 6 bags. How many cookies are in each bag?

A 12

B 18

C 24

D 30

22 Use fraction strips to answer the question.

$\frac{1}{6}$	$\frac{1}{6}$	$\frac{1}{6}$	$\frac{1}{6}$	$\frac{1}{6}$	$\frac{1}{6}$

Odessa is making pancakes. She measures $\frac{4}{6}$ cup of sugar. She spills $\frac{1}{6}$ cup on the floor. How much sugar does she have now?

F $\frac{1}{6}$ cup

G $\frac{3}{6}$ cup

H $\frac{4}{6}$ cup

J $\frac{5}{6}$ cup

23 For a party, Cameron makes a 2-foot long sandwich containing 2,832 calories. He divides the sandwich into 8 equal pieces. How many calories are in each piece?

A 300 calories

B 304 calories

C 350 calories

D 354 calories

CHAPTER
3

Geometry and Measurement

Perimeter and Area

The distance around a plane figure is its **perimeter**. You can find the perimeter of a rectangle by adding the length of all its sides.

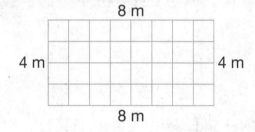

Perimeter = length + width + length + width

Perimeter = 8 + 4 + 8 + 4 = 24 meters

You can also use a **formula** to find the perimeter of a rectangle. A formula is an equation that shows how to find an amount like the perimeter or area of a figure. The formula for finding the perimeter of a rectangle is:

$$P = 2 \times l + 2 \times w$$

Perimeter   length   width

$P = 2 \times 8 + 2 \times 4$

$P = 16 + 8 = 24$ meters

The amount of space a figure covers is called its **area**. The formula for finding the area of a rectangle is:

$$A = l \times w$$

Area   length   width

$A = 8 \times 4 = 32$ square meters

Example 1

Ben's house is shaped like a rectangle that is 46 feet long and 28 feet wide. What is the distance around Ben's house?

Strategy   Use the formula for the perimeter of a rectangle.

Step 1   Write the formula.

$$P = 2 \times l + 2 \times w$$

Step 2   Replace the unknowns.

Replace l and w with the length and width of the rectangle.

The length is 46 feet. The width is 28 feet.

$$P = 2 \times 46 + 2 \times 28$$

Step 3   Multiply. Then add.

Remember to write the unit in your answer.

$$P = 92 + 56$$

$$P = 148 \text{ feet}$$

Solution   **The perimeter of Ben's house is 148 feet.**

Example 2

A bulletin board is 36 inches long and 24 inches wide. What is the area of the bulletin board?

Strategy   Use the formula for the area of a rectangle.

Step 1   Write the formula.

$$A = l \times w$$

Step 2   Replace the unknowns.

Replace l with 36 inches and w with 24 inches.

$$A = 36 \times 24$$

Step 3   Multiply to find the value of A.

Label the area in square units.

$$A = 36 \times 24$$

$$A = 864 \text{ square inches}$$

Solution   **The area of the bulletin board is 864 square inches.**

Example 3

The perimeter of a rectangular swimming pool is 34 yards. The pool is 5 yards wide. What is the length of the pool?

Strategy   Use the formula for the perimeter of a rectangle.

Step 1   Write the formula.

$$P = 2 \times l + 2 \times w$$

Step 2   Replace the unknowns.

You know the perimeter of the pool is 34 yards. Replace P with 34.

You know the width of the pool is 5 yards. Replace w with 5.

$$34 = 2 \times l + 2 \times 5$$

Step 3   Multiply.

$$34 = 2 \times l + 10$$

Step 4   Work backward.

Some number plus 10 is 34.

$$34 = (2 \times l) + 10$$

$$34 = ? + 10$$

$24 + 10 = 34$, so $2 \times l$ must be equal to 24.

$$24 = 2 \times l$$

Now you can divide to find l.

$24 \div 2 = 12$ Remember, division is the opposite of multiplication.

$24 = 2 \times 12$ So, $l = 12$.

Solution   **The length of the swimming pool is 12 yards.**

A photograph is 8 centimeters wide and has an area of 96 square centimeters. What is the length of the photograph?

Use the formula for the _____ of a rectangle.

$A =$ _____ $\times$ _____

Replace the unknowns and rewrite the equation.

Replace A with _____.

Replace w with _____.

The equation with the replaced values is _____ $=$ _____ $\times$ _____.

To find l, think: What number times 8 $=$ _____?

To find the answer, I can divide _____ by _____.

_____ $\div$ _____ $=$ _____

$l =$ _____ cm

The length of the photograph is _____ centimeters.

1 What are the perimeter and area of a rectangle with a length of 16 inches and a width of 20 inches?

   A. $P = 36$ in.; $A = 32$ sq. in.

   B. $P = 72$ in.; $A = 320$ sq. in.

   C. $P = 640$ in.; $A = 56$ sq. in.

   D. $P = 320$ in.; $A = 72$ sq. in.

2 Which rectangle has an area of 16 square units?

   A.

   B.

   C.

   D.

3 A rectangle has a perimeter of 58 meters and a length of 17 meters. What is the width of the rectangle?

   A. 3 m

   B. 12 m

   C. 24 m

   D. 41 m

4 A flowerbed is 40 feet long. It has a perimeter of 130 feet. Which statement about the flowerbed is true?

   A. The width of the flowerbed is 90 feet.

   B. All 4 sides of the flowerbed are the same length.

   C. The area of the flowerbed is 160 square feet.

   D. The flowerbed has two sides that are each 25 feet long.

5 Nora has 100 feet of fencing to use for a rabbit cage. For which cage does Nora have enough fencing?

   A. Cage A: $l = 24$ ft; $w = 20$ ft

   B. Cage B: $l = 10$ ft; $A = 500$ sq. ft

   C. Cage C: $l = 8$ ft; $A = 480$ sq. ft

   D. Cage D: $l = 20$ ft; $w = 35$ ft

6 Nick's room is in the shape of a rectangle. The perimeter of his room is 48 feet. The area of his room is 140 square feet. What are the measurements of his room?

   A. $l = 16$ ft; $w = 8$ ft

   B. $l = 14$ ft; $w = 10$ ft

   C. $l = 12$ ft; $w = 12$ ft

   D. $l = 8$ ft; $w = 6$ ft

Use the information below for questions 7–9.

Silas is going to put a fence around 3 sides of his rectangular garden. The fourth side runs along the side of his rectangular shed. Silas draws a diagram of his shed and garden.

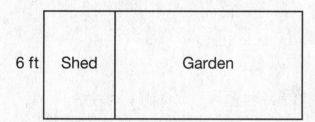

Silas will use 30 feet of fence for his fence project.

7 How many feet long is Silas's garden?

A. 5 ft

C. 12 ft

B. 28 ft

D. 14 ft

8 What is the area of Silas's garden?

A. 144 sq. ft

B. 72 sq. ft

C. 36 sq. ft

D. 30 sq. ft

9 The width of the shed is 3 ft. What is the perimeter around the combined shed and garden?

A. 33 ft   C. 39 ft

B. 36 ft   D. 42 ft

10 Which equation calculates the area of this square?

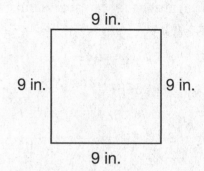

A. $2 \times 9 = 18$ sq. in.

B. $9 \times 4 = 36$ sq. in.

C. $9 \times 9 = 81$ sq. in.

D. $4 \times 4 = 16$ sq. in.

11 Rosa hung a picture that measures 16 inches long and 12 inches wide on the bulletin board hanging above her desk. The length and width of the bulletin board are shown below.

How many square inches of the bulletin board are **not** covered by the poster?

A. 240 sq. in.

B. 432 sq. in.

C. 192 sq. in.

D. 48 sq. in.

12 A rectangle has an area of 72 square yards. It has a perimeter of 36 yards. What are the length and width of the rectangle?

A. l = 12 yards; w = 6 yards

B. l = 36 yards; w = 2 yards

C. l = 6 yards; w = 6 yards

D. l = 9 yards; w = 4 yards

13 The area of a rectangle is 336 square centimeters. The rectangle has a width of 8 centimeters. What is the length of the rectangle?

A. 328 cm

B. 164 cm

C. 42 cm

D. 21 cm

14 What are the area and perimeter of a desk that has the measurements shown?

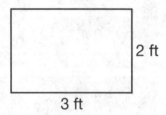

2 ft

3 ft

A. A = 10 ft; P = 6 sq. ft

B. A = 10 sq. ft; P = 6 ft

C. A = 6 ft; P = 10 sq. ft

D. A = 6 sq. ft; P = 10 ft

15 José's laptop has a screen that is 8 inches wide. The screen has an area of 112 square inches. What is the perimeter of the laptop screen?

A. 104 in.

B. 37 in.

C. 44 in.

D. 74 in.

16 Omar wants to tape two same-sized poster boards together along their lengths. The poster boards are 9 inches wide.

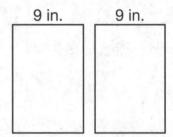

9 in.   9 in.

The area of each poster board is 144 square inches. How many inches of tape does Omar need?

Record your answer and fill in the bubbles. Be sure to use the correct place value.

			.		
⓪	⓪	⓪		⓪	⓪
①	①	①		①	①
②	②	②		②	②
③	③	③		③	③
④	④	④		④	④
⑤	⑤	⑤		⑤	⑤
⑥	⑥	⑥		⑥	⑥
⑦	⑦	⑦		⑦	⑦
⑧	⑧	⑧		⑧	⑧
⑨	⑨	⑨		⑨	⑨

LESSON **22**

Identifying Figures

1 **GETTING THE IDEA**

A **point** is a location in space. A capital letter is used to name a point. This point is named X.

Points are the building blocks of geometry. Other geometric figures are made up of points.

A **line** is made of many points and extends without end in opposite directions. A line has no thickness. This line is $\overleftrightarrow{AB}$ or $\overleftrightarrow{BA}$.

A **line segment** is part of a line. It is made up of two **endpoints** and all the points between the endpoints. This segment is $\overline{CD}$ or $\overline{DC}$.

A **ray** is also part of a line. It has one endpoint and extends without end in one direction. This ray is $\overrightarrow{EF}$.

Example 1

Draw $\overrightarrow{PQ}$.

Strategy   **Draw the endpoint. Then draw a ray from the endpoint.**

   Step 1   Identify what you need to draw.

       The symbol → means ray.

   Step 2   Draw the endpoint, P.

   Step 3   Draw a different point, Q.

   Step 4   Draw the ray.

       Start at endpoint P. Draw a line through Q. Draw an arrowhead to show that the ray continues.

Solution   One way to draw $\overrightarrow{PQ}$ is shown in Step 4.

Lesson 22: Identifying Figures **189**

An **angle** is a figure made up of two rays that share an endpoint. The **vertex** of an angle is that endpoint. This angle can be named ∠K, ∠JKL, or ∠LKJ.

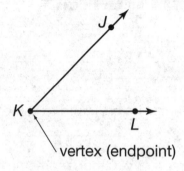

vertex (endpoint)

Angles are measured in units called **degrees**. The symbol for degrees is [°]. You can classify an angle by its measure.

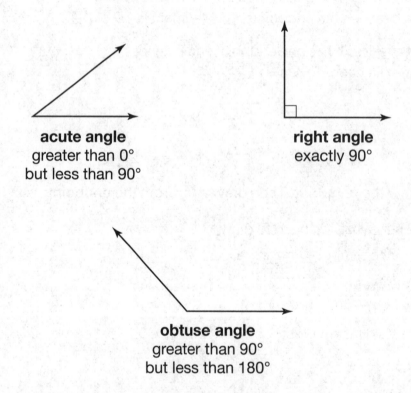

acute angle
greater than 0°
but less than 90°

right angle
exactly 90°

obtuse angle
greater than 90°
but less than 180°

Notice the box symbol in the right angle above. This symbol shows that the right angle measures exactly 90°. A right angle is shaped like the letter L.

An angle can be formed by two line segments that share an endpoint.

Example 2

Classify each angle of *STUV* as acute, right, or obtuse.

Explain your reasoning.

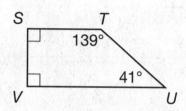

Strategy   Use the measure of each angle to classify it.

Step 1   Classify ∠S.

The box symbol indicates that the measure of ∠S is 90°.

So ∠S is a right angle.

Step 2   Classify ∠T.

The measure of ∠T is 139°, which is between 90° and 180°.

So ∠T is an obtuse angle.

Step 3   Classify ∠U.

The measure of ∠U is 41°, which is between 0° and 90°.

So ∠U is an acute angle.

Step 4   Classify ∠V.

The box symbol indicates that the measure of ∠V is 90°.

So ∠V is a right angle.

Solution   ∠S is a right angle, ∠T is an obtuse angle, ∠U is an acute angle, and ∠V is a right angle.

Two lines that intersect to form right angles are **perpendicular lines**.
$\overleftrightarrow{AB}$ is perpendicular to $\overleftrightarrow{CD}$. This is written as $\overleftrightarrow{AB} \perp \overleftrightarrow{CD}$.

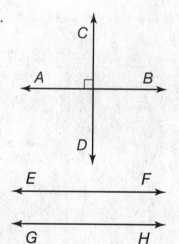

Two lines that never intersect are **parallel lines**.
$\overleftrightarrow{EF}$ is parallel to $\overleftrightarrow{GH}$. This is written as $\overleftrightarrow{EF} \parallel \overleftrightarrow{GH}$.

Example 3

This figure shows an overhead view of the four streets that surround the local high school. Identify one pair of parallel lines and one pair of perpendicular lines.

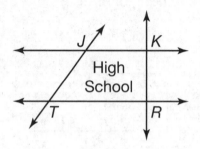

Strategy Identify lines that do not intersect and lines that form a right angle.

Step 1 Find two lines that do **not** intersect.

$\overleftrightarrow{JK}$ and $\overleftrightarrow{TR}$ do not intersect, so $\overleftrightarrow{JK}$ and $\overleftrightarrow{TR}$ are parallel. No matter how far you extend $\overleftrightarrow{JK}$ and $\overleftrightarrow{TR}$ they will never intersect.

The parts of $\overleftrightarrow{KR}$ and $\overleftrightarrow{JT}$ shown do not intersect. But if you extend these lines, they will eventually intersect. So $\overleftrightarrow{KR}$ and $\overleftrightarrow{JT}$ are not parallel.

Step 2 Find two lines that intersect to form a right angle.

$\angle R$ and $\angle K$ make corners like the corner of a sheet of paper. These are right angles. $\overleftrightarrow{TR}$ and $\overleftrightarrow{KR}$ intersect to form $\angle R$. So $\overleftrightarrow{TR}$ and $\overleftrightarrow{KR}$ are perpendicular. $\overleftrightarrow{JK}$ and $\overleftrightarrow{KR}$ intersect to form $\angle K$. So $\overleftrightarrow{JK}$ and $\overleftrightarrow{KR}$ are also perpendicular.

Solution $\overleftrightarrow{JK} \parallel \overleftrightarrow{TR}; \overleftrightarrow{TR} \perp \overleftrightarrow{KR}$

Example 4

Name the following parts of square *ABCD*.

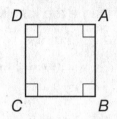

- Points

- Line segments

- Angles

- Parallel segments

- Perpendicular segments

Strategy   Use the definition of each figure.

Step 1   Identify the points that make up *ABCD*.

There are many points that make up square *ABCD*, but only 4 points are labeled: *A*, *B*, *C*, and *D*.

Step 2   Identify the line segments that make up *ABCD*.

There are 4 line segments that make up square *ABCD*: $\overline{AB}$, $\overline{BC}$, $\overline{CD}$, and $\overline{AD}$.

Step 3   Identify the angles of *ABCD*.

There are 4 angles in *ABCD*: $\angle A$, $\angle B$, $\angle C$, and $\angle D$.

Step 4   Identify parallel segments in *ABCD*.

$\overline{AB}$ and $\overline{CD}$ do **not** intersect, so $\overline{AB}$ and $\overline{CD}$ are parallel segments.

$\overline{AD}$ and $\overline{BC}$ do **not** intersect, so $\overline{AD}$ and $\overline{BC}$ are also parallel segments.

Step 5   Identify perpendicular segments in *ABCD*.

A square always has 4 right angles. You can see that the corners are all square corners. So every pair of segments that intersect are perpendicular. $\overline{AB} \perp \overline{AD}$, $\overline{AB} \perp \overline{BC}$, $\overline{BC} \perp \overline{CD}$, and $\overline{AD} \perp \overline{CD}$.

Solution   The parts of square *ABCD* are shown in each step above.

Name the following parts of the figure.

- Points
- Line segments
- Rays
- Angles
- Parallel segments
- Perpendicular segments

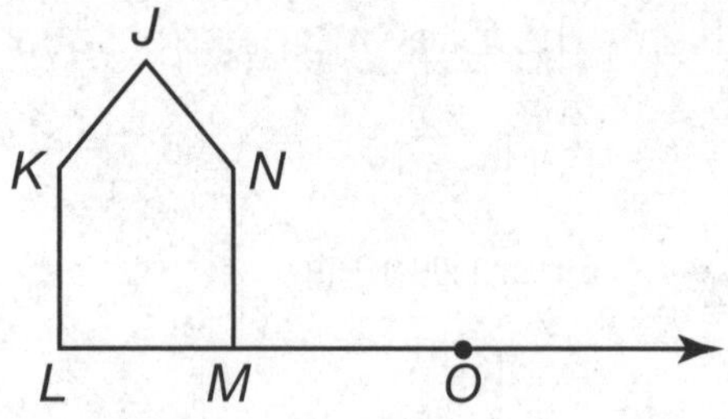

A point is a _____ in space. Name the labeled point(s) in the figure.

_____

A line segment is part of a line. It has _____ endpoint(s). Name the line segment(s) in the figure.

_____

A ray is part of a line. It has _____ endpoint(s). Name the ray(s) in the figure.

_____

An angle is formed by 2 line segments or rays that share _____ endpoint(s). Name the angle(s) in the figure.

_____

Parallel lines are lines that _____. Name the parallel line segments in the figure.

_____

Perpendicular lines are lines that form _____.

Name the perpendicular line segments in the figure.

_____

The parts of the figure are:

- Points: _____
- Line segments: _____
- Rays: _____
- Angles: _____
- Parallel segments: _____
- Perpendicular segments: _____

1 Which statement is true?

  A. A ray has two endpoints.

  B. A point is a location in space.

  C. A line segment is made up of exactly two points.

  D. A line can have any thickness.

2 Charlene drew the figure shown.

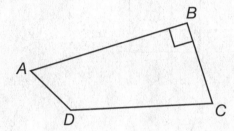

Which angle in the figure is an obtuse angle?

  A. ∠A

  B. ∠B

  C. ∠C

  D. ∠D

3 What does C in the diagram show?

  A. A point on a line

  B. An endpoint on a line

  C. An endpoint of a ray

  D. An endpoint on a line segment

Use rectangle *WXYZ* for questions 4 and 5.

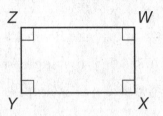

4 Which term best describes $\overline{WX}$ and $\overline{YZ}$?

  A. points

  B. parallel line segments

  C. right angles

  D. line segments

5 In *WXYZ*, which pair of line segments is **not** perpendicular?

  A. $\overline{WZ}$ and $\overline{WX}$

  B. $\overline{WX}$ and $\overline{XY}$

  C. $\overline{XY}$ and $\overline{YZ}$

  D. $\overline{YZ}$ and $\overline{XW}$

6 Which of the following is a way to draw $\overleftrightarrow{ST}$?

  A.
  ◄————•————————•
        S   T

  B.
      •————————————•
      S   T

  C.
      •————————————•———►
      S   T

  D.
  ◄——•————————————•——►
      S   T

7 Which statement is true?

    A. An angle is a figure made up of two rays.

    B. An angle has two endpoints.

    C. An angle is measured in meters.

    D. The vertex of an angle is a ray.

8 What is the measure of a right angle?

    A. 180°

    B. Greater than 90°

    C. 90°

    D. Less than 90°

9 What is the measure of an acute angle?

    A. 180°

    B. Greater than 90°

    C. 90°

    D. Less than 90°

10 Which lines appear to be parallel in the figure?

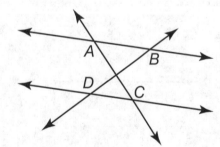

    A. $\overleftrightarrow{AB}$ and $\overleftrightarrow{DC}$

    B. $\overleftrightarrow{AC}$ and $\overleftrightarrow{DC}$

    C. $\overleftrightarrow{AC}$ and $\overleftrightarrow{DB}$

    D. $\overleftrightarrow{DC}$ and $\overleftrightarrow{DB}$

11 Keira drew a figure with the following properties.

- At least one pair of parallel line segments
- At least 4 angles
- No perpendicular line segments

Which figure could be Keira's figure?

    A.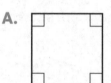

    B.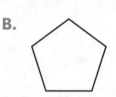

    C.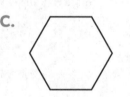

    D.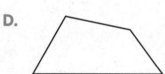

12 Which is **not** the measure of an obtuse angle?

    A. 91°

    B. 105°

    C. 150°

    D. 180°

13 Which of the following is a right angle in the figure below?

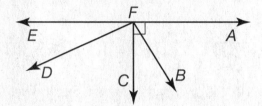

A. ∠DFC

B. ∠AFC

C. ∠BFE

D. ∠BFC

14 Marci is looking at part of a map shown below.

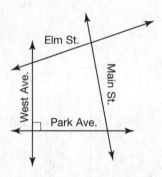

Elm St.

West Ave.

Main St.

Park Ave.

Which statement is **not** true about the streets on the map?

A. West Ave. is perpendicular to Park Ave.

B. Park Ave. is parallel to Elm St.

C. West Ave. and Main St. are not parallel.

D. Main St. and Park Ave. are not perpendicular.

15 Diego drew a figure with the following properties.

- $\overline{KL} \perp \overline{IK}$ and $\overline{KL} \parallel \overline{IJ}$.
- $\overleftrightarrow{LJ}$ intersects $\overline{KL}$ and $\overline{IJ}$.
- The measure of ∠KLJ is 60° and the measure of ∠IJL is 120°.

Which statement is true about Diego's figure?

A. ∠KLJ is obtuse.

B. ∠KIJ is acute.

C. ∠IKL measures 90°.

D. ∠KLJ is a right angle.

16 How many pairs of parallel line segments are in the figure?

Record your answer and fill in the bubbles. Be sure to use the correct place value.

			.		
⓪	⓪	⓪		⓪	⓪
①	①	①		①	①
②	②	②		②	②
③	③	③		③	③
④	④	④		④	④
⑤	⑤	⑤		⑤	⑤
⑥	⑥	⑥		⑥	⑥
⑦	⑦	⑦		⑦	⑦
⑧	⑧	⑧		⑧	⑧
⑨	⑨	⑨		⑨	⑨

Identifying Lines of Symmetry

A figure has **symmetry** if it can be folded on a line so that the two parts match exactly. The fold line is the **line of symmetry**.

The triangle below has a line of symmetry. When the triangle is folded on the dashed line, the two parts match exactly.

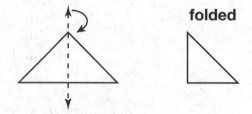

folded

Example 1

Is the line in each figure a line of symmetry?

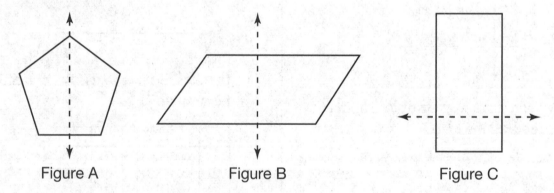

Figure A   Figure B   Figure C

Strategy   Imagine folding each figure along the line.

Look at the fold line on each figure. Imagine folding the figure along the line.

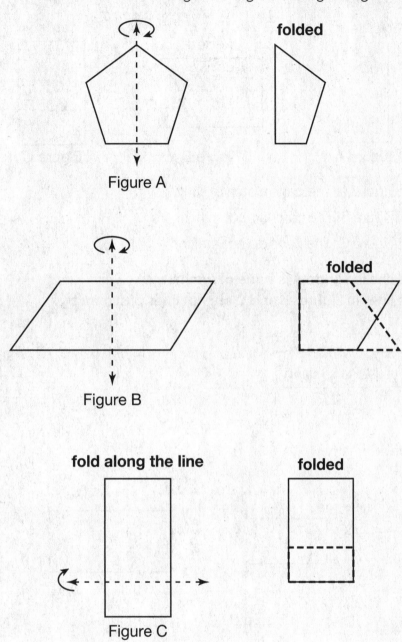

folded

Figure A

folded

Figure B

fold along the line

folded

Figure C

Check each folded figure to see if the parts match exactly.

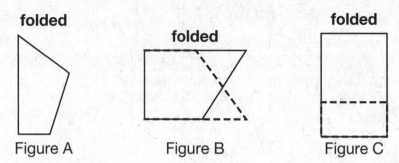

Figure A   Figure B   Figure C

Figure A: The parts match exactly.

Figure B: The parts do not match.

Figure C: The parts do not match.

Solution   **The line in Figure A is a line of symmetry.**
The lines in Figures B and C are not lines of symmetry.

A figure has symmetry if you can draw a line of symmetry for the figure. A line of symmetry can be vertical, horizontal, or on a slant.

Example 2

Which figures have symmetry?

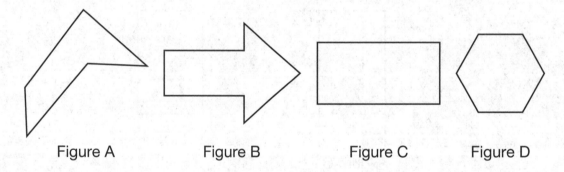

Figure A   Figure B   Figure C   Figure D

Strategy   **Use the definition of symmetry.**

Try to draw a line in each figure that would make the parts match.

Figure A

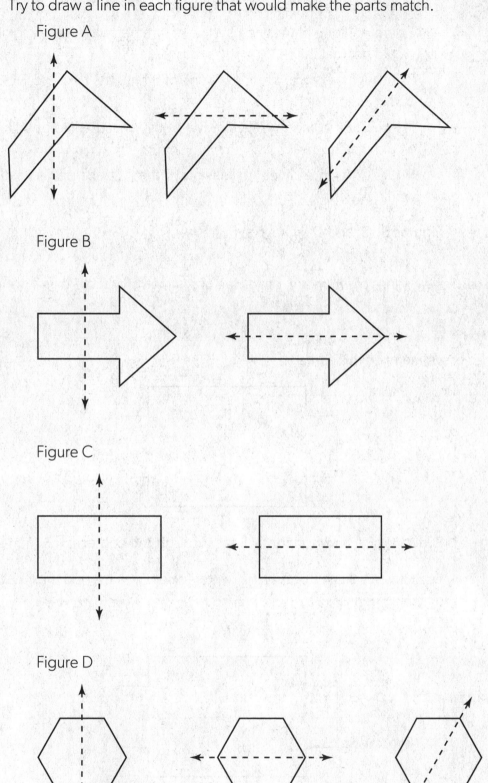

Figure B

Figure C

Figure D

Check if the lines are lines of symmetry.

Figure A: None of the lines is a line of symmetry, because if folded, the parts would not match.

Figure B: The horizontal line is a line of symmetry, because if folded, the parts would match.

Figure C: Both lines are lines of symmetry, because if folded, the parts would match.

Figure D: All three lines are lines of symmetry, because if folded, the parts would match.

Solution **Figures B, C, and D all have symmetry.**

A figure can have no lines of symmetry, only 1 line of symmetry, or more than 1 line of symmetry.

Example 3

Draw lines of symmetry on this figure.

Strategy **Draw vertical and horizontal lines through the center.**

Step 1 Draw a vertical line through the center to separate the figure into 2 equal and matching parts.

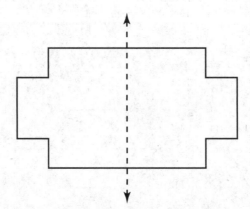

Step 2   Draw a horizontal line through the center.

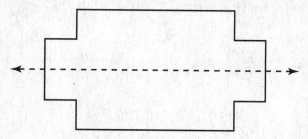

Step 3   Count the number of lines of symmetry the figure has.

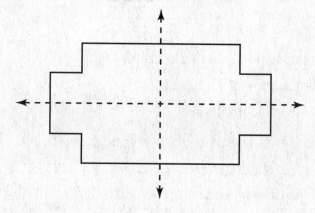

Solution   The figure has two lines of symmetry as shown above.

Draw the line(s) of symmetry for this figure.

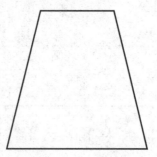

A line of symmetry goes through the _____ of the figure.

Think about drawing a vertical line through the center of the figure.

Is a vertical line a line of symmetry? _____

Draw the line if it is a line of symmetry.

Think about drawing a horizontal line through the center of the figure.

Is the horizontal line a line of symmetry? _____

Draw the line if it is a line of symmetry.

The figure has _____ line(s) of symmetry as shown above.

1. Which figure shows a line of symmetry?

A.
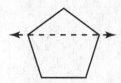

B.
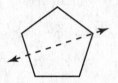

C.
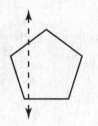

D.
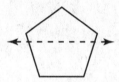

2. How many lines of symmetry does the figure have?

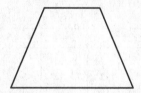

A. 4
B. 3
C. 2
D. 1

3. How many lines of symmetry does the triangle have?

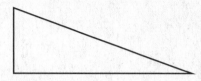

A. 3
B. 2
C. 1
D. 0

4. Which lists all of the letters shown that have symmetry?

A. A, C, D, and E
B. A, D, and E
C. A, C, E, and F
D. C, D, and F

5. How many lines of symmetry does the figure have?

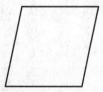

A. 0
B. 1
C. 2
D. 4

6 Which statement is true about the figures below?

 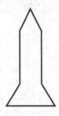

Figure 1   **Figure 2**   **Figure 3**   **Figure 4**

A. Each figure has symmetry.

B. Figure 1 has 2 lines of symmetry.

C. Figure 3 has 1 line of symmetry.

D. Figure 4 has 4 lines of symmetry.

---

7 Four students were asked to draw all the lines of symmetry for a figure. Their work is shown in the table

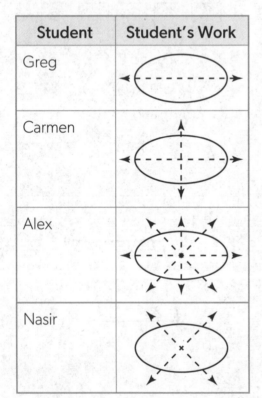

Student	Student's Work
Greg	
Carmen	
Alex	
Nasir	

Which student's work correctly shows all the lines of symmetry?

A. Greg

B. Carmen

C. Alex

D. Nasir

8 How many lines of symmetry does the figure have?

Record your answer and fill in the bubbles. Be sure to use the correct place value.

			.		
⓪	⓪	⓪		⓪	⓪
①	①	①		①	①
②	②	②		②	②
③	③	③		③	③
④	④	④		④	④
⑤	⑤	⑤		⑤	⑤
⑥	⑥	⑥		⑥	⑥
⑦	⑦	⑦		⑦	⑦
⑧	⑧	⑧		⑧	⑧
⑨	⑨	⑨		⑨	⑨

9 How many lines of symmetry does a square have?

A. 1

B. 2

C. 3

D. 4

10 Lorena says a circle has no lines of symmetry. Brandon disagrees. He says a circle has many lines of symmetry.

Who is correct and why?

A. Lorena is correct, because a circle has no angles.

B. Lorena is correct, because a circle has no straight lines.

C. Brandon is correct, because any line through the center of a circle is a line of symmetry.

D. Brandon is correct, because a circle has no straight lines.

Use the following information for questions 11 and 12.

Leila folded a piece of paper in half. She drew this shaded figure on one half of the paper.

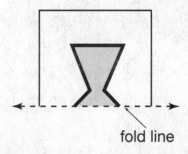

fold line

11 How many lines of symmetry does the shaded figure have?

A. 2　　　　C. 1

B. 0　　　　D. 3

12 Leila cuts along the edges of the shaded figure and then unfolds the paper. How many lines of symmetry does the new figure have?

Record your answer and fill in the bubbles. Be sure to use the correct place value.

0	0	0	.	0	0
1	1	1		1	1
2	2	2		2	2
3	3	3		3	3
4	4	4		4	4
5	5	5		5	5
6	6	6		6	6
7	7	7		7	7
8	8	8		8	8
9	9	9		9	9

4.6(C), 4.6(D)

Classifying Two-Dimensional Figures

 GETTING THE IDEA -

You can classify figures by angles and by sides.

You can classify triangles by the size of the angles.

  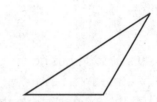

Right triangle	**Acute triangle**	**Obtuse triangle**
Has a right angle.	Has three acute angles.	Has an obtuse angle.

You can also classify quadrilaterals. Some quadrilaterals have special names.

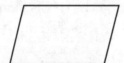 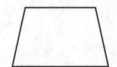

Parallelogram	**Trapezoid**
Has two pairs of parallel sides.	Has only one pair of parallel sides.

Rectangle	**Square**	**Rhombus**
Parallelogram with four right angles.	Parallelogram with four right angles and all sides the same length.	Parallelogram with all sides the same length.

Example 1

Which triangles are right triangles?

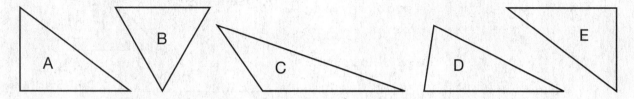

Strategy   Look for right angles in the triangles.

Step 1   Determine what you are looking for.

A right triangle always has 1 right angle. A right angle looks like a square corner.

Step 2   Look at each triangle to see if it has a right angle.

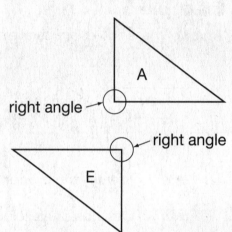

Triangle A has a right angle.

Triangle B has no right angles.

Triangle C has no right angles.

Triangle D has no right angles.

Triangle E has has a right angle.

Solution   Triangles A and E are right triangles.

Example 2

Which triangles are obtuse triangles?

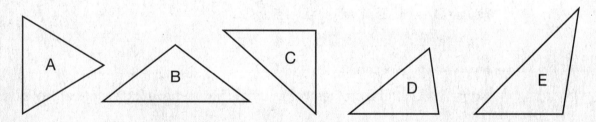

Strategy   Look for obtuse angles in the triangles.

Step 1   Determine what you are looking for.

The measure of an obtuse angle is greater than 90°.

Step 2	Compare each angle with the square corner of a right angle.

Triangle A has no obtuse angles.

Triangle B has an obtuse angle.

Triangle C has no obtuse angles.

Triangle D has no obtuse angles.

Triangle E has an obtuse angle.

Solution **Triangles B and E are obtuse triangles.**

Figures can be classified in other ways. Some figures have parallel lines or perpendicular lines.

Example 3

Which of these figures are parallelograms?

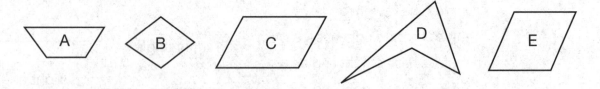

Strategy **Identify the properties of a parallelogram.**

Step 1	Describe a parallelogram.

A parallelogram has 2 pairs of parallel sides.

Step 2	Compare the figures with your description.

Figure A has 1 pair of parallel sides.

Figure B has 2 pairs of parallel sides.

Figure C has 2 pairs of parallel sides.

Figure D has no pairs of parallel sides.

Figure E has 2 pairs of parallel sides.

Step 3	Identify the parallelograms.

Figures B, C, and E are parallelograms. They all have 2 pairs of parallel sides.

Solution **Figures B, C, and E are parallelograms.**

Example 4

Which of these figures are **not** parallelograms?

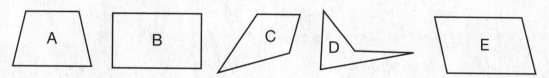

Strategy   Identify the properties of a parallelogram.

Step 1   Describe a parallelogram.

A parallelogram has 2 pairs of parallel sides. So a figure that is not a parallelogram will not have 2 pairs of parallel sides.

Step 2   Compare the figures with your description.

Figure A has 1 pair of parallel sides.

Figure B has 2 pairs of parallel sides.

Figure C has no pairs of parallel sides.

Figure D has no pairs of parallel sides.

Figure E has 2 pairs of parallel sides.

Step 3   Identify the figures that are not parallelograms.

Figures A, C, and D are **not** parallelograms. They do not have 2 pairs of parallel sides.

Solution   Figures A, C, and D are not parallelograms.

Example 5

Which of these figures are trapezoids?

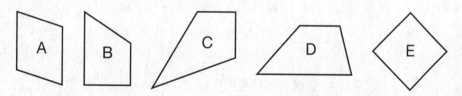

Strategy   Identify the properties of a trapezoid.

Step 1   Describe a trapezoid.

A trapezoid has only 1 pair of parallel sides.

Step 2	Compare the figures with your description.
	Figure A has 2 pairs of parallel sides.
	Figure B has only 1 pair of parallel sides.
	Figure C has no pairs of parallel sides.
	Figure D has only 1 pair of parallel sides.
	Figure E has 2 pairs of parallel sides.
Step 3	Identify the trapezoids.
	Figures B and D are trapezoids. They each only have 1 pair of parallel sides.
Solution	**Figures B and D are trapezoids.**

② COACHED EXAMPLE

Which of these triangles are acute triangles?

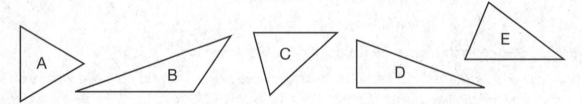

An acute triangle has _____ acute angles.

Triangle A has _____ acute angles.

Triangle B has _____ acute angles.

Triangle C has _____ acute angles.

Triangle D has _____ acute angles.

Triangle E has _____ acute angles.

Triangles _____, _____, and _____ are acute triangles.

1 Which triangle is a right triangle?

A.

B.

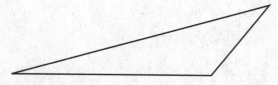

C.

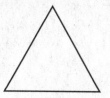

D.

2 Which term best describes a four-sided figure with only two right angles?

A. Parallelogram

B. Trapezoid

C. Rhombus

D. Square

3 Look at the figure below.

Which statement is **not** true?

A. The figure has at least one right angle.

B. The figure is a quadrilateral.

C. The figure has at least one acute angle.

D. The figure has two pairs of parallel sides.

4 Look at the figure below.

How many right angles does the figure have?

Record your answer and fill in the bubbles. Be sure to use the correct place value.

			.		
⓪	⓪	⓪		⓪	⓪
①	①	①		①	①
②	②	②		②	②
③	③	③		③	③
④	④	④		④	④
⑤	⑤	⑤		⑤	⑤
⑥	⑥	⑥		⑥	⑥
⑦	⑦	⑦		⑦	⑦
⑧	⑧	⑧		⑧	⑧
⑨	⑨	⑨		⑨	⑨

5 Look at the figure below.

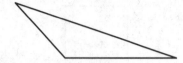

Which term best describes the figure?

A. Right triangle

B. Acute triangle

C. Obtuse triangle

D. Parallelogram

6 Jenna drew this figure.

Which statement correctly describes Jenna's figure?

A. The figure is a triangle.

B. The figure is a trapezoid.

C. The figure has right angles.

D. The figure is a parallelogram.

7 Which figure has four sides that are the same length and no right angles?

A. Rhombus

B. Rectangle

C. Parallelogram

D. Quadrilateral

8 Cedric drew a shape with the following properties.

• 4 right angles

• 4 sides of equal length

Which shape did Cedric draw?

A. Right triangle

B. Rectangle

C. Rhombus

D. Square

9 Which figure is **not** a parallelogram?

A.

B.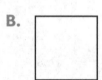

C.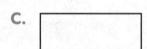

D.

10 Which of the following is a property of an acute triangle?

A. 4 sides

B. All sides the same length

C. 2 pairs of parallel sides

D. 3 acute angles

11 Jasmine says that all squares are rectangles. Ricky says that a square is not a rectangle. Who is correct?

A. Jasmine, because squares and rectangles both have four sides.

B. Jasmine, because a square has four right angles.

C. Ricky, because a square has four sides that are the same length and a rectangle does not.

D. Ricky, because all squares are rhombuses.

12 Look at the properties listed below.

• 3 sides

• 1 pair of perpendicular sides

Which figure has both of these properties?

A. Acute triangle

B. Right triangle

C. Obtuse triangle

D. Square

13 Which statement comparing right triangles and acute triangles is **not** true?

A. Right triangles and acute triangles have 3 sides.

B. Right triangles and acute triangles have at least 2 acute angles.

C. An acute triangle has 3 acute angles, but a right triangle has 3 right angles.

D. A right triangle has 2 perpendicular sides, but an acute triangle has no perpendicular sides.

14 Look at the figure below.

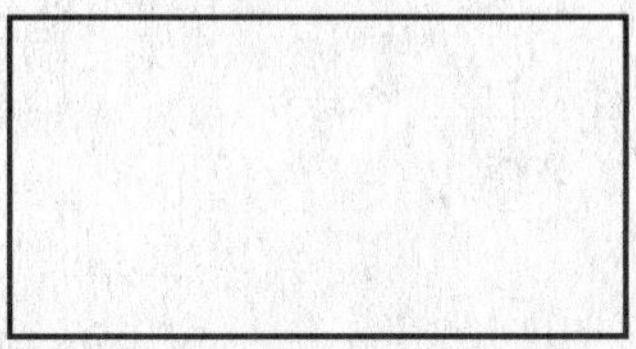

Which term could **not** be used to describe the figure?

A. Quadrilateral

B. Parallelogram

C. Rectangle

D. Square

4.7(C), 4.7(D)

Measuring and Drawing Angles

1 GETTING THE IDEA

A **protractor** is a tool used to measure and draw angles. A full-circle protractor is marked to show 360°. A half-circle protractor shows 180°.

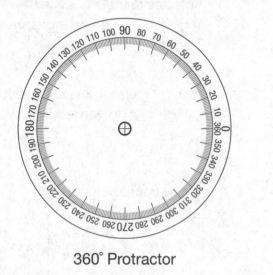

360° Protractor

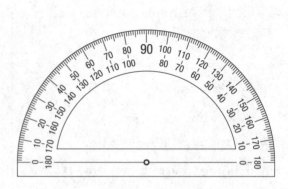

180° Protractor

Either type of protractor can be used to measure and draw angles.

A half-circle protractor may have a single set of marks from 0° to 180°.

A half-circle protractor may also have a double set of marks from 0° to 180° in reverse order along the inside arc of the protractor.

The **vertex** of an angle is the point where the two sides, or **rays**, of the angle meet. A protractor measures the number of degrees between the two rays of an angle.

Example 1

What is the measure of the angle?

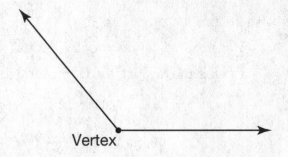

Vertex

Strategy   **Use a protractor to measure the angle in degrees.**

Step 1   Place the center of the protractor on the vertex of the angle.

Line up one ray of the angle with the 0° mark on the right side of the protractor.

You may need to extend the ray of the angle.

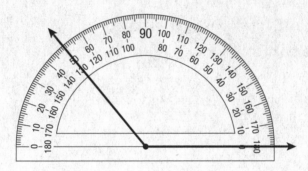

Step 2   Find the measure of the angle.

Read the measure of the angle where the other ray crosses the scale on the protractor.

You may also have to extend this ray.

The angle is greater than 90°.

Use the inner scale to read the angle measure.

The ray passes through the 130° mark on the protractor.

Solution   **The measure of the angle is 130°.**

Example 2

Draw an angle that measures 75°.

Strategy   **Use a protractor to draw the angle.**

Step 1   Draw one ray of the angle.

The endpoint of the ray will be the vertex of the angle.

Step 2   Use the protractor.

Place the center point of the protractor on the endpoint of the ray.

Line up the ray with the 0° mark on the protractor.

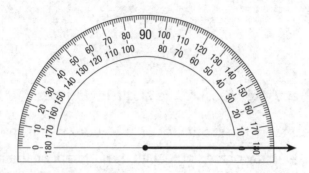

Step 3   Find 75° on the protractor.

The angle is less than 90°.

Use the 75° mark on the inner scale.

Mark a point at 75°.

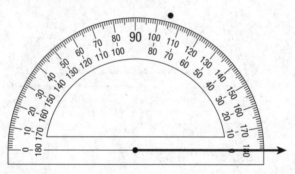

Step 4   Draw the angle.

Remove the protractor.

Draw a line to connect the endpoint of the first ray and the point you marked at the 75° mark.

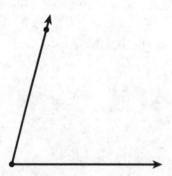

Solution   An angle that measures 75° is shown in Step 4.

Draw an angle that measures 140°.

Use the protractor below.

    Draw one _____ of the angle.

    Line up the endpoint of the ray with the _____° mark on the protractor.

Find _____° on the protractor.

    The angle is _____ than 90°.

    Mark a point at _____°.

Draw a line to connect the endpoint of the first ray and the point you marked.

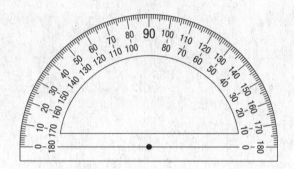

1 Look at the angles shown below.

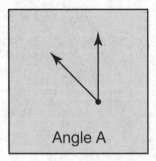

Angle A	Angle B	Angle C

Which shows the angles listed in order from least to greatest measurement?

A. Angle A, Angle B, Angle C   **C.** Angle B, Angle A, Angle C

B. Angle A, Angle C, Angle B   **D.** Angle C, Angle B, Angle A

2 Which angle measures 105°?

A.

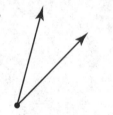

B.

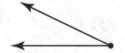

C.

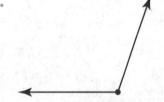

D.

3 What units are used to measure an angle?

A. Inches   **C.** Rays

B. Arcs   **D.** Degrees

4 Look at the angle below.

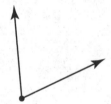

Which statement best describes the measure of the angle?

A. Less than 70°

B. Equal to 70°

C. Greater than 70°

D. The measure of the angle cannot be determined.

5 Look at Angle A below.

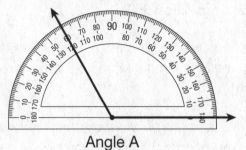

Angle A

Which statement is true?

A. Angle A measures 60°.

B. Angle A measures 120°.

C. The measure of Angle A is between 50° and 70°.

D. The measure of Angle A is between 60° and 120°.

6 What is the measure of Angle B?

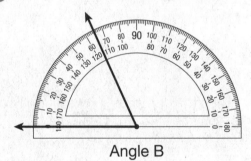

Angle B

Record your answer and fill in the bubbles. Be sure to use the correct place value.

			.		
⓪	⓪	⓪		⓪	⓪
①	①	①		①	①
②	②	②		②	②
③	③	③		③	③
④	④	④		④	④
⑤	⑤	⑤		⑤	⑤
⑥	⑥	⑥		⑥	⑥
⑦	⑦	⑦		⑦	⑦
⑧	⑧	⑧		⑧	⑧
⑨	⑨	⑨		⑨	⑨

7 Which angle measures 35°?

A.

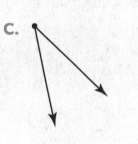

B.

C.

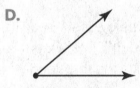

D.

8 What is the name of the point where two sides of an angle meet?

A. Vertex

B. Ray

C. Protractor

D. Degree

9 The hands of a clock form an angle at exactly 4:00.

What is the measure of the angle?

A. 60°

B. 90°

C. 120°

D. 150°

10 The window below is shaped like a half circle. It is split into unequal panes. The panes form the three angles shown.

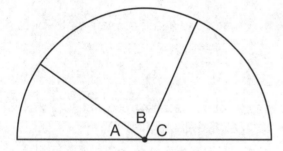

Which statement about the measures of the angles is **not** true?

A. The measure of Angle A is 35°.

B. The measure of Angle B is 115°.

C. The measure of Angle C is 65°.

D. The measure of the angle formed by Angles B and C is 145°.

Use the information below for questions 11 and 12.

The needle of a compass makes an angle with the North mark on the compass.

11 The figure below shows what a heading of NE (Northeast) looks like on the compass.

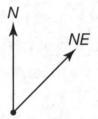

What is the measure of this angle?

A. 45°

B. 55°

C. 135°

D. 145°

12 When the compass shows a heading of SW (Southwest), the needle is pointing in the exact opposite direction as the NE needle. What is the measure of the angle between an arrow pointing North and an arrow pointing Southwest?

A. 45°

B. 55°

C. 135°

D. 150°

Finding Angle Measures

1 ▶ GETTING THE IDEA

You can add and subtract angle measures.

The measure of the whole angle formed by the two outer rays is the sum of the smaller angles.

$50° + 20° = 70°$

The measure of the whole angle is 70°.

Notice that the smaller angles do not overlap.

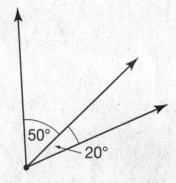

Example 1

What is the measure of the unknown angle?

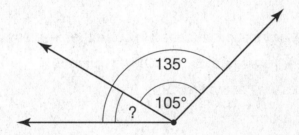

Strategy   Write an equation.

> **Step 1**   Write an equation to represent the total angle measure.
>
> Let m represent the measure of the unknown angle.
>
> Add the measures of the smaller angles to get the measure of the larger angle.
>
> $m + 105 = 135$

> **Step 2**   Subtract to solve the equation for m.
>
> $$m + 105 = 135$$
> $$m + 105 - 105 = 135 - 105$$
> $$m = 30$$

Solution   **The measure of the angle is 30°.**

Example 2

A gear rotates 150° in two turns. For the first turn, the gear rotates 70°. How many degrees does the gear rotate during the second turn?

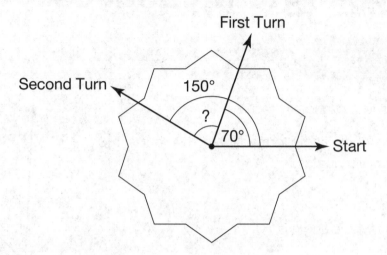

Strategy   Write an equation to represent the problem.

Step 1   Determine what the problem asks you to find.

You have to find how many degrees the gear rotates during the second turn.

Step 2   Identify the information you need to solve the problem.

The gear rotates a total of 150° in two turns.

It rotates 70° for the first turn.

Step 3   Write an equation.

The two turns rotate the gear a total of 150°.

Let m represent the degree measure of the second turn.

$70 + m = 150$

Step 4   Solve the equation.

$$70 + m = 150$$
$$70 - 70 + m = 150 - 70$$
$$m = 80$$

Solution   The gear rotates 80° during the second turn.

Two angles are **complementary angles** if the sum of their measures is 90°. Two angles are **supplementary angles** if the sum of their measures is 180°.

Complementary Angles	Supplementary Angles

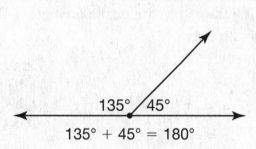

30° + 60° = 90°   135° + 45° = 180°

Example 3

The two angles in the figure are complementary. What is the measure of the unknown angle?

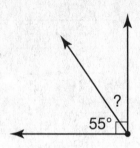

Strategy   Write an equation.

Step 1   Write an equation to represent the total angle measure.

Let m represent the measure of the unknown angle.

The angles are complementary. So the sum of the measures of the smaller angles is 90°.

$m + 55 = 90$

Step 2   Subtract to solve the equation for m.

$$m + 55 = 90$$
$$m + 55 - 55 = 90 - 55$$
$$m = 35$$

Solution   The measure of the angle is 35°.

A robotic arm rotates 107°. The arm pauses to pick up an object. It continues the rotation until it sets down the object. The two angles formed by the rotation of the robotic arm are supplementary angles, as shown in the diagram. How many degrees does the robotic arm rotate from the position where it picks up the object to the position where it sets the object down?

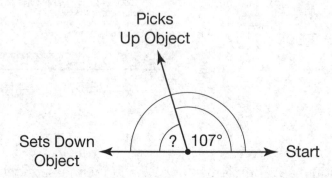

The problem asks me to find _____

_____.

The information I need to solve this problem is:

_____

_____

I can write an addition _____ to solve the problem.

Let *m* represent the number of _____ the arm rotates from the position where it picks up the object to the position where it sets the object down.

Write the equation. _____

Solve the equation.

The robotic arm rotates _____ degrees from the position where it picks up the object to the position where it sets the object down.

1 Which figure shows two angles that combine to make an angle with a total measure of 110°?

A.

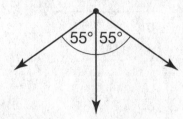

B.

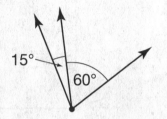

C.

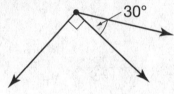

D.

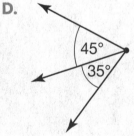

2 Which angle measures are of supplementary angles?

A. 84° and 84°

B. 34° and 56°

C. 73° and 107°

D. 29° and 92°

3 Look at the figure below.

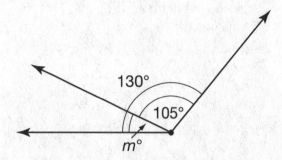

What is the measure of the missing angle?

A. 20°

B. 25°

C. 30°

D. 235°

4 Look at the figure below.

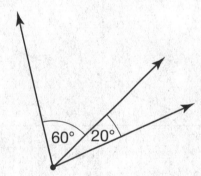

Which equation does **not** relate to the measures of the angles in the figure?

A. 20° + 60° = 80°

B. 80° − 20° = 60°

C. 80° − 60° = 20°

D. 60° − 20° = 40°

5 The angles in the figure below are complementary angles.

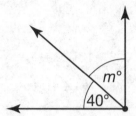

What is the missing measure, $m°$?

A. 140°

B. 40°

C. 50°

D. 90°

6 The sides of a rectangle form 4 right angles.

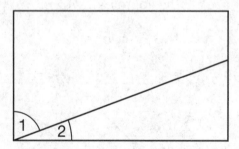

The measure of angle 1 is 70°. What is the measure of angle 2?

A. 20°

B. 50°

C. 90°

D. 160°

7 In which figure does the value of m equal 90?

A.

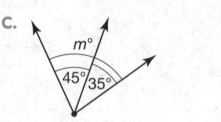

B.

C.

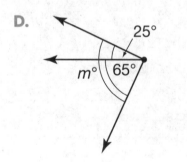

D.

8 A camera rotates 15° and then stops to take a picture. Then it rotates 5° to take another picture. This makes up one rotation cycle, so the camera takes two pictures in each rotation cycle.

How many cycles does the camera lens go through to reach 100°?

Record your answer and fill in the bubbles. Be sure to use the correct place value.

			.		
⓪	⓪	⓪		⓪	⓪
①	①	①		①	①
②	②	②		②	②
③	③	③		③	③
④	④	④		④	④
⑤	⑤	⑤		⑤	⑤
⑥	⑥	⑥		⑥	⑥
⑦	⑦	⑦		⑦	⑦
⑧	⑧	⑧		⑧	⑧
⑨	⑨	⑨		⑨	⑨

9 Which statement is true?

A. Two acute angles may be complementary.

B. Two acute angles may be supplementary.

C. Two obtuse angles may be complementary.

D. Two obtuse angles may be supplementary.

10 Angles 1 and 2 are complementary angles. The measure of angle 1 is 78°. What is the measure of angle 2?

A. 12°

B. 22°

C. 102°

D. 282°

Use this information and diagram for questions 11 and 12.

The diagram shows a window made of 6 triangles that are the exact same size.

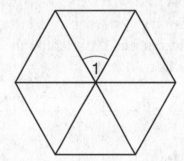

11 What equation can you use to find the measure of angle 1?

A. $60 \div 3 = m$

B. $120 \div 3 = m$

C. $180 \div 3 = m$

D. $360 \div 3 = m$

12 What is the measure of angle 1?

A. 120°

B. 60°

C. 40°

D. 20°

Units of Measure

You use measurements to describe the amount, weight, or length of an object or event. The units you use depend on the nature and size of what you're measuring. For example, seconds and days are units of time. Seconds are used to describe very short amounts of time, and days are used to describe longer amounts of time. The units used to measure time are **second (sec)**, **minute (min)**, **hour (hr)**, and **day (d)**.

Two different systems of measurement can be used to measure length, capacity, weight, and mass. Remember, **capacity** is the amount a container can hold when it is completely filled. **Mass** is the amount of matter in an object.

The **customary system** is used in the United States to measure length, capacity, and weight. The **metric system** is used throughout the world to measure length, capacity, and mass. Each system has its own units.

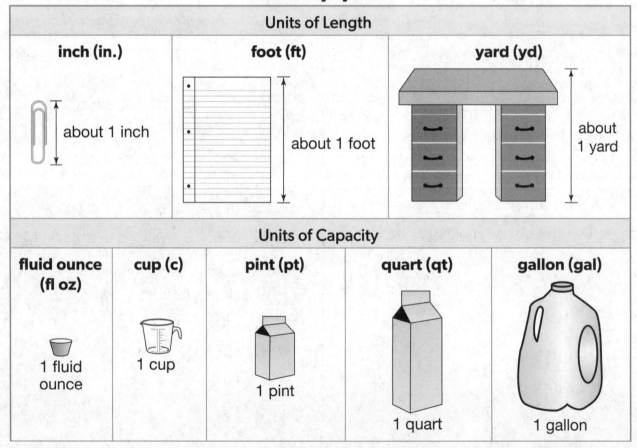

Customary System

Units of Length		
inch (in.)	**foot (ft)**	**yard (yd)**
about 1 inch	about 1 foot	about 1 yard

Units of Capacity				
fluid ounce (fl oz)	**cup (c)**	**pint (pt)**	**quart (qt)**	**gallon (gal)**
1 fluid ounce	1 cup	1 pint	1 quart	1 gallon

Units of Weight

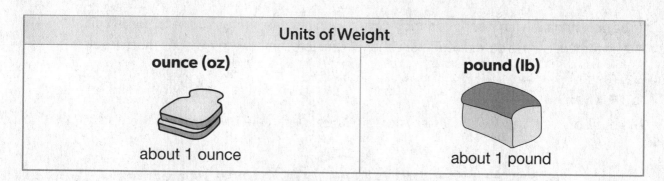

ounce (oz)	pound (lb)
about 1 ounce	about 1 pound

Metric System

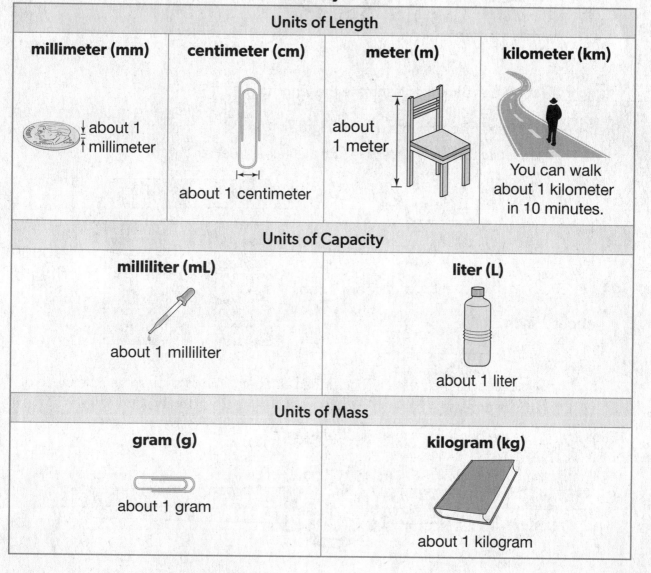

Units of Length

millimeter (mm)	centimeter (cm)	meter (m)	kilometer (km)
about 1 millimeter	about 1 centimeter	about 1 meter	You can walk about 1 kilometer in 10 minutes.

Units of Capacity

milliliter (mL)	liter (L)
about 1 milliliter	about 1 liter

Units of Mass

gram (g)	kilogram (kg)
about 1 gram	about 1 kilogram

A **benchmark** is a familiar or common object with a measurement close to some unit. A benchmark can be compared to another object to estimate the object's measurement.

Example 1

Marcus bought a new watch. Use customary units to estimate the length of the watch.

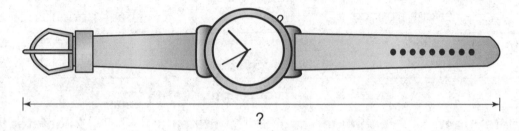

?

Strategy   Use a benchmark to estimate the length.

Step 1   Choose an appropriate unit of length.

The customary units of length are inches, feet, and yards.

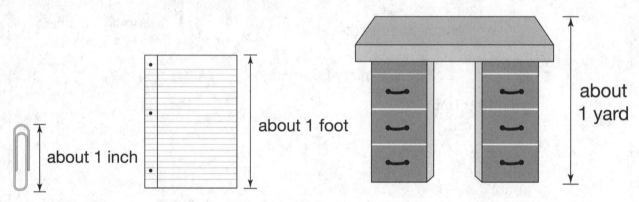

about 1 inch

about 1 foot

about 1 yard

Because the watch is longer than a paper clip and shorter than the piece of paper, use a paper clip to estimate the length of the watch.

Step 2   Use the benchmark to estimate the length.

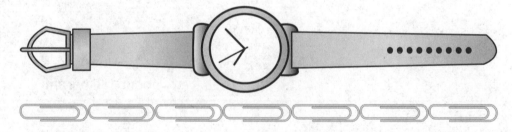

7 paper clips long, or about 7 inches

Solution   The estimated length of the watch is about 7 inches.

Example 2

Jamie is a judge in a pumpkin-growing contest. She needs to find the mass of the pumpkins. She begins with the pumpkin below. What is the mass of this pumpkin?

Strategy   **Choose a unit of mass. Use a scale to measure the mass.**

Step 1   Choose an appropriate unit of mass.

Mass is measured using grams or kilograms.

about 1 gram   about 1 kilogram

Because the mass of a pumpkin is much greater than the mass of a paper clip, use kilograms.

Step 2   Use a scale to find the mass.

The mass of the pumpkin is between 9 and 10 kilograms. Because there are 10 marks between 9 and 10, each mark represents one tenth. So the arrow on the scale points to 9.8.

Solution   The mass of the pumpkin is 9.8 kilograms.

Example 3

Steve estimates that the water bottle holds 2 quarts of water. Is Steve's estimate reasonable?

Strategy   **Use benchmarks to determine whether the estimate is reasonable.**

Step 1   Look at the benchmarks for different units of capacity.

1 fluid ounce   1 cup   1 pint   1 quart   1 gallon

The quart is between the size of the pint and the gallon. Circle the quart.

Step 2   Compare the benchmark to the estimate.

The two containers of milk hold much more liquid than the water bottle.

Solution   **Steve's estimate is not reasonable.**

Inez pours milk into a measuring cup for a recipe. How much milk is she using for the recipe?

Look at the measuring cup.

The measurement units on the cup are _____.

Look at the top of the milk in the measuring cup.

Does the top of the milk line up with a number on the measuring cup? _____

The top of the milk line falls between the numbered marks for _____ milliliters and _____ milliliters.

What number is halfway between 300 and 400? _____

Inez used _____ of milk for the recipe.

1 Ben used a scale to find the mass of a quarter. Choose the number that makes the statement reasonable.

The mass of Ben's quarter is about _____ grams.

A. 6

B. 60

C. 600

D. 6,000

2 Gail is measuring the length of her classroom. Which is the most reasonable measurement for her classroom?

A. 3 inches

B. 3 feet

C. 30 inches

D. 30 feet

3 Choose the unit of measure that makes the statement reasonable.

Juan's cell phone is 5 _____ long.

A. Feet

B. Inches

C. Kilometers

D. Yards

4 Choose the unit of measure that makes the statement reasonable.

Likang's bike is 5 _____ long.

A. Centimeters

B. Feet

C. Inches

D. Meters

5 Eli is making plaster for an art project. He fills the measuring cup with the amount of water he needs to mix with the dry plaster.

How much water did Eli put in the measuring cup?

A. 400 mL

B. 425 mL

C. 450 mL

D. 500 mL

6 Which unit is a unit of mass?

A. Ounce

B. Pound

C. Kilogram

D. Liter

7 Which statement can **not** be true?

 A. The capacity of a bathtub is 5,000 gallons.

 B. The capacity of a water pitcher is 2 quarts.

 C. The capacity of a soup bowl is 2 cups.

 D. The capacity of a large aquarium is 48 gallons.

8 Which statement is true?

 A. One yard is less than one inch.

 B. One pint is less than one cup.

 C. One gram is less than one kilogram.

 D. One gallon is less than one pint.

9 Choose the phrase that makes the statement reasonable.

 One foot is _____ one yard.

 A. Less than

 B. Equal to

 C. Greater than

 D. About the same as

10 Kim bought a bag of apples.

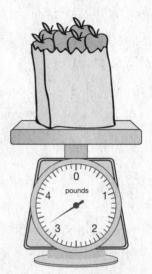

According to the scale, how many pounds of apples did Kim buy?

Record your answer and fill in the bubbles. Be sure to use the correct place value.

⓪	⓪	⓪	.	⓪	⓪
①	①	①		①	①
②	②	②		②	②
③	③	③		③	③
④	④	④		④	④
⑤	⑤	⑤		⑤	⑤
⑥	⑥	⑥		⑥	⑥
⑦	⑦	⑦		⑦	⑦
⑧	⑧	⑧		⑧	⑧
⑨	⑨	⑨		⑨	⑨

11 Which metric unit of length would be best to measure the distance from your home to a shopping mall?

 A. Millimeter

 B. Centimeter

 C. Meter

 D. Kilometer

12 Choose the unit of capacity that makes the statement reasonable.

A chef filled a large cooking pot with 6 _____ of water.

A. Cups

B. Gallons

C. Fluid ounces

D. Quarts

13 Choose the unit of capacity that makes the statement reasonable.

Ramon filled a children's swimming pool with 90 _____ of water.

A. Cups

B. Gallons

C. Pints

D. Quarts

14 Choose the unit of capacity that makes the statement reasonable.

Nina filled an ice cube tray with 1 _____ of water.

A. Fluid ounce

B. Gallon

C. Pint

D. Quart

Use the information and diagram for questions 15 and 16.

Cole used a paper clip to estimate the length of a leaf.

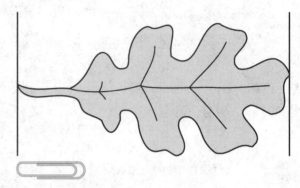

15 Which number correctly completes the following sentence?

The leaf is about _____ paper clips long.

A. 1

B. 2

C. 3

D. 4

16 Using what you know about benchmark measurements, about how long is the leaf?

A. 1 inch

B. 4 inches

C. 1 foot

D. 4 feet

4.8(B)

Converting Customary Units of Measure

① GETTING THE IDEA

The table shows the relationships between different related units of the customary system and different units of time.

Length	Capacity	Weight	Time
1 yd = 3 ft	1 gal = 4 qt	1 lb = 16 oz	1 d = 24 hr
1 yd = 36 in.	1 gal = 8 pt		1 hr = 60 min
1 ft = 12 in.	1 gal = 16 c		1 hr = 3,600 sec
	1 qt = 2 pt		1 min = 60 sec
	1 qt = 4 c		
	1 pt = 2 c		
	1 c = 8 fl oz		

You can change a measurement from one unit to another unit when solving a problem. For example, you might need to know how many minutes are in 3 hours. To find the number of minutes, you can **convert** the number of hours to minutes.

When you convert a measurement from a larger unit to a smaller unit, you use multiplication.

When you convert a measurement from a smaller unit to a larger unit, you use division.

Example 1

Julia is enclosing her rectangular garden with a fence. She needs 7 yards of fencing. Fencing is sold in feet. How many feet of fencing does Julia need?

Strategy   Use multiplication to convert the measurement.

Step 1   Identify the units being converted.

7 yards = ? feet

Step 2	Write the number of feet equal to 1 yard.

1 yard = 3 feet

Step 3	Multiply the number of yards by the number of feet in 1 yard.

$7 \times 3 = 21$ feet

Step 4	Use addition to check your answer.

Because there are 3 feet in 1 yard and there are 7 yards, you can add 3 feet seven times to check your answer.

7 yards = 1 yard + 1 yard + 1 yard + 1 yard + 1 yard + 1 yard + 1 yard

= 3 feet + 3 feet + 3 feet + 3 feet + 3 feet + 3 feet + 3 feet

= 21 feet

Solution   Julia needs 21 feet of fencing.

Example 2

Juan made this table to show how gallons and pints are related. Find the missing numbers.

Number of Gallons	Number of Pints
3	24
6	
7	56
9	
10	80

Strategy   Use multiplication to convert the measurements.

Step 1	Identify the units being converted.

Start with the top unknown measurement.

6 gallons = ? pints

Step 2	Write the number of pints equal to 1 gallon.

1 gallon = 8 pints

Step 3	Multiply the number of gallons by the number of pints in 1 gallon.

$6 \times 8 = 48$ pints

Step 4   Use the number of pints in 1 gallon to convert the second unknown measurement.

$$9 \text{ gallons} = ? \text{ pints}$$
$$9 \times 8 = 72 \text{ pints}$$

Solution   The missing numbers in the table are 48 and 72.

Example 3

A punch bowl can hold 20 quarts of punch. How many gallons does the punch bowl hold?

Strategy   Use division to convert the measurement.

Step 1   Identify the units being converted.

$$20 \text{ quarts} = ? \text{ gallons}$$

Step 2   Write the number of quarts equal to 1 gallon.

$$4 \text{ quarts} = 1 \text{ gallon}$$

Step 3   Divide the number of quarts by the number of quarts in 1 gallon.

$$20 \text{ quarts} \div 4 = 5 \text{ gallons}$$

Step 4   Use addition to check your answer.

Because there are 4 quarts in 1 gallon, and there are 5 gallons, you can add 4 quarts five times to check your answer.

$$5 \text{ gallons} = 1 \text{ gallon} + 1 \text{ gallon} + 1 \text{ gallon} + 1 \text{ gallon} + 1 \text{ gallon}$$
$$= 4 \text{ quarts} + 4 \text{ quarts} + 4 \text{ quarts} + 4 \text{ quarts} + 4 \text{ quarts}$$
$$= 20 \text{ quarts}$$

Solution   The punch bowl holds 5 gallons.

It took Timothy and his family 17 hours to drive from Boston, Massachusetts, to Atlanta, Georgia. How many minutes did it take Timothy and his family to drive from Boston to Atlanta?

Identify the units being converted.

_____ hours = ? _____

Write the number of minutes equal to 1 hour.

1 hour = _____ minutes

To convert hours to minutes, multiply the number of _____ by the number of minutes in 1 hour.

17 hours × _____ = _____ minutes

It took Timothy and his family _____ minutes to drive from Boston to Atlanta.

1. Ki ran one mile in 7 minutes. How many seconds did it take her to run the mile?

   A. 700

   B. 420

   C. 70

   D. 42

2. Eli measures 16 cups of milk to make ice cream. He states that he is using 4 pints of milk. Is Eli right?

   A. No, 1 pint = 2 cups. So, 16 cups ÷ 2 = 8 pints.

   B. No, 1 cup = 2 pints. So, 16 cups × 2 = 32 pints.

   C. Yes, 1 pint = 4 cups, and 16 ÷ 4 = 4.

   D. Yes, 16 cups = 1 gallon, 4 cups = 1 quart, and 16 ÷ 4 = 4.

3. Which of the statements below is **not** true?

   A. 4 lb = 64 oz

   B. 5 ft = 60 in.

   C. 4 gal = 8 qt

   D. 8 min = 480 sec

4. The table shows the weights of apples two people bought.

   Apples Bought

Person	Weight of Apples
Sara	3 pounds
Neal	40 ounces

   Which statement is true?

   A. Neal bought more because $40 \text{ oz} > \frac{3}{16} \text{ oz}$.

   B. Sara bought less because $\frac{3}{10} \text{ oz} < 40 \text{ oz}$.

   C. Neal bought more because 40 oz > 30 oz.

   D. Sara bought more because 48 oz > 40 oz.

5. Roberto's parents stated that it would take exactly 3 days to use a garden hose to fill the family's pool. Roberto calculated the number of hours it would take to fill the pool like this:

   $$3 \text{ days} \times 24 = 72 \text{ hours}$$

   Did Roberto find the number of hours correctly?

   A. No, 1 day = 60 hours. So, 3 days × 60 = 180 hours.

   B. Yes, 24 days = 1 hour. So, 24 days × 3 = 72 days.

   C. Yes, 1 day = 24 hours. So, 3 days × 24 = 72 hours.

   D. No, 1 day = 24 hours. So, 24 hours ÷ 3 = 8 hours.

6 Which quantity is less than 3 gallons?

A. 16 quarts

B. 16 pints

C. 24 pints

D. 12 quarts

7 The table shows the heights of 4 sunflowers in Lauren's garden.

Lauren's Sunflowers

Sunflower	Height
1	80 inches
2	5 feet
3	50 inches
4	7 feet
5	72 inches

Which list shows the sunflowers in order from shortest to tallest?

A. Sunflower 3, Sunflower 2, Sunflower 5, Sunflower 1, Sunflower 4

B. Sunflower 3, Sunflower 2, Sunflower 5, Sunflower 4, Sunflower 1

C. Sunflower 2, Sunflower 3, Sunflower 5, Sunflower 1, Sunflower 4

D. Sunflower 4, Sunflower 1, Sunflower 5, Sunflower 2, Sunflower 3

8 A football player ran 120 feet. How many yards did the football player run?

A. 12   C. 360

B. 40   D. 1,440

9 Which length is greater than 72 inches?

A. 3 yards

B. 6 feet

C. 60 inches

D. 2 yards

10 Which statement is **not** true?

A. 2 days = 36 hours

B. 36 hours = 2,160 minutes

C. 72 minutes = 4,320 seconds

D. 1 day = 1,440 minutes

11 It took Sarah 14 minutes to run 1 mile. How many seconds did it take Sarah to run 1 mile?

Record your answer and fill in the bubbles. Be sure to use the correct place value.

Use the information below for questions 12 and 13.

Martin bought 4 yards of fabric for a project. After finishing the project, he has 2 feet of fabric left over.

12 How many inches of fabric does Martin have left over?

A. 72   C. 20

B. 24   D. 8

13 How much fabric did Martin use for his project?

A. 2 yards

B. 3 yards

C. 10 feet

D. 12 feet

14 A certain blue whale is 83 feet long. How long is the blue whale in inches?

Record your answer and fill in the bubbles. Be sure to use the correct place value.

			.		
⓪	⓪	⓪		⓪	⓪
①	①	①		①	①
②	②	②		②	②
③	③	③		③	③
④	④	④		④	④
⑤	⑤	⑤		⑤	⑤
⑥	⑥	⑥		⑥	⑥
⑦	⑦	⑦		⑦	⑦
⑧	⑧	⑧		⑧	⑧
⑨	⑨	⑨		⑨	⑨

Use the information below for questions 14–16.

The table shows the amount of water some people brought to a game.

Water Brought to Game

Person	Amount of Water
Beth	2 gallons
Ramon	6 quarts
Theo	8 cups
Coach	4 pints

15 How much water did Beth bring to the game?

A. 4 quarts

B. 8 pints

C. 10 cups

D. 16 pints

16 How many cups of water did Ramon bring to the game?

A. 48   C. 24

B. 36   D. 12

17 Who brought the most water to the game?

A. Beth

B. Ramon

C. Theo

D. Coach

LESSON **29**

4.8(B)

Converting Metric Units of Measure

1 GETTING THE IDEA

The table shows the relationships between different related units in the metric system.

Units of Length	Units of Capacity	Units of Mass
1 km = 1,000 m	1 L = 1,000 mL	1 kg = 1,000 g
1 m = 100 cm		
1 m = 1,000 mm		
1 cm = 10 mm		

As with customary units, you use multiplication to **convert** a measurement from a larger unit to a smaller unit.

You use division to convert a measurement from a smaller unit to a larger unit.

Example 1

Damon's dog has a mass of 5 kilograms. What is the mass of his dog in grams?

Strategy   Use multiplication to convert the measurement.

Step 1   Identify the units being converted.

5 kilograms = ? grams

Step 2   Write the number of grams in 1 kilogram.

1 kilogram = 1,000 grams

Step 3   Multiply the number of kilograms by the number of grams in 1 kilogram.

5 × 1,000 = 5,000 grams

Solution   Damon's dog has a mass of **5,000 grams.**

Example 2

Make a table that relates metric units of capacity.

Strategy Convert each measurement with a larger unit into a measurement with a smaller unit.

Step 1 Identify the units that are related.

The metric units of capacity are liters and milliliters.

Since 1 liter = 1,000 milliliters, liters are the larger unit.

Step 2 **Write the numbers of liters in the table.**

Use the numbers 1, 2, 3, 4, and 5.

Number of Liters	Number of Milliliters
1	
2	
3	
4	
5	

Step 3 Multiply each number of liters by the number of milliliters in 1 liter.

$1 \times 1,000 = 1,000$ milliliters

$2 \times 1,000 = 2,000$ milliliters

$3 \times 1,000 = 3,000$ milliliters

$4 \times 1,000 = 4,000$ milliliters

$5 \times 1,000 = 5,000$ milliliters

Step 4 Complete the table.

Number of Liters	Number of Milliliters
1	1,000
2	2,000
3	3,000
4	4,000
5	5,000

Solution **The table shows the relationship between the metric units of capacity.**

Example 3

A maple tree is 900 centimeters tall. What is the height of the tree in meters?

Strategy Use division to convert the measurement.

Step 1 Identify the units being converted.

900 centimeters = ? meters

Step 2 Write the number of centimeters in 1 meter.

100 centimeters = 1 meter

Step 3 Divide the number of centimeters by the number of centimeters in 1 meter.

$900 \div 100 = ?$

Think: How many hundreds are in 900? There are 9 hundreds in 900.

$900 \div 100 = 9$ meters

Solution The maple tree is 9 meters tall.

The distance from Abe's house to school is 12 kilometers. What is the distance from Abe's house to school in meters?

Identify the units being converted.

_____ kilometers = ? _____

Write the number of meters equal to 1 kilometer.

1 kilometer = _____ meters

To convert kilometers to meters, multiply the number of _____ by the number of meters in 1 kilometer.

12 kilometers × _____ = _____ meters

The distance from Abe's house to school is _____ meters.

1 Kyle bought a 2-liter carton of orange juice. How many milliliters of juice are in the carton?

A. 2

B. 20

C. 200

D. 2,000

2 How can you convert 300 centimeters to millimeters?

A. Multiply 300 by 10.

B. Multiply 300 by 100.

C. Divide 300 by 10.

D. Divide 300 by 100.

3 Malia bought a sofa that is 2 meters long. She says that the sofa is 2,000 centimeters long.

Which explains why Malia's statement is incorrect?

A. 1 meter = 10 centimeters, so 2 meters = 20 centimeters

B. 1 meter = 100 centimeters, so 2 meters = 200 centimeters

C. 1 meter = 10 millimeters, so 2 meters = 20 millimeters

D. 1 meter = 100 millimeters, so 2 meters = 200 millimeters

4 Which equation is **not** true?

A. 400 mm = 40 cm

B. 5 kg = 5,000 g

C. 15 L = 1,500 mL

D. 800 cm = 8 m

Use the information below for questions 5 and 6.

The table shows the distances Ivan ran in the last two weeks.

Distances Ivan Ran

Week	Distance
1	3,000 meters
2	4 kilometers

5 How many kilometers did Ivan run in Week 1?

A. 4

B. 3

C. 40

D. 30

6 How many meters did Ivan run in Week 2?

A. 4,000

B. 3,000

C. 400

D. 300

7 Jana caught three fish. The mass of each fish is shown below.

| 2 kg | 1,200 g | 2,560 g |

Which list shows the measurements in order from greatest to least?

A. 2,560 g; 2 kg; 1,200 g

B. 2,560 g; 1,200 g; 2 kg

C. 1,200 g; 2,560 g; 2 kg

D. 1,200 g; 2 kg; 2,560 g

8 Zach's school building is 30 meters tall. Which measurement is equivalent to 30 meters?

A. 300 cm

B. 300 mm

C. 3,000 mm

D. 3,000 cm

9 Peyton's garden is 400 centimeters wide. How could you describe the width of Peyton's garden by using a larger unit of measure?

A. 4 m

B. 4,000 mm

C. 40,000 m

D. 4,000 cm

10 Ana is making soup. Her recipe makes 9 liters. She has a pot that holds 8,000 milliliters. Should Ana use this pot to make the soup?

A. Yes, 9 liters is less than 8,000 milliliters, so the pot will hold all of the soup.

B. Yes, 9 liters is the same as 8,000 milliliters, so the pot will hold exactly all of the soup.

C. No, 9 liters is greater than 8,000 milliliters, so the pot won't hold all of the soup.

D. No, 9 liters is much less than 8,000 milliliters, so the pot is much too large for making the soup.

11 The table below shows the relationship between millimeters and another metric unit of length.

Number of Millimeters	Number of _____
30	3
50	5
70	7
90	9

What is the other metric unit of length?

A. meters

B. millimeters

C. centimeters

D. kilometers

Use this information for questions 12 and 13.

Frank planted a tree that is 3 meters tall.

12 How many centimeters tall is the tree?

Record your answer and fill in the bubbles. Be sure to use the correct place value.

			.		
⓪	⓪	⓪		⓪	⓪
①	①	①		①	①
②	②	②		②	②
③	③	③		③	③
④	④	④		④	④
⑤	⑤	⑤		⑤	⑤
⑥	⑥	⑥		⑥	⑥
⑦	⑦	⑦		⑦	⑦
⑧	⑧	⑧		⑧	⑧
⑨	⑨	⑨		⑨	⑨

13 What is the tree's height in millimeters?

A. 3

B. 30

C. 300

D. 3,000

14 How can you convert a mass of 8,000 grams to kilograms?

A. Multiply 8,000 by 100.

B. Multiply 8,000 by 1,000.

C. Divide 8,000 by 10.

D. Divide 8,000 by 1,000.

Use this information for questions 15–17.

The table shows the amount of water four friends brought on their hike.

Water Brought on Hike

Hiker	Amount of Water
Kenny	2,000 milliliters
Jane	3 liters
Joe	3,000 milliliters
Zoe	4 liters

15 How many liters of water did Kenny bring on the hike?

A. 2

B. 20

C. 200

D. 2,000

16 How many milliliters of water did Zoe bring on the hike?

A. 4

B. 40

C. 400

D. 4,000

17 Which statement is true?

A. Kenny brought more water than Jane.

B. Jane and Joe brought the same amount of water.

C. Zoe brought less water than Joe.

D. Jane brought 100 less milliliters of water than Zoe.

Solving Measurement Problems

To solve a measurement problem, you sometimes have to convert a measurement to a different unit.

To find the number of 1-cup servings you can get from a 2-quart bottle of milk, you need to convert 2 quarts to cups.

1 quart = 4 cups	There are 4 cups in 1 quart.
2 quarts = 2 × 4 cups	Multiply to find the number of cups in 2 quarts.
2 quarts = 8 cups	

You can get eight 1-cup servings from a 2-quart bottle of milk.

Example 1

Gretchen has 8 yards of fabric. She is cutting it into 2-foot pieces to make flags. How many flags can she make?

Strategy   Convert larger units to smaller units.

Step 1   Find the number of feet equal to 8 yards.

One yard is equal to 3 feet. So, multiply 8 yards by 3.

$8 \times 3 = 24$

8 yards is equal to 24 feet.

Step 2   Find the number of 2-foot pieces Gretchen can cut from 24 feet of fabric.

Divide 24 feet by 2 feet.

$24 \div 2 = 12$

Solution   **Gretchen can make 12 flags.**

Example 2

One batch of Mateo's fruit punch recipe calls for 800 milliliters of apple juice. He plans on making 5 batches of fruit punch for a party. How many liters of apple juice does Mateo need?

Strategy   **Find how much apple juice is needed in all. Then convert smaller units to larger units.**

Step 1   Write a multiplication expression.

800×5 The amount of apple juice needed for 1 batch multiplied by 5 batches

Step 2   Find the product.

$800 \times 5 = 4{,}000$

Mateo needs 4,000 milliliters of apple juice.

Step 3   To convert the number of milliliters to liters, divide the number of milliliters by 1,000.

$4{,}000 \div 1{,}000 = 4$

Solution   **Mateo needs 4 liters of apple juice.**

Example 3

Penelope's dog has an 8-ounce serving of dog food for dinner every night. How many servings are in a 6-pound bag of dog food?

Strategy   **Convert the larger unit to the smaller unit.**

Step 1   Use a number line to find the number of ounces equal to 6 pounds.

1 pound = 16 ounces

Complete the number line for pounds and ounces.

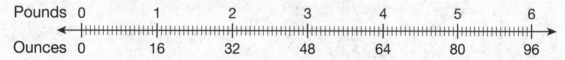

6 pounds are equal to 96 ounces.

Step 2   Find the number of 8-ounce servings in 96 ounces.

Divide 96 ounces by 8.

96 ÷ 8 = 12

Solution   **There are 12 servings in a 6-pound bag of dog food.**

Example 4

Amy and Andy want to buy a toy that costs $8.63.

Amy has:

Andy has:

They will combine their money to buy the toy. Do they have enough money?

Strategy   Find how much money they have in all. Then compare it to $8.63.

Step 1   Combine the money amounts.

There are 7 dollars and 17 dimes.

Step 2   Regroup dimes as dollars.

10 dimes = 1 dollar

So, 17 dimes = 1 dollar and 7 dimes.

Step 3   Count the money.

There are 8 dollars and 7 dimes, or $8.70.

Step 4   Compare $8.70 and $8.63.

$8.70 > $8.63

$8.70 is more than $8.63.

Solution   Amy and Andy have enough money for the toy.

Elizabeth scooped out 1 cup of yogurt from a brand-new container of yogurt. The container holds 2 pints of yogurt. How much yogurt is left?

Convert the _____ units to _____ units.

There are _____ cups in 1 pint.

The yogurt container holds 2 pints. Convert 2 pints into cups.

_____ cups × _____ = _____ cups

Write a subtraction expression to represent the word problem using the measurements in cups.

_____ − ☐

Subtract.

☐ − ☐ = ☐

There are ☐ **cup(s) of yogurt left.**

1 Fiona ran 6 laps around a track. Each lap was 500 meters. How far did Fiona run?

   A. 300 meters

   B. 30 meters

   C. 30 kilometers

   D. 3 kilometers

2 Cecelia needs a total of 96 ounces of grapes. She finds one bag of grapes that weighs 4 pounds. She needs to find another bag of grapes. How much should it weigh?

   A. $\frac{1}{2}$ pound

   B. 1 pound

   C. 2 pounds

   D. 4 pounds

3 Jeremy needs 16 yards of fencing. The fencing comes in 8-foot panels. Each panel costs $100. Jeremy finds the total cost of the fencing he needs. Which of these steps would Jeremy **not** have used?

   A. Multiply 16 yards by 3.

   B. Divide 16 yards by 8.

   C. Divide 48 feet by 8.

   D. Multiply 6 panels by $100.

4 Keith has 2 snakes, Wiggle and Squiggle. Wiggle is 34 inches long. Squiggle is 3 feet long. Which statement is true?

   A. Wiggle is 31 inches longer than Squiggle.

   B. Squiggle is 2 inches longer than Wiggle.

   C. Squiggle is 31 feet shorter than Wiggle.

   D. Wiggle is 4 inches shorter than Squiggle.

5 Darpan drinks 2 quarts of milk every 4 days. If he drinks the same amount of milk each day, how many cups of milk does Darpan drink in 1 day?

Record your answer and fill in the bubbles. Be sure to use the correct place value.

			.		
⓪	⓪	⓪		⓪	⓪
①	①	①		①	①
②	②	②		②	②
③	③	③		③	③
④	④	④		④	④
⑤	⑤	⑤		⑤	⑤
⑥	⑥	⑥		⑥	⑥
⑦	⑦	⑦		⑦	⑦
⑧	⑧	⑧		⑧	⑧
⑨	⑨	⑨		⑨	⑨

Use the information below for questions 6–8.

For 3 hours after school, Rob and Kim practice their instruments, do homework, and do chores. Each student keeps track of the time spent on each activity.

Rob
- 80 minutes practicing tuba
- 35 minutes doing homework
- the rest of the time doing chores

Kim
- 90 minutes practicing violin
- 1 hour doing homework
- the rest of the time doing chores

6 How many more minutes does Kim practice her instrument than Rob?

    A. 10

    B. 20

    C. 30

    D. 35

7 How many minutes does Rob do chores?

    A. 35

    B. 45

    C. 65

    D. 90

8 How many more minutes does Rob do chores than Kim?

    A. 10

    B. 20

    C. 30

    D. 35

9 Colton and Nevae each built a tower using 2-inch blocks. Nevae's tower is 40 inches tall. If the two towers are stacked together, they are 6 feet tall.

Which of the following statements is **not** true?

    A. Colton used 20 blocks to make his tower.

    B. Nevae's tower is 8 inches taller than Colton's.

    C. Colton and Nevae used a total of 36 blocks.

    D. Nevae used 4 more blocks than Colton.

10 Parker needs 2 liters of broth to make soup. He has two 750-milliliter cans of broth. How many more milliliters of broth does he need?

    A. 500 mL

    B. 748 mL

    C. 1,250 mL

    D. 1,498 mL

Use the information below for questions 11 and 12.

The map shows the lengths of roads between four cities.

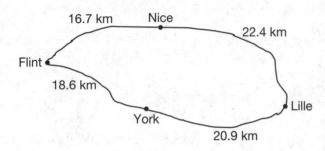

11 What is the shortest route from Flint to Lillie?

A. 16,700 meters

B. 22,400 meters

C. 39,100 meters

D. 39,500 meters

12 What is the difference in meters between the shorter route and the longer route from York to Nice?

A. 400 meters

B. 8,000 meters

C. 35,300 meters

D. 43,300 meters

13 Ana is knitting a scarf. She wants it to be 2 meters long. If Ana knits 10 centimeters each day, how many days will it take her to complete the scarf?

A. 2   C. 200

B. 20   D. 2,000

Use the table for questions 14–16.

Gift Sale

Item	Price
Monkey puzzle	$24.50
Glitter shoelaces	$14.25
Jewelry box	$34.90
Bicycle clock	$43.50
Butterfly light	$16.70
Globe	$58.95

14 Ellie buys glitter shoelaces and a butterfly light. She gives the clerk a $20-bill, a $10-bill, and a $5-bill. How much change should Ellie receive?

A. $30.95   C. $4.05

B. $5.95   D. $0.95

15 Javier bought two items. He spent a total of $59.40. What two items did he buy?

A. Monkey puzzle and glitter shoelaces

B. Monkey puzzle and jewelry box

C. Jewelry box and butterfly light

D. Glitter shoelaces and bicycle clock

16 Lupita gave the clerk $80.00. She received $6.80 in change. Which two items could she have bought?

A. Monkey puzzle and jewelry box

B. Jewelry box and bicycle clock

C. Jewelry box and butterfly light

D. Glitter shoelaces and globe

1 The model represents a rectangular backyard.

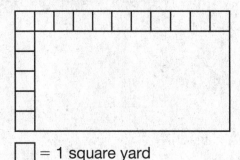

= 1 square yard

What is the area of the backyard?

A 15 square yards

B 50 square yards

C 55 square yards

D 66 square yards

2 Which is a reasonable estimate for the mass of a watermelon?

F 5 grams

G 50 grams

H 5 kilograms

J 50 kilograms

3 Maggie has fabric that is 4 meters long. How can she convert the length to centimeters?

A Multiply 4 by 1.

B Multiply 4 by 10.

C Multiply 4 by 100.

D Multiply 4 by 1,000.

4 Which figure is a trapezoid?

F

G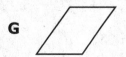

H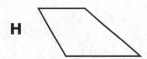

J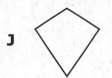

5 Mrs. Kennedy has 6 feet of fabric. How many 4-inch strips can she make?

    A 10 strips

    B 18 strips

    C 24 strips

    D 72 strips

6 Which of the figures represents an obtuse angle?

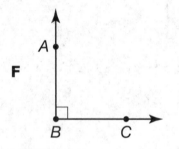

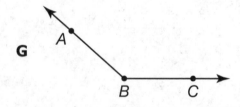

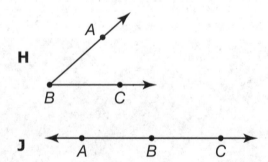

7 Each side of this triangle is the same length. How many lines of symmetry does the triangle have?

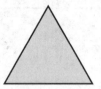

    A 1

    B 2

    C 3

    D 6

8 Parker threw the ball 54 feet. How many yards did he throw the ball?

Record your answer and fill in the bubbles. Be sure to use the correct place value.

			.		
⓪	⓪	⓪		⓪	⓪
①	①	①		①	①
②	②	②		②	②
③	③	③		③	③
④	④	④		④	④
⑤	⑤	⑤		⑤	⑤
⑥	⑥	⑥		⑥	⑥
⑦	⑦	⑦		⑦	⑦
⑧	⑧	⑧		⑧	⑧
⑨	⑨	⑨		⑨	⑨

9 Which figure is an obtuse triangle?

A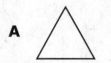

B

C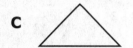

D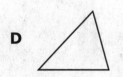

10 A rectangle has a length of 24 inches. The perimeter of the rectangle is 60 inches. What is the width in inches?

Record your answer and fill in the bubbles. Be sure to use the correct place value.

			.		
⓪	⓪	⓪		⓪	⓪
①	①	①		①	①
②	②	②		②	②
③	③	③		③	③
④	④	④		④	④
⑤	⑤	⑤		⑤	⑤
⑥	⑥	⑥		⑥	⑥
⑦	⑦	⑦		⑦	⑦
⑧	⑧	⑧		⑧	⑧
⑨	⑨	⑨		⑨	⑨

11 Which pair of lines appears to be parallel?

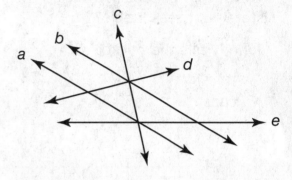

A Lines *a* and *b*

B Lines *c* and *d*

C Lines *b* and *e*

D Lines *d* and *e*

12 Use a protractor.

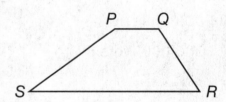

Which angle measures 55°?

F ∠P

G ∠Q

H ∠R

J ∠S

13 Johnny is washing his parents' car. He fills a bucket with water. Which unit of capacity makes the statement reasonable?

Johnny fills the bucket with 2 _____ of water.

   A cups

   B pints

   C quarts

   D gallons

14 Shondra brought 3,000 milliliters of water for the hike. How many liters did she bring?

   F 3 liters

   G 30 liters

   H 30,000 liters

   J 300,000 liters

15 Carli made 4 gallons of lemonade to sell. How many quarts of lemonade did she make?

   A 1 quart

   B 4 quarts

   C 8 quarts

   D 16 quarts

16 What is the unknown angle measure?

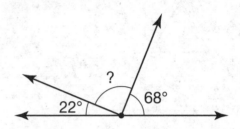

   F 80°

   G 90°

   H 100°

   J 110°

17 Daniel has 4 feet of rope. He cuts it into 6 equal length pieces. How long is each piece in inches?

Record your answer and fill in the bubbles. Be sure to use the correct place value.

⓪	⓪	⓪		⓪	⓪
①	①	①		①	①
②	②	②		②	②
③	③	③		③	③
④	④	④		④	④
⑤	⑤	⑤		⑤	⑤
⑥	⑥	⑥		⑥	⑥
⑦	⑦	⑦		⑦	⑦
⑧	⑧	⑧		⑧	⑧
⑨	⑨	⑨		⑨	⑨

18 Which figure shows an angle measuring 120°?

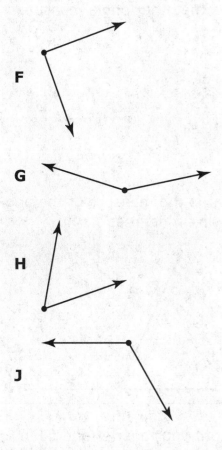

19 What is the unknown angle measure?

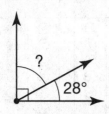

A 62°

B 52°

C 28°

D 90°

20 The table shows the prices of various items.

Item	Price
Puzzle book	$10.30
Video game	$19.75
Board game	$22.85
Toy train set	$12.40

Danica bought two items. She gave the cashier $40 and received $6.85 in change. Which two items did Danica buy?

F Puzzle book and video game

G Puzzle book and board game

H Video game and toy train set

J Board game and toy train set

21 The area of a rectangle is 72 square units. The length of the rectangle is 12 units. What is the perimeter of the rectangle?

A 34 units

B 18 units

C 36 units

D 17 units

22 Which figure has exactly 4 lines of symmetry?

F

G

H

J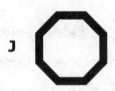

23 Which statement does **NOT** describe the figure?

A   The figure is a parallelogram.

B   The figure is a quadrilateral.

C   The figure is a trapezoid.

D   The figure is a square.

24 Two angles are supplementary. One angle measures 55°. What does the other angle measure?

F   25°

G   35°

H   125°

J   135°

25 What is the measure of the angle shown, in degrees?

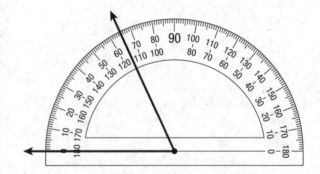

Record your answer and fill in the bubbles. Be sure to use the correct place value.

			.		
⓪	⓪	⓪		⓪	⓪
①	①	①		①	①
②	②	②		②	②
③	③	③		③	③
④	④	④		④	④
⑤	⑤	⑤		⑤	⑤
⑥	⑥	⑥		⑥	⑥
⑦	⑦	⑦		⑦	⑦
⑧	⑧	⑧		⑧	⑧
⑨	⑨	⑨		⑨	⑨

CHAPTER 4

Data Analysis and Personal Financial Literacy

Representing Data

1 GETTING THE IDEA

A **dot plot** is a way of showing data on a number line. **Data** are information collected about people or things.

A frequency table can help to organize the data for a dot plot. The frequencies in this table tell the numbers of sunflowers that grew each number of inches in two weeks.

In the dot plot below, each dot represents one sunflower's growth in two weeks. There are as many dots above a number of inches as the frequency for that number of inches in the table.

Sunflower Growth

Inches	Frequency
0	0
1	1
2	4
3	3

This dot plot shows the number of sunflowers that grew 0, 1, 2, or 3 inches in two weeks.

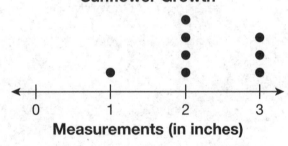

Sunflower Growth

Measurements (in inches)

You can draw a dot plot that shows data in whole numbers or fractional units. The frequency table and dot plot below show the number of daffodils that grew 0, $\frac{1}{4}$, $\frac{2}{4}$, or $\frac{3}{4}$ inch in two weeks:

Daffodil Growth

Inches	Frequency
0	0
$\frac{1}{4}$	1
$\frac{2}{4}$	3
$\frac{3}{4}$	2

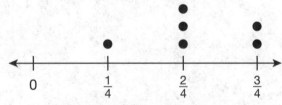

Daffodil Growth

Measurements (in inches)

Example 1

Students in a cooking class recorded the number of teaspoons of salt in each recipe of a cookbook.

| $\frac{2}{8}$ | $\frac{8}{8}$ | $\frac{8}{8}$ | $\frac{3}{8}$ | $\frac{4}{8}$ | $\frac{4}{8}$ | $\frac{8}{8}$ | $\frac{2}{8}$ | $\frac{6}{8}$ | $\frac{6}{8}$ | $\frac{8}{8}$ | $\frac{8}{8}$ | $\frac{6}{8}$ | $\frac{8}{8}$ | $\frac{8}{8}$ | $\frac{4}{8}$ | $\frac{6}{8}$ | $\frac{2}{8}$ | $\frac{6}{8}$ | $\frac{8}{8}$ |

Draw a dot plot for the data.

Strategy   **Mark a dot on the number line for each measurement.**

Step 1   Organize the data. Count the number of times each measurement shows in the data. A frequency table can help.

Teaspoons of Salt	Frequency
$\frac{2}{8}$	3
$\frac{3}{8}$	1
$\frac{4}{8}$	3
$\frac{5}{8}$	0
$\frac{6}{8}$	5
$\frac{7}{8}$	0
$\frac{8}{8}$	8

Step 2   Label the units on a number line.
Mark the number line in equal units of $\frac{1}{8}$, from $\frac{2}{8}$ to $\frac{8}{8}$. These are the least and greatest measurements in the data.

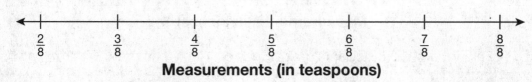

Measurements (in teaspoons)

Step 3	Draw dots on the number line.

Make one dot for each measurement in the table.

There are no recipes with $\frac{5}{8}$ or $\frac{7}{8}$ teaspoon of salt, so leave the space above those fractions on the number line blank.

Salt in Recipes

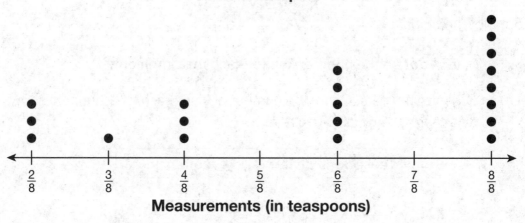

Measurements (in teaspoons)

Solution The dot plot of the data is shown in Step 3.

Example 2

A teacher measured her students' heights. The dot plot shows how much they grew in six months.

Student Growth

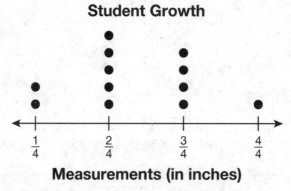

Measurements (in inches)

How many more students grew $\frac{1}{4}$ inch or $\frac{2}{4}$ inch than grew $\frac{3}{4}$ inch?

Strategy Use the data to find the number of students that grew each amount, and subtract.

Step 1   Find the number of students who grew $\frac{1}{4}$ inch or $\frac{2}{4}$ inch.

          2 dots above $\frac{1}{4}$ means 2 students grew $\frac{1}{4}$ inch.

          5 dots above $\frac{2}{4}$ means 5 students grew $\frac{2}{4}$ inch.

          $2 + 5 = 7$, so 7 students grew $\frac{1}{4}$ inch or $\frac{2}{4}$ inch.

Step 2   Find the number of students who grew $\frac{3}{4}$ inch.

          4 dots above $\frac{3}{4}$ means 4 students grew $\frac{3}{4}$ inch.

Step 3   Find the difference.

          $7 - 4 = 3$

Solution   3 more students grew $\frac{1}{4}$ inch or $\frac{2}{4}$ inch than grew $\frac{3}{4}$ inch.

Stem-and-leaf plots are tables that are used to display numerical data that have more than one digit. The plots have one column each for "stems" and "leaves." The key shows how to read the data by showing the place value of the stem and the leaf. The stem-and-leaf plot below shows the data set 17, 18, 19, 20, 28, 28, 37.

Stem	Leaf
1	7 8 9
2	0 8 8
3	7

Key: 1 | 7 = 17

Example 3

The stem-and-leaf plot shows the scores for 26 students on a recent math test.

Math Test Scores

Stem	Leaf
5	9
6	
7	0 1 2 4 5 7
8	0 1 2 3 4 4 4 9 9
9	0 0 2 3 6 6 7
10	0 0 0

Key: 5 | 9 = 59

An A is a score of 90 or better and a B is a score of 80–89. How many students scored either an A or a B on the test?

Strategy   Count the leaves.

Step 1   Count the number of leaves for each stem that is 8 or greater.

There are 9 leaves for the stem 8.

There are 7 leaves for the stem 9.

There are 3 leaves for the stem 10.

Step 2   Add the number of leaves for the 3 stems.

$9 + 7 + 3 = 19$

Solution   **19 students scored either an A or a B on the test.**

Low temperatures for every day in June in one city were recorded. The stem-and-leaf plot shows the temperatures.

Low Temperatures in June (in degrees Fahrenheit)

Stem	Leaf
4	0 2 4 7 7 8 9 9 9
5	0 0 1 2 2 2 3 4 4 4 4 5 6 6 6 6 7 8
6	1 3 3

Key: 4 | 0 = 40°F

How many more low temperatures were in the 50s than in the 40s or the 60s?

The number of temperatures in the 50s is _____.

The number of temperatures in the 40s is _____.

The number of temperatures in the 60s is _____.

The number of temperatures in the 40s or the 60s is _____ + _____ = _____.

Write an equation to find how many more temperatures were in the 50s than in the 40s or the 60s.

_____ ◯ _____ = _____

There were _____ more low temperatures in the 50s than in the 40s or the 60s.

1 Several students were tested on the distances they could run in 5 minutes. The data shows the results in miles.

$\frac{3}{8}$	$\frac{3}{8}$	$\frac{4}{8}$	$\frac{4}{8}$	$\frac{3}{8}$	$\frac{5}{8}$
$\frac{4}{8}$	$\frac{5}{8}$	$\frac{6}{8}$	$\frac{4}{8}$	$\frac{2}{8}$	$\frac{4}{8}$

Which dot plot correctly shows this data?

A.

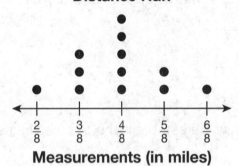

C.

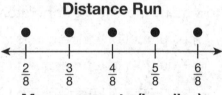

B.

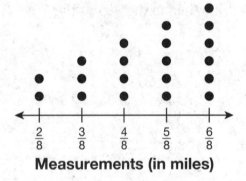

D.

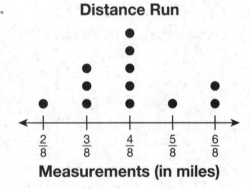

2 Sammi studied baby caterpillars for a science project. The dot plot shows the lengths of the baby caterpillars she found in her backyard.

Baby Caterpillar Lengths

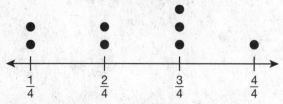

Measurements (in inches)

If all of the baby caterpillars were lined up end-to-end, how long would the line be?

A. 8 inches

B. $2\frac{1}{2}$ inches

C. $4\frac{3}{4}$ inches

D. $3\frac{3}{4}$ inches

3 The stem-and-leaf plot shows Linda's homework scores in her math class.

Homework Scores

Stem	Leaf
8	5 5 7
9	1 5 5 9
10	0 0 0

Key: 8 | 5 = 85

How many more scores above 90 did Linda get than scores below 90?

A. 1   C. 0

B. 4   D. 7

4 Carlos is an artist who paints watercolors. The widths of his brushes are shown in the dot plot.

Paintbrush Widths

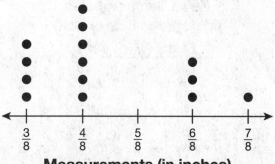

Measurements (in inches)

Carlos is planning to buy two brushes that are $\frac{5}{8}$ inch wide. How many brushes will Carlos have in all after he buys the new brushes?

A. 16   C. 2

B. 14   D. 5

5 The stem-and-leaf plot shows the number of snow cones Davis sold at his refreshment stand during each of the last eight weeks.

Snow Cones Sold Each Week

Stem	Leaf
25	1 5 6
26	
27	0 1 2 2 2

Key: 25 | 1 = 251

Which is a number of snow cones that Davis sold in one week?

A. 26   C. 250

B. 260   D. 270

6 Andre recorded the temperature at noon each day for a week. The stem-and-leaf plot shows the temperatures.

**Noon Temperatures
(in degrees Fahrenheit)**

Stem	Leaf
9	6 7 9 9
10	2 3 4

Key: 9 | 6 = 96°F

How many degrees warmer was the highest temperature that Andre recorded than the lowest temperature?

A. 2 degrees   C. 3 degrees

B. 10 degrees   D. 8 degrees

7 An elementary school principal asked 10 of her students how much time they usually spend on homework each week. The stem-and-leaf plot shows the results.

**Time Spent on Homework
(in hours)**

Stem	Leaf
0	3 3 4 5 6 9
1	0 0 1 1 1

Key: 0 | 3 = 3 hours

How many students spent less than 5 hours or more than 10 hours on homework?

A. 10

B. 6

C. 11

D. 9

Use the information below for questions 8 and 9.

Nicole uses stickers for her scrapbook. The dot plot shows the lengths of her stickers.

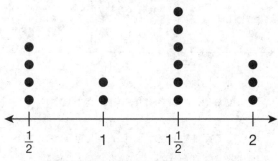

Sticker Lengths

Measurements (in inches)

8 How many stickers longer than 1 inch does Nicole have?

A. 2   C. 9

B. 11   D. 15

9 Nicole places her three longest stickers in a line and her four shortest stickers in a line. How much longer, in inches, is her line of longest stickers than her line of shortest stickers?

Record your answer and fill in the bubbles. Be sure to use the correct place value.

			.		
⓪	⓪	⓪		⓪	⓪
①	①	①		①	①
②	②	②		②	②
③	③	③		③	③
④	④	④		④	④
⑤	⑤	⑤		⑤	⑤
⑥	⑥	⑥		⑥	⑥
⑦	⑦	⑦		⑦	⑦
⑧	⑧	⑧		⑧	⑧
⑨	⑨	⑨		⑨	⑨

Fixed and Variable Expenses

1 GETTING THE IDEA

Expenses are costs of things that you spend money on. Some expenses are fixed expenses and others are variable expenses.

Fixed expenses are expenses that do not change for a given period of time. Rent is a fixed monthly expense for many people. It stays the same from month to month.

Variable expenses are expenses that can change from day to day. The cost of food is a variable expense. It changes whenever you buy different food items.

Mr. Alva's expenses for last month are shown in the circle graph.

His fixed expenses are rent, phone, utilities, and insurance.

His variable expenses are food, entertainment, transportation, and clothing.

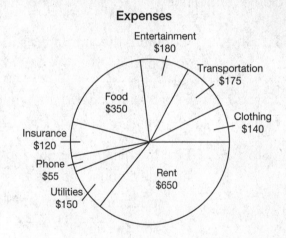

Expenses

Example 1

Ms. Banner's fixed expenses for each month are shown in the table. She has $1,800 to spend this month. How much does Ms. Banner have left for variable expenses?

Expense	Amount
Rent	$700
Phone and utilities	$132
Insurance	$90
Fitness club membership	$35

Strategy   Calculate the difference between how much Ms. Banner has for spending and her fixed expenses.

Step 1   Find the sum of Ms. Banner's fixed expenses.

$$\$700 + \$132 + \$90 + \$35 = \$957$$

Ms. Banner's fixed expenses are $957.

Step 2   Subtract Ms. Banner's fixed expenses from the amount she has for spending.

$$\$1,800 - \$957 = \$843$$

Ms. Banner has $843 left.

Solution   **Ms. Banner has $843 for variable expenses.**

Example 2

This month, Ms. Banner has already spent $320 for groceries, $150 for gas, and $200 for entertainment, all of which are variable expenses. Ms. Banner still wants to spend $160 for new clothes and $30 to go out to dinner with her friends. Does Ms. Banner have enough money for clothes and dinner?

Strategy   **Compare the amount Ms. Banner has left to spend to the amount she wants to spend.**

Step 1   Find the amount Ms. Banner has already spent on variable expenses.

$$\$320 + \$150 + \$200 = \$670$$

Step 2   Find the difference between the amount Ms. Banner has for variable expenses and the amount she has already spent.

In Example 1, you found that Ms. Banner has $843 for variable expenses.

$$\$843 - \$670 = \$173$$

Ms. Banner has $173 left to spend.

Step 3   Find the amount Ms. Banner wants to spend.

$$\$160 + \$30 = \$190$$

Ms. Banner wants to spend $190.

Step 4   Compare the amount Ms. Banner has left to the amount she wants to spend.

$$\$173 < \$190$$

The amount Ms. Banner has left is less than the amount she wants to spend.

Solution   **Ms. Banner does not have enough money for clothes and dinner.**

One month, Ms. Banner has $1,900 for all her expenses. Her fixed expenses remain the same as shown in Example 1. For her variable expenses, she has budgeted $400 for food, $120 for transportation, $200 for entertainment, and $150 for clothing. She also has an unexpected $350 car repair. Does Ms. Banner have enough money to pay for the car repair? If not, how could she change her budget to have enough money?

The amount of Ms. Banner's fixed expenses is $_____.

To find the amount Ms. Banner has for her variable expenses, subtract

her _____ expenses from how much she has to spend this month.

variable expenses = $ _____ $\bigcirc$ $_____

= $ _____

To find the amount Ms. Banner has budgeted for variable expenses, add

the amounts for_____, _____, _____, and _____.

amount budgeted = $_____ $\bigcirc$ $ _____ $\bigcirc$ $_____ $\bigcirc$ $_____

= $_____

To find the amount Ms. Banner has left for other variable expenses, _____ the

amount she has budgeted for variable expenses from the total she has to spend for

all _____ expenses.

amount left for other variable expenses = $_____ $\bigcirc$ $_____

= $_____

Compare the cost of car repairs to the amount _____.

$_____ $\bigcirc$ $_____

Ms. Banner _____ enough money to pay for car repairs.

She could change her budget by _____
_____.

1 Which of the following describes a variable expense?

   A. Mr. Davison pays home owner association dues every three months.

   B. Ms. Fernandez pays for membership to her health club every month.

   C. Mr. Graham rents a movie and buys snacks for family movie night on some weekends.

   D. Ms. Jensen makes a payment on her car lease on the second Tuesday of every month.

2 Jason spent $2,200 last month. His fixed expenses were $550 for rent, $180 for utilities, and $128 for insurance. He also spent $48 on movie tickets. Which expression is equal to the amount he could spend on variable expenses last month?

   A. $2,200 − $550 − $180 − $128

   B. $550 + $180 + $128 + $48

   C. $550 + $180 + $128

   D. $2,200 − $550 − $180 − $128 − $48

3 Which of the following describes a fixed expense?

   A. Every month, Kim has dinner at a new restaurant.

   B. Cassidy buys a $20 bus pass each month to get to work.

   C. Nicole goes shopping with her friends every month.

   D. Paul goes to the arcade with his friends on Fridays.

4 Mr. Kim's monthly fixed expenses are listed in the table.

Expense	Amount
Rent	$720
Phone	$40
Insurance	$85
Utilities	$172

He has $2,000 to spend. How many dollars does he have for variable expenses?

Record your answer and fill in the bubbles. Be sure to use the correct place value.

Use the information for questions 5 and 6.

The circle graph shows Ms. Malone's June expenses. Her fixed expenses are rent, utilities, phone, and insurance.

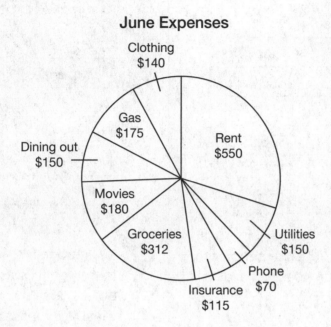

June Expenses

Clothing $140
Gas $175
Dining out $150
Movies $180
Rent $550
Groceries $312
Utilities $150
Phone $70
Insurance $115

5 How many dollars did Ms. Malone spend on fixed expenses?

Record your answer and fill in the bubbles. Be sure to use the correct place value.

			.		
⓪	⓪	⓪		⓪	⓪
①	①	①		①	①
②	②	②		②	②
③	③	③		③	③
④	④	④		④	④
⑤	⑤	⑤		⑤	⑤
⑥	⑥	⑥		⑥	⑥
⑦	⑦	⑦		⑦	⑦
⑧	⑧	⑧		⑧	⑧
⑨	⑨	⑨		⑨	⑨

6 In July, Ms. Malone has the same amount to spend as in June. She has the same fixed expenses. She wants to buy a new TV for $325. How could Ms. Malone change her spending from June to July so she can buy the TV?

A. She could not go to the movies or buy clothes.

B. She could spend $320 on groceries but not dine out or go to the movies.

C. She could spend $150 on gas. She could spend $317 on groceries but not dine out or go to the movies.

D. She could spend $150 on gas. She could also spend $340 on groceries and $220 on rent.

Use the information below for questions 7 and 8.

The table shows all of Mr. Parker's monthly fixed expenses.

Expense	Amount
Rent	$680
Phone	$50
Insurance	$90
Utilities	$135
Car payment	$230

7 Mr. Parker has $2,000 to spend each month. How much does he have for variable expenses?

A. $1,185

B. $885

C. $1,115

D. $815

8 In September, Mr. Parker spends $400 on groceries and $200 on gas. Which of the following can he also do in September?

A. He can spend $120 to dine out and pay $100 to service his car.

B. He can buy his mother a present for $50. He can go out 4 times and spend $40 each time.

C. He can spend $90 to go to the movies. He can spend $140 on books.

D. He can buy 5 video games for $32 each. He can spend $60 on clothes.

Use the information below for questions 9 and 10.

Ms. Smith has $1,750 to spend each month. Her monthly fixed expenses are listed in the table.

Expense	Amount
Rent	$550
Phone	$65
Health club	$45
Utilities	$120

9 In October, Ms. Smith takes her dog to the vet. It costs $265. How many dollars does she have left for her other variable expenses?

A. $705

B. $970

C. $1,485

D. $2,265

10 In November, Ms. Smith's rent increases by $100 each month. How does this affect the amount Ms. Smith has to spend on variable expenses?

A. It increases by $100.

B. It increases by $650.

C. It stays the same.

D. It decreases by $100.

LESSON 33

Calculating Profit

1 GETTING THE IDEA

Profit is the difference between what a business earns and what it spends.

The money that a business earns is called **revenue**. The money that it spends on different things is its **expenses**. Expenses include the cost of supplies.

Mark sells 24 cups of hot chocolate for $1 each at a football game. The cocoa powder, sugar, and milk used to make the hot chocolate cost $8.

revenue = $1 × 24 = $24

expenses = $8

profit = revenue − expenses

$\qquad$ = 24 − 8

$\qquad$ = $16

Mark made a profit of $16 selling hot chocolate.

Example 1

A class is raising money by selling animal key chains. For each key chain, the animal design costs $1.25 and the chain and ring cost $0.50. The class sells each key chain for $4.00. What is the profit from selling each key chain?

Strategy   Calculate the difference between revenue and expenses.

Step 1   Find the revenue for each key chain.

The revenue is the selling price for each key chain.

revenue = $4.00

Step 2   Find the expenses for each key chain.

The expenses are the cost of the animal design plus the cost of the chain and ring.

$$
\begin{array}{r}
1.2\,5 \\
+\ 0.5\,0 \\
\hline
1.7\,5
\end{array}
$$

expenses = $1.75

Step 3   Subtract the expenses from the revenue.

$$
\begin{array}{r}
\text{revenue} \quad \overset{\scriptscriptstyle 9}{}\,\overset{\scriptscriptstyle 3\ \,\cancel{10}\ 10}{4.0\ 0} \\
-\ \text{expenses} \quad -\ 1.7\ 5 \\
\hline
\text{profit} \quad 2.2\ 5
\end{array}
$$

Solution   **The profit for each key chain is $2.25.**

Another expense that businesses have to consider is the cost of labor. The **cost of labor** is the amount paid to employees.

Example 2

A company makes hand-crafted wooden puzzles. One worker can make three puzzles in an hour. The company pays the worker $20 an hour. The cost of the materials to make three puzzles is $9. Each puzzle sells for $15. What is the profit for three puzzles?

Strategy   **Calculate the difference between revenue and expenses.**

Step 1   Find the revenue for three puzzles.

Each puzzle sells for $15. Multiply 3 by 15.

$3 \times 15 = 45$

revenue = $45

Step 2   Find the expenses for three puzzles.

The cost of labor is $20. The cost of supplies is $9. Add 20 and 9.

$20 + 9 = 29$

expenses = $29

Step 3   Subtract the expenses from the revenue.

profit = revenue − expenses

$= 45 - 29$

$= 16$

Solution   **The profit for three puzzles is $16.**

Jada opens a lemonade stand. She buys a bag of lemons for $5, sugar for $3, and bottles of water for $3. She pays her sister $8 to help make the lemonade. Jada sells 40 servings of lemonade for $1 per serving. What is her profit?

To find Jada's revenue, multiply the cost of each serving by _____.

    revenue = _____ ☐ _____

           = $_____

Find Jada's expenses.

    Jada's cost of labor is $_____.

    To find the cost of supplies, add the costs for lemons, _____, and _____.

    cost of supplies = _____ ☐ _____ ☐ _____

                  = $_____

    Add the cost of labor and the cost of _____.

    expenses = _____ ☐ _____

           = $_____

Profit is equal to the _____ minus the _____.

    profit = _____ ☐ _____

          = $_____

Jada's profit for selling 40 servings of lemonade is $_____.

1 Jason builds toy race cars. He sells them to his friends for $10 each. The table shows the cost for parts needed to build one car.

Part	Cost
Body	$3.50
Wheels	$1.30
Decorations	$0.80

What is Jason's profit for selling one car?

A. $5.60

B. $4.40

C. $5.40

D. $4.60

2 Nina charges $80 to clean one house. On Saturday, she cleaned 3 houses. She paid $45 for all her cleaning supplies. What was Nina's profit for cleaning three houses?

A. $65

B. $105

C. $195

D. $240

3 Marcus sells his old comics books for $105. He originally bought the comic books for $38. How much profit did he make selling his comic books?

A. $33

B. $67

C. $105

D. $143

4 Juanita buys old toys, fixes them up, and then resells them. She bought 10 old toys for $8 each. Her supplies to fix up the toys cost $12. She resells the old toys for $15 each. What is her profit in dollars?

Record your answer and fill in the bubbles. Be sure to use the correct place value.

			.		
⓪	⓪	⓪		⓪	⓪
①	①	①		①	①
②	②	②		②	②
③	③	③		③	③
④	④	④		④	④
⑤	⑤	⑤		⑤	⑤
⑥	⑥	⑥		⑥	⑥
⑦	⑦	⑦		⑦	⑦
⑧	⑧	⑧		⑧	⑧
⑨	⑨	⑨		⑨	⑨

5 A company sells handmade napkin holders for $15 each. The material for one napkin holder costs $2.25. The cost for a worker to make a napkin holder is $5.35. What is the profit for selling one napkin holder?

A. $7.40

B. $9.35

C. $7.50

D. $8.40

6 Kori has a car washing service. Her prices for washing different types of cars are shown in the table.

Car	Cost
Compact	$6.00
Sedan	$8.00
Minivan	$12.00

Kori paid her friend $40 to help. In one day, they washed 5 compacts, 10 sedans, and 3 minivans. The cost of her cleaning supplies for that day were $28. What was her profit?

A. $146

B. $118

C. $106

D. $78

7 Charlie charges $9 to trim the nails of one dog. He bought nail clippers for $15. Charlie trimmed the nails of 8 dogs. Which equation shows how to calculate Charlie's profit?

A. Profit = $(8 \times 15) - 9$

B. Profit = $(8 \times 9) - 15$

C. Profit = $(8 + 9) - 15$

D. Profit = $15 - 9$

8 Renee sold two paintings. One sold for $150 and the other sold for $125. She spent $87 on painting supplies. What is her profit, in dollars, for the two paintings?

Record your answer and fill in the bubbles. Be sure to use the correct place value.

			.		
⓪	⓪	⓪		⓪	⓪
①	①	①		①	①
②	②	②		②	②
③	③	③		③	③
④	④	④		④	④
⑤	⑤	⑤		⑤	⑤
⑥	⑥	⑥		⑥	⑥
⑦	⑦	⑦		⑦	⑦
⑧	⑧	⑧		⑧	⑧
⑨	⑨	⑨		⑨	⑨

9 For a fund-raising project, Ms. Lee's class ordered custom T-shirts to sell. They bought 50 T-shirts for $150. They sold the T-shirts for $8 each. They sold 40 of the T-shirts and gave the remaining T-shirts away. What was the class's profit?

A. $250

B. $400

C. $320

D. $170

10 Mo bought the ingredients shown in the table to make granola bars.

Ingredient	Cost
Flour	$3.25
Oats	$2.25
Eggs	$2.00
Sugar	$3.15
Baking soda	$0.85
Butter	$1.50

Using all of the ingredients, he made 24 bars. He sold each bar for $2. What was Mo's profit?

A. $48

B. $35

C. $13

D. $11

11 Nick baked a peach pie for the bake sale. The ingredients to bake the pie cost $8.30. The pie had eight slices. He sold each slice for $3. What was Nick's profit?

A. $15.70

B. $11.30

C. $15.30

D. $5.30

12 Mr. Powers paid Brandon $150 to paint his deck. Brandon bought painting supplies for $38. He also paid a friend $50 to help him. What was Brandon's profit, in dollars, for painting the deck?

Record your answer and fill in the bubbles. Be sure to use the correct place value.

Understanding Financial Institutions

 GETTING THE IDEA -

Financial institutions are businesses that make money by managing the money of people and other businesses. Some examples of financial institutions are banks, credit unions, and credit card companies.

You save your money in a bank. You might know someone who has borrowed money from a bank or credit union. Every time people use their credit cards, they are getting a loan from the credit card company.

Many people keep their money in bank accounts. Banks hold the money, so it is safe from being stolen or lost. When you put money in a bank account, you are making a **deposit**. When you take money from a bank account, you are making a **withdrawal**.

Example 1

At the beginning of March, Mrs. Vance had $200 in her bank account. The table shows all the deposits and withdrawals she made to her account during the month. How much money does Mrs. Vance have in her account at the end of March?

Date	Transaction	Amount
March 3	Withdrawal	$80
March 6	Deposit	$135
March 11	Deposit	$40
March 16	Withdrawal	$70
March 22	Deposit	$120

Strategy   Add deposits to the account and subtract withdrawals from the account.

Step 1   Find the sum of Mrs. Vance's deposits.

$135 + $40 + $120 = $295

Mrs. Vance's deposits total $295.

Step 2	Find the sum of Mrs. Vance's withdrawals.

$80 + $70 = $150

Mrs. Vance's withdrawals total $150.

Step 3	Add the deposits and subtract the withdrawals from the amount Mrs. Vance had in her account at the beginning of March.

$200 + $295 − $150 = $345

Mrs. Vance has $345 in her account.

Solution **At the end of March, Mrs. Vance has $345 in her account.**

When a person borrows money from a bank or credit card company, the bank or company charges interest. **Interest** is a fee. The amount of interest a person pays depends on the amount borrowed and how long it takes to pay the money back.

Example 2

Ms. Winters buys a new couch for $504. To buy the couch, she uses a credit card that charges no interest for the first 6 months after the purchase. She wants to pay back the money with equal monthly payments over 6 months before interest is charged. What will Ms. Winter's monthly payment be?

Strategy	**Divide to find the monthly payment.**

Step 1	Write a division equation representing the problem.

The cost of the couch in dollars divided by the number of months equals the monthly payment.

$504 \div 6 = m$

Step 2	Find the value of m.

$$
\begin{array}{r}
84 \\
6\overline{)504} \\
-48 \\
\hline
24 \\
-24 \\
\hline
0
\end{array}
$$

Solution **Ms. Winter's monthly payment will be $84.**

Ms. Winters also buys a new bed for $856 at the same time using the same credit card. She decides to pay back the money for both purchases with 4 equal monthly payments. What will Ms. Winter's monthly payment be?

The amount Ms. Winters borrows is the sum of the cost of the couch and the cost

of the _____.

amount she borrows = $_____ ◯ $_____

= $ _____

To find her monthly payment, divide the amount in dollars that she borrows by the

number of _____.

_____ ◯ _____ = m

Find the value of m. Show your work here.

Ms. Winter's monthly payment will be $ _____.

1 At the beginning of August, Kendra had $320 in her bank account. The table shows all her deposits and withdrawals for the month of August.

Kendra's Bank Account

Date	Transaction	Amount
August 2	Withdrawal	$65
August 6	Withdrawal	$160
August 17	Deposit	$180
August 22	Withdrawal	$80
August 23	Deposit	$120
August 29	Deposit	$100

How much is in Kendra's account at the end of August?

A. $225

B. $415

C. $95

D. $395

2 Macey makes a purchase with a credit card that charges no interest for 6 months. Her monthly payment will be $60 for 6 months. Which of the following could be her purchase?

A. 2 dresses for $60 each and a TV for $300

B. 3 book cases for $120 each

C. 2 stereos for $150 each and a night stand for $50

D. 1 vacuum cleaner for $200 and 4 pillows for $30 each

3 Jackson buys a laptop for $588 with his credit card. He wants to pay back the money with 6 equal monthly payments. His credit card company will charge him $24 in interest over the 6 months. How much will his monthly payment be?

A. $98

B. $94

C. $102

D. $122

4 At the beginning of December, Ms. Cortez had $240 in her bank account. At the end of December, she has $400 in her account. During December Ms. Cortez made deposits of $350. How much money, in dollars, did she withdraw from her account during December?

Record your answer and fill in the bubbles. Be sure to use the correct place value.

			.		
⓪	⓪	⓪		⓪	⓪
①	①	①		①	①
②	②	②		②	②
③	③	③		③	③
④	④	④		④	④
⑤	⑤	⑤		⑤	⑤
⑥	⑥	⑥		⑥	⑥
⑦	⑦	⑦		⑦	⑦
⑧	⑧	⑧		⑧	⑧
⑨	⑨	⑨		⑨	⑨

5 Mr. Anderson had $500 in his bank account at the beginning of June. For the month of June, he made deposits totaling $320, and he made withdrawals totaling $400. Which statement best describes his account at the end of June compared to the beginning of June?

A. He has $80 more in his account.

B. He has the same amount in his account.

C. He has $420 less in his account.

D. He has $80 less in his account.

6 Iona buys new clothes for $348 with her credit card. She wants to pay back the money with 4 equal monthly payments. Her credit card company will charge her $24 in interest over the 4 months. How much will her monthly payment be, in dollars?

Record your answer and fill in the bubbles. Be sure to use the correct place value.

⓪	⓪	⓪	.	⓪	⓪
①	①	①		①	①
②	②	②		②	②
③	③	③		③	③
④	④	④		④	④
⑤	⑤	⑤		⑤	⑤
⑥	⑥	⑥		⑥	⑥
⑦	⑦	⑦		⑦	⑦
⑧	⑧	⑧		⑧	⑧
⑨	⑨	⑨		⑨	⑨

Use the information below for questions 7 and 8.

Amelia is thinking about making the following purchases with her credit card. Her card charges no interest for the first 6 months after purchase.

Item	Price
Bed	$300
Desk	$180
Dresser	$150
Nightstand	$120

7 Which purchase would result in 6 monthly payments of $55?

A. 1 bed

B. 1 desk and 1 nightstand

C. 1 desk and 1 dresser

D. 3 nightstands

8 Amelia wants to make 6 equal monthly payments less than $70. Which of these purchases is the most expensive that she could make?

A. 1 bed and 1 nightstand

B. 2 desks

C. 2 dressers

D. 1 dresser and 1 nightstand

Use the information below for questions 9 and 10.

Mrs. Moran had $560 in her bank account at the beginning of July. The table shows all her transactions for the month of July.

Mrs. Moran's Account

Date	Transaction	Amount
July 2	Withdrawal	$80
July 6	Deposit	$165
July 9	Withdrawal	$150
July 12	Deposit	$210
July 18	Deposit	$100
July 22	Withdrawal	$185

9 How much was in Mrs. Moran's account on July 15?

    A. $480

    B. $145

    C. $620

    D. $705

10 Which best describes the change in Mrs. Moran's account from the beginning of July to the end of July?

    A. Her account has $60 less.

    B. Her account has $60 more.

    C. Her account has $145 less.

    D. Her account has $145 more.

Use the information below for questions 11 and 12.

Marcus buys a surfboard for $428 and a stereo for $282 with a credit card that charges no interest over the first 6 months after purchase. He wants to pay back the cost of the surfboard and stereo with 5 monthly payments.

11 Suppose Marcus wants to make equal monthly payments. How much will his monthly payment be, in dollars?

Record your answer and fill in the bubbles. Be sure to use the correct place value.

12 Suppose Marcus makes a payment of $170 the first month. He will make the remaining payments equal. How much will each of the remaining monthly payments be?

    A. $135

    B. $108

    C. $540

    D. $220

Use the information and circle graph below for questions 1 and 2.

The circle graph shows Mr. Khullar's expenses for April. His fixed expenses are rent, club membership, utilities, and insurance.

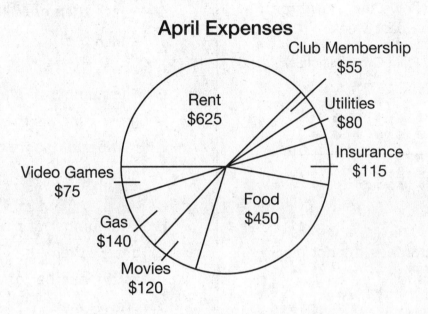

April Expenses

1   How much did Mr. Khullar spend on variable expenses, in dollars?

Record your answer and fill in the bubbles. Be sure to use the correct place value.

2   In May, Mr. Khullar has the same amount to spend as in April. He has the same fixed expenses. He wants to buy a desk for $220. Which of the following changes can he make to his expenses from April so he can buy a desk?

F   He does not spend money on video games and movies.

G   He spends $300 on food and does not spend money on video games.

H   He spends $360 on food and does not spend money on movies.

J   He spends $380 on food and $100 on gas. He does not spend money on video games.

Use the information below for questions 3 and 4.

Janet is growing 14 tomato plants. The dot plot shows the growth of the plants over the past week.

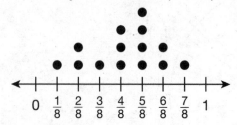

Weekly Plant Growth (inches)

3 Which data does the dot plot represent?

A $\frac{2}{8}, \frac{7}{8}, \frac{5}{8}, \frac{3}{8}, \frac{4}{8}, \frac{4}{8}, \frac{6}{8}, \frac{5}{8}, \frac{2}{8}, \frac{5}{8}, \frac{1}{8},$
   $\frac{4}{8}, \frac{6}{8}, \frac{5}{8}$

B $\frac{2}{8}, \frac{7}{8}, \frac{5}{8}, \frac{3}{8}, \frac{4}{8}, \frac{4}{8}, \frac{6}{8}, \frac{5}{8}, \frac{1}{8}, \frac{5}{8}, \frac{1}{8},$
   $\frac{4}{8}, \frac{6}{8}, \frac{5}{8}$

C $\frac{2}{8}, \frac{7}{8}, \frac{5}{8}, \frac{3}{8}, \frac{4}{8}, \frac{4}{8}, \frac{6}{8}, \frac{4}{8}, \frac{2}{8}, \frac{5}{8}, \frac{1}{8},$
   $\frac{4}{8}, \frac{6}{8}, \frac{5}{8}$

D $\frac{3}{8}, \frac{7}{8}, \frac{5}{8}, \frac{3}{8}, \frac{4}{8}, \frac{3}{8}, \frac{6}{8}, \frac{5}{8}, \frac{2}{8}, \frac{5}{8}, \frac{1}{8},$
   $\frac{5}{8}, \frac{6}{8}, \frac{5}{8}$

4 Which statement is **NOT** true?

F More plants grew more than $\frac{5}{8}$ inch than grew less than $\frac{3}{8}$ inch.

G The number of plants that grew $\frac{4}{8}$ inch is the same as the number of plants that grew either $\frac{1}{8}$ or $\frac{2}{8}$ inch.

H The number of plants that grew either $\frac{3}{8}$ or $\frac{4}{8}$ is the same as the number of plants that grew $\frac{5}{8}$ inch.

J More plants grew more than $\frac{4}{8}$ inch than grew less than $\frac{4}{8}$ inch.

5 A company sells bookcases for $225 each. The material for one bookcase costs $30. It takes two workers to build a bookcase. The company pays each worker $40 for a bookcase. What is the company's profit for selling one bookcase?

A $115

B $145

C $155

D $185

Use the information below for questions 6 and 7.

Cooper is thinking about making the following purchases with his credit card. His card charges no interest over the first 3 months after purchase.

Item	Price
Compact disc	$15
Video game	$30
Book	$10
Board game	$25

6 Which purchase results in 3 monthly payments of $50?

   F 6 books and 5 compact discs

   G 6 compact discs and 2 board games

   H 4 board games and 2 video games

   J 4 video games and 3 books

7 Which purchase results in 3 monthly payments of $40?

   A 2 board games and 6 books

   B 5 compact discs and 5 books

   C 2 books and 4 board games

   D 3 video games and 1 board game

8 Which of the following describes a variable expense?

   F Mr. Rogers buys a bus pass every month so he can go to work.

   G Ms. Kelly pays her car insurance every two months.

   H Mrs. Wiggins goes to dinner with her friends occasionally.

   J Mr. Tavares pays his cable bill every month.

9 Janice makes puppets. She sells them for $30 each. The table shows the cost for parts needed to build a puppet.

Part	Cost
Wood	$4.50
Fabric	$3.30
Paint	$2.60
String	$1.80

What is Janice's profit for selling one puppet?

   A $12.20

   B $17.80

   C $13.20

   D $16.80

10 At the beginning of October, Kendra had $250 in her bank account. The table shows all her deposits and withdrawals for the month of October.

Date	Transaction	Amount
October 3	Withdrawal	$125
October 8	Deposit	$180
October 15	Deposit	$120
October 21	Withdrawal	$200
October 25	Deposit	$140

How much money is in Kendra's account at the end of October?

F $115

G $135

H $250

J $365

---

11 Harrison has a house cleaning service. His prices are shown in the table.

House	Price
One bedroom	$80
Two bedrooms	$120
Three bedrooms	$150

He pays an assistant $125 each day. In 2 days, they cleaned 3 one-bedroom houses, 1 two-bedroom house, and 2 three-bedroom houses. The cost of his cleaning supplies for the two days was $45. What was his profit?

A $350

B $365

C $410

D $490

12 Alex uses a credit card to buy some business supplies for $540. He wants to pay back the money with equal monthly payments over 5 months. His credit card company will charge him $25 in interest over the 5 months. How much will his monthly payment be, in dollars?

Record your answer and fill in the bubbles. Be sure to use the correct place value.

			.		
⓪	⓪	⓪		⓪	⓪
①	①	①		①	①
②	②	②		②	②
③	③	③		③	③
④	④	④		④	④
⑤	⑤	⑤		⑤	⑤
⑥	⑥	⑥		⑥	⑥
⑦	⑦	⑦		⑦	⑦
⑧	⑧	⑧		⑧	⑧
⑨	⑨	⑨		⑨	⑨

13 Robbie made a frequency table to record how far a number of students ran over the weekend.

Miles	Frequency
1	1
2	3
3	2
4	4
5	1
6	1

Which dot plot shows Robbie's data?

A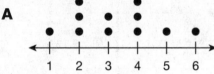

B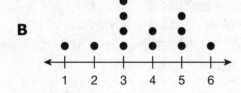

C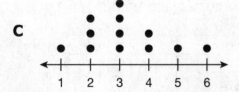

D

14 Shaun makes a purchase with a credit card that charges no interest for 6 months. His monthly payment is $55 for 6 months. Which of the following could be his purchase?

F He buys 2 chairs for $30 each and a bed for $300.

G He buys 3 bookcases for $120 each.

H He buys 2 dressers for $140 each and a nightstand for $50.

J He buys a table for $200 and 4 chairs for $30 each.

15 Mr. Gomes paid Hector $120 to landscape the yard. Hector bought some tools for $38 and paid a friend $30 to help him. What was Hector's profit in dollars?

Record your answer and fill in the bubbles. Be sure to use the correct place value.

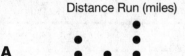

Use the information below for questions 16 and 17.

The stem and leaf plot shows the quiz scores for 16 students.

Quiz Scores

Stem	Leaf
1	6 7 7 8 9
2	2 3 4 4 5 6 7
3	1 2 2 5

Key: 1 | 6 = 16

16 How many students scored more than 25 points on the quiz?

F 5   **H** 8

G 6   **J** 11

17 Which of following statements is true?

A More students scored above 25 points than scored below 25 points.

B The number of students scoring 17 or 18 points is the same as the number of students scoring 24 or 25 points.

C More students scored above 30 points than scored below 20 points.

D The number of students scoring 23 points is the same as the number of students scoring 32 points.

18 Heidi sells necklaces for $12 each. Last week, she sold 9 necklaces. She paid $45 for materials to make the necklaces. What was Heidi's profit?

F $108

G $33

H $63

J $53

19 Mr. Lee's monthly fixed expenses are listed in the table.

Expense	Amount
Rent	$575
Phone	$55
Insurance	$110
Utilities	$127

He has $1,600 to spend for the month. How much money, in dollars, does he have left for variable expenses?

Record your answer and fill in the bubbles. Be sure to use the correct place value.

GLOSSARY

acute angle an angle with a measure greater than 0° but less than 90° (Lesson 22)

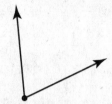

acute triangle a triangle with three angles that each measure less than 90° (Lesson 24)

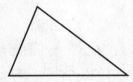

addend a number added to one or more other numbers to find a sum (Lesson 12)

$$7 + 3 = 10$$
↑   ↑
addends

angle a figure formed by two rays that share the same endpoint (Lesson 22)

area the amount of space that a figure covers (Lesson 21)

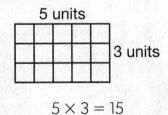

5 units

3 units

$$5 \times 3 = 15$$

The area of the rectangle is 15 square units.

benchmark an object that can be used to compare and estimate a measurement (Lesson 27)

about 1 gram   about 1 kilogram

benchmark fraction a common fraction that can be compared with other fractions (Lesson 11)

$$\frac{1}{4}, \frac{1}{2}, \frac{3}{4}$$

capacity the amount a container can hold (Lesson 27)

1 cup   1 pint

about 1 milliliter

centimeter (cm) a metric unit of measure for length (Lesson 27)

100 centimeters (cm) = 1 meter (m)

about 1 centimeter

common denominator a shared multiple of the denominators of two or more fractions (Lesson 10)

> 12 is a multiple of 4 and 6.
>
> So, a common denominator of $\frac{3}{4}$ and $\frac{5}{6}$ is 12.

common numerator a shared multiple of the numerators of two or more fractions (Lesson 10)

> 15 is a multiple of 3 and 5.
>
> So, a common numerator of $\frac{3}{4}$ and $\frac{5}{6}$ is 15.

compatible numbers numbers that are close to the numbers in a problem but are easier to compute mentally (Lesson 17)

> Actual numbers: $47 \div 7$
>
> Compatible numbers: $49 \div 7 = 7$

complementary angles two angles whose measures have a sum of 90° (Lesson 26)

Complementary Angles

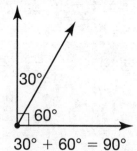

$$30° + 60° = 90°$$

convert to change a measurement given in one unit to an equivalent measure using a larger or smaller unit (Lessons 28, 29)

> 1 foot (ft) = 12 inches (in.)

cost of labor the amount a business pays to its employees (Lesson 33)

cup (c) a customary unit of measure for capacity (Lesson 27)

> 2 cups (c) = 1 pint (pt)

customary system of measurement the system of measurement used in the United States to measure length, capacity, and weight (Lesson 27)

> length: inch (in.), foot (ft), yard (yd)
>
> capacity: fluid ounce (fl oz), cup (c), pint (pt), quart (qt), gallon (gal)
>
> weight: ounce (oz), pound (lb)

data information collected about people or things (Lesson 31)

day (d) a unit of time (Lesson 27)

> 1 day (d) = 24 hours (hr)

decimal a number with a decimal point (Lessons 2, 5, 7)

> 0.4 is a decimal.

decimal point a symbol that separates the ones from the tenths in a decimal (Lesson 5)

> decimal: 0.6
> ↑
> decimal point

decompose to break a fraction into smaller parts (Lesson 8)

> $\frac{3}{4}$ can be decomposed into the sum $\frac{2}{4} + \frac{1}{4}$.

degree (°) a unit for measuring angles (Lesson 22)

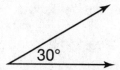

denominator the bottom number of a fraction—it tells how many equal parts are in the whole (Lesson 8)

$\frac{2}{3}$ has a denominator of 3.

deposit money put into a bank account (Lesson 34)

difference the result of a subtraction problem (Lesson 12)

$$12 - 7 = 5$$
$$\uparrow$$
difference

dividend the number that is divided by another number in a division problem (Lesson 16)

$$20 \div 4 = 5$$
$$\uparrow$$
dividend

divisor the number by which another number is divided in a division problem (Lesson 16)

$$18 \div 3 = 6$$
$$\uparrow$$
divisor

dot plot a graph that uses dots to show data on a number line (Lesson 31)

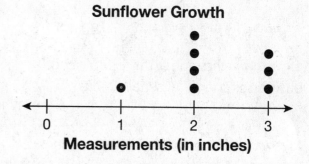

endpoint a point marking the end of a line segment or ray (Lesson 22)

endpoint

equal to (=) a symbol that is used to compare two numbers or expressions, and that means they have an equivalent value (Lesson 3)

$$2 + 4 = 6$$

2 plus 4 is equal to 6.

equivalent two numbers, such as a fraction and decimal, that name the same value (Lesson 7)

$\frac{6}{10}$ and 0.6 are equivalent.

equivalent fractions two or more fractions that name the same part of the same or equivalent wholes using different numerators and denominators (Lesson 9)

$\frac{1}{2}$ and $\frac{4}{8}$ are equivalent fractions.

estimate to find about how many or about how much (Lesson 17)

expanded form a way of writing a number as a sum of the values of its digits (Lessons 1, 2)

$$2,781 = 2,000 + 700 + 80 + 1$$

expenses the money that people and businesses spend on certain things (Lessons 32, 33)

factor a number multiplied by another number to find a product (Lesson 15)

$$5 \times 7 = 35$$
$$\uparrow \quad \uparrow$$
$$\text{factors}$$

financial institution a business that manages the money of people and other businesses (Lesson 34)

fixed expense an expense that does not change for a given period of time (Lesson 32)

fluid ounce a customary unit of measure for capacity (Lesson 27)

$$8 \text{ fluid ounces (fl oz)} = 1 \text{ cup (c)}$$

foot (ft) a customary unit of measure for length (Lesson 27)

$$1 \text{ foot (ft)} = 12 \text{ inches (in.)}$$

formula an equation that shows how to find an amount like the perimeter or area of a figure (Lesson 21)

$$A = l \times w$$

$$\text{Area} = \text{length} \times \text{width}$$

fraction a number that names part of a whole or part of a group (Lesson 7)

$\frac{1}{4}$ is a fraction.

gallon (gal) a customary unit of measure for capacity (Lesson 27)

$$1 \text{ gallon (gal)} = 4 \text{ quarts (qt)}$$

gram (g) a metric unit of measure for mass (Lesson 27)

$$1,000 \text{ grams (g)} = 1 \text{ kilogram (kg)}$$

greater than (>) a symbol that is used to compare two numbers and that means that the first number is greater than the second number (Lesson 3)

$$12 > 7$$

12 is greater than 7.

hour (hr) a unit of time (Lesson 27)

$$1 \text{ hour (hr)} = 60 \text{ minutes (min)}$$

inch (in.) a customary unit of measure for length (Lesson 27)

$$12 \text{ inches (in.)} = 1 \text{ foot (ft)}$$

interest a fee charged by financial institutions for loans (Lesson 34)

kilogram (kg) a metric unit of measure for mass (Lesson 27)

$$1 \text{ kilogram (kg)} = 1,000 \text{ grams (g)}$$

kilometer (km) a metric unit of measure for length (Lesson 27)

$$1 \text{ kilometer (km)} = 1,000 \text{ meters (m)}$$

less than (<) a symbol that is used to compare two numbers and that means the first number is less than the second number (Lesson 3)

$$6 < 8$$

6 is less than 8.

line a figure that has many points and extends without end in opposite directions (Lesson 22)

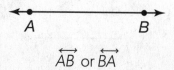

$$\overleftrightarrow{AB} \text{ or } \overleftrightarrow{BA}$$

line of symmetry an imaginary line drawn on a figure so that when the figure is folded along the line, the two parts match exactly (Lesson 23)

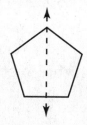

line segment a figure that is made of two endpoints and all the points between them (Lesson 22)

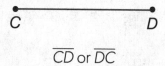

$$\overline{CD} \text{ or } \overline{DC}$$

liter (L) a metric unit of measure for capacity (Lesson 27)

1 liter (L) = 1,000 milliliters (mL)

lowest terms the form of a fraction in which the only number that will divide evenly into both the numerator and denominator is 1 (Lesson 9)

$\frac{4}{5}$ is in lowest terms because 1 is the only number that divides evenly into 4 and 5.

mass the amount of matter in an object (Lesson 27)

This object has a mass of about 4 kilograms.

meter (m) a metric unit of measure for length (Lesson 27)

1 meter (m) = 100 centimeters (cm)

metric system of measurement a system of measurement used throughout the world to measure length, capacity, and mass (Lesson 27)

length: millimeter (mm), centimeter (cm), meter (m), kilometer (km)

capacity: milliliter (mL), liter (L)

mass: gram (g), kilogram (kg)

milliliter (mL) a metric unit of measure for capacity (Lesson 27)

1,000 milliliters (mL) = 1 liter (L)

millimeter (mm) a metric unit of measure for length (Lesson 27)

1,000 millimeters (mm) = 1 meter (m)

minuend the number that another number is subtracted from in a subtraction problem (Lesson 12)

$$15 - 7 = 8$$
$$\uparrow$$
minuend

minute (min) a unit of time (Lesson 27)

60 minutes (min) = 1 hour (hr)

multiple the product of a number and any whole number (Lesson 10)

multiples of 8: 8, 16, 24, 32, 40, 48, 56, 64, 72, . . .

numerator the top number of a fraction—it tells how many equal parts of the whole are shaded or counted (Lesson 8)

$\frac{5}{8}$ has a numerator of 5.

obtuse angle an angle with a measure greater than 90° but less than 180° (Lesson 22)

obtuse triangle a triangle with an obtuse angle (Lesson 24)

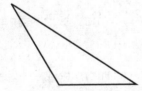

ounce (oz) a customary unit of measure for weight (Lesson 27)

16 ounces (oz) = 1 pound (lb)

parallel lines two lines that never intersect (Lesson 22)

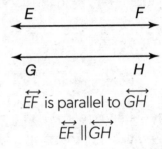

$\overleftrightarrow{EF}$ is parallel to $\overleftrightarrow{GH}$

$\overleftrightarrow{EF} \parallel \overleftrightarrow{GH}$

parallelogram a quadrilateral that has 2 pairs of parallel sides (Lesson 24)

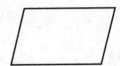

partial products the products of digits of factors (Lesson 15)

$$6 \times 23 = 6 \times 20 + 6 \times 3$$
$$= 120 + 18$$
$$\uparrow \qquad \uparrow$$
partial products

pattern an ordered set of numbers that follows a rule (Lesson 20)

3, 6, 12, 24, 48, . . .

rule: multiply by 2

perimeter the distance around a plane figure (Lesson 21)

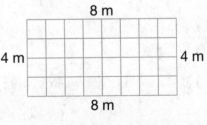

$$4 + 8 + 4 + 8 = 24$$

The perimeter of the rectangle is 24 meters.

perpendicular lines two lines that intersect to form right angles (Lesson 22)

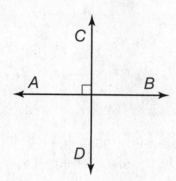

$\overleftrightarrow{AB}$ is perpendicular to $\overleftrightarrow{CD}$

$$\overleftrightarrow{AB} \perp \overleftrightarrow{CD}$$

pint (pt) a customary unit of measure for capacity (Lesson 27)

1 pint (pt) = 2 cups (c)

place value the value of a digit based on its position in a number (Lesson 1)

point a location in space (Lesson 22)

P

pound (lb) a customary unit of measure for weight (Lesson 27)

1 pound (lb) = 16 ounces (oz)

product the result of multiplying two or more numbers (Lesson 15)

$$8 \times 2 = 16$$
↑
product

profit the difference between what a business earns and what it spends (Lesson 33)

protractor a tool used to measure and draw angles (Lesson 25)

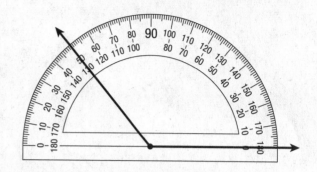

quart (qt) a customary unit of measure for capacity (Lesson 27)

1 quart (qt) = 4 cups (c)

quotient the result of dividing one number by another (Lessons 16, 18)

$$12 \div 6 = 2$$
↑
quotient

ray a figure that has one endpoint and extends without end in one direction (Lessons 22, 25)

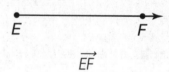

$$\overrightarrow{EF}$$

rectangle a parallelogram with 4 right angles (Lesson 24)

remainder a whole number that is left over when a dividend cannot be divided evenly (Lessons 16, 18)

remainder

revenue the money a business earns (Lesson 33)

rhombus a parallelogram with all sides the same length (Lesson 24)

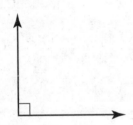

right angle an angle that measures exactly 90° (Lesson 22)

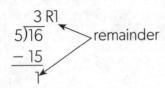

right triangle a triangle with a right angle (Lesson 24)

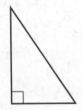

round to adjust a number to a given place value (Lessons 4, 17)

138 rounded to the nearest ten is 140.
138 rounded to the nearest hundred is 100.

rule an instruction or set of instructions to follow when forming a pattern (Lesson 20)

92, 83, 74, 65, 56, 47, . . .

rule: subtract 9

second (sec) a unit of time (Lesson 27)

60 seconds (sec) = 1 minute (min)

square a parallelogram with 4 right angles and all sides the same length (Lesson 24)

standard form a way of writing numbers using the digits 0–9, with each digit having a place value (Lessons 1, 2)

1,257

stem-and-leaf plot a table that is used to display numerical data that have more than one digit (Lesson 31)

Math Test Scores

Stem	Leaf
5	9
6	
7	0 1 2 4 5 7
8	0 1 2 3 4 4 4 9 9
9	0 0 2 3 6 6 7
10	0 0 0

Key: 5 | 9 = 59

subtrahend the number being subtracted from another number in a subtraction problem (Lesson 12)

$16 - 9 = 7$

subtrahend

sum the result of adding two or more numbers (Lesson 12)

$$5 + 3 = 8$$

$\uparrow$

sum

supplementary angles two angles whose measures have a sum of 180° (Lesson 26)

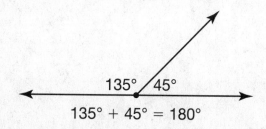

$$135° + 45° = 180°$$

symmetry quality possessed by a figure that can be folded on a line so that the two parts match exactly (Lesson 23)

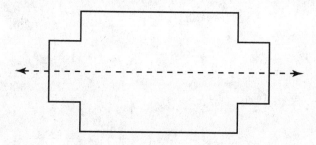

term each number in a pattern (Lesson 20)

2, 4, 6, 8, 10, 12, 14, . . .

The number pattern has 7 terms.

trapezoid a quadrilateral that has only 1 pair of parallel sides (Lesson 24)

unit fraction a fraction that has 1 as the numerator (Lesson 8)

$\frac{1}{8}$ and $\frac{1}{3}$ are unit fractions.

variable expense an expense that can change from one period to another (Lesson 32)

vertex a common endpoint of two rays (Lessons 22, 25)

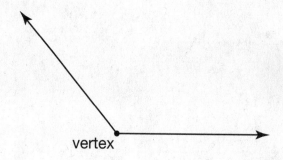

vertex

whole number 0 or any of the counting numbers (Lesson 1)

0, 1, 2, 3, 4, . . .

withdrawal money taken out of a bank account (Lesson 34)

word form a way of writing numbers using words (Lessons 1, 2)

215 = two hundred fifteen

yard (yd) a customary unit of measure for length (Lesson 27)

1 yard (yd) = 3 feet (ft)

Practice Test 1

Name: _____

DIRECTIONS

Read each question carefully. For a multiple-choice question, determine the best answer to the question from the four answer choices provided. For a griddable question, determine the best answer to the question. Then fill in the answer.

1 The estimated population of a city is 2,096,802. Which expression has the same value as 2,096,802?

A   2,000,000 + 900,000 + 60,000 + 800 + 20

B   2,000,000 + 900,000 + 6,000 + 800 + 20

C   2,000,000 + 90,000 + 6,000 + 800 + 2

D   2,000,000 + 90,000 + 6,000 + 80 + 2

GO ON

2 Francine made a frequency table to record the distances that some snails traveled in 1 minute.

Distance (feet)	Frequency
0	3
$\frac{1}{4}$	2
$\frac{2}{4}$	7
$\frac{3}{4}$	5
1	2

Which dot plot displays the data Francine recorded?

Distance Traveled (feet)

F

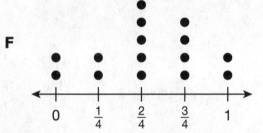

Distance Traveled (feet)

H

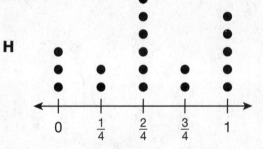

Distance Traveled (feet)

G

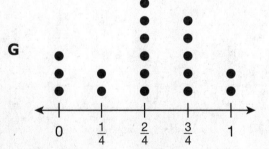

Distance Traveled (feet)

J

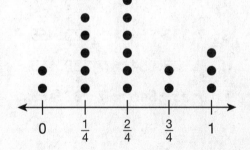

GO ON

3 Shannon models the difference $\frac{7}{12} - \frac{2}{12}$ with fraction strips. Which model represents the difference?

A
| $\frac{1}{12}$ | $\frac{1}{12}$ | $\frac{1}{12}$ | $\frac{1}{12}$ | $\frac{1}{12}$ | $\frac{1}{12}$ | $\frac{1}{12}$ | $\frac{1}{12}$ | $\frac{1}{12}$ | $\frac{1}{12}$ | $\frac{1}{12}$ | $\frac{1}{12}$ |

B
| $\frac{1}{12}$ | $\frac{1}{12}$ | $\frac{1}{12}$ | $\frac{1}{12}$ | $\frac{1}{12}$ | $\frac{1}{12}$ | $\frac{1}{12}$ | $\frac{1}{12}$ | $\frac{1}{12}$ | $\frac{1}{12}$ | $\frac{1}{12}$ | $\frac{1}{12}$ |

C
| $\frac{1}{12}$ | $\frac{1}{12}$ | $\frac{1}{12}$ | $\frac{1}{12}$ | $\frac{1}{12}$ | $\frac{1}{12}$ | $\frac{1}{12}$ | $\frac{1}{12}$ | $\frac{1}{12}$ | $\frac{1}{12}$ | $\frac{1}{12}$ | $\frac{1}{12}$ |

D
| $\frac{1}{12}$ | $\frac{1}{12}$ | $\frac{1}{12}$ | $\frac{1}{12}$ | $\frac{1}{12}$ | $\frac{1}{12}$ | $\frac{1}{12}$ | $\frac{1}{12}$ | $\frac{1}{12}$ | $\frac{1}{12}$ | $\frac{1}{12}$ | $\frac{1}{12}$ |

4 Which comparison is true?

F 7,232,465 < 7,232,456

G 7,332,564 > 7,323,465

H 7,323,654 > 7,332,456

J 7,233,546 < 7,233,465

GO ON

5 Nathan has 2 pounds of sugar. He divides it into 8 equal portions. How many ounces does each portion weigh?

    A 2 ounces

    B 4 ounces

    C 10 ounces

    D 126 ounces

6 What is the missing angle measure?

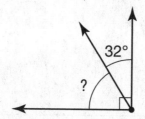

32°

?

    F 68°

    G 58°

    H 48°

    J 148°

GO ON

7 Dena draws a diagram to model a math problem.

258

n	138

x	x	x	x

Which problem could Dena be modeling?

A Will has $258. He receives $138 as a gift. He donates the total to 4 charities. Each charity receives an equal amount. How much does each charity get?

B Will donates $258 to one charity. He also donates $138 each to 4 other charities. How much does he donate in total?

C Will has $258. He spends $138. He donates the remainder to 4 charities. Each charity receives an equal amount. How much does each charity get?

D Will has $258. He donates $138 to 4 charities. Each charity receives an equal amount. How much does he have left?

---

8 Audra made a pot of soup. The soup has 2,898 calories. She divided the soup into 6 equal servings. How many calories are in each serving?

F 483

G 408

H 500

J 480

GO ON ➡

9 The models below are shaded to represent two different fractions.

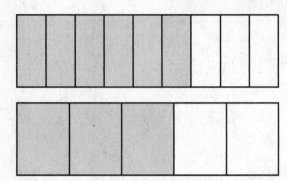

Which statement correctly compares the fractions?

A $\frac{2}{3} < \frac{3}{6}$

B $\frac{3}{5} > \frac{6}{9}$

C $\frac{6}{9} > \frac{3}{5}$

D $\frac{2}{5} < \frac{3}{9}$

---

10 Nathan is saving money to buy a surfboard. He has already saved $18. He decides to save $15 each week. How much money will he have after 12 weeks?

F $180

G $216

H $198

J $231

GO ON

11 Use the number lines to help answer the question.

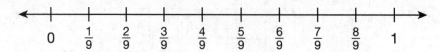

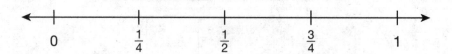

Which statement is true?

A $\frac{2}{9} + \frac{3}{9}$ is close to $\frac{1}{4}$.

B $\frac{2}{9} + \frac{3}{9}$ is close to $\frac{1}{2}$.

C $\frac{2}{9} + \frac{3}{9}$ is close to $\frac{3}{4}$.

D $\frac{2}{9} + \frac{3}{9}$ is close to 1.

---

12 Bonnie paid for a necklace with $40. Her change was $13.74. What was the price, in dollars, of the necklace?

Record your answer and fill in the bubbles. Be sure to use the correct place value.

			.		
⓪	⓪	⓪		⓪	⓪
①	①	①		①	①
②	②	②		②	②
③	③	③		③	③
④	④	④		④	④
⑤	⑤	⑤		⑤	⑤
⑥	⑥	⑥		⑥	⑥
⑦	⑦	⑦		⑦	⑦
⑧	⑧	⑧		⑧	⑧
⑨	⑨	⑨		⑨	⑨

GO ON

13 A business purchases 8 computers. Each computer costs $1,257. What was the total cost for 8 computers?

    A $9,056

    B $10,056

    C $10,006

    D $9,656

---

14 The model represents a rectangular room.

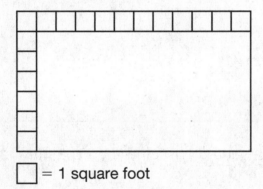

= 1 square foot

Which of the following could be used to find the room's perimeter?

    F Add 12 and 6. Then multiply the sum by 2.

    G Add 12 and 7. Then multiply the sum by 2.

    H Add 11 and 6. Then multiply the sum by 2.

    J Add 11 and 7. Then multiply the sum by 2.

GO ON

15 Which of the following could be used to find the missing output in the table below?

Input	Output
20	12
22	14
33	25
36	28
41	

A Add 8 to 40.

B Add 3 to 28.

C Subtract 8 from 28.

D Subtract 8 from 41.

---

16 What number is represented by point *M* on the number line?

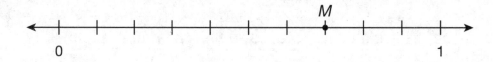

F 0.7

G 0.3

H 0.73

J 0.07

GO ON

17 Zoe buys $\frac{2}{3}$ pound of peanuts, $\frac{3}{5}$ pound of pecans, $\frac{3}{4}$ pound of hazel nuts, and $\frac{7}{12}$ pound of pistachios. Which statement is **NOT** true?

   A Zoe buys more peanuts than pecans.

   B Zoe buys less hazel nuts than peanuts.

   C Zoe buys more pecans than pistachios.

   D Zoe buys less pistachios than hazel nuts.

---

18 At the beginning of November, Kendall has $520 in his bank account. The table shows all his deposits and withdrawals for the month of November.

Date	Transaction	Amount
November 3	Withdrawal	$150
November 9	Deposit	$180
November 11	Withdrawal	$140
November 18	Deposit	$125
November 23	Deposit	$135
November 29	Withdrawal	$200

How much money is in Kendall's account at the end of November?

   F $490

   G $570

   H $440

   J $470

GO ON

19 The model is shaded to represent a number greater than 1.

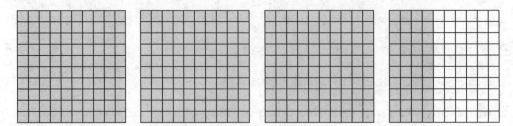

Which fraction and decimal are represented by this model?

A $3\frac{4}{10}$ and 30.04

B $3\frac{4}{100}$ and 3.04

C $300\frac{4}{100}$ and 300.04

D $3\frac{4}{10}$ and 3.4

---

20 Kenji is a baker. He filled orders for 13 boxes of assorted muffins. The table shows the number of each type of muffin in a box.

Box of Assorted Muffins

Muffin	Number in a Box
Chocolate chip	12
Blueberry	14
Cream cheese	18

Which equation could be used to find the total number of muffins, m, that Kenji put in the boxes?

F $13 \times (12 + 14 + 18) = m$

G $13 + (12 \times 14 \times 18) = m$

H $13 + 12 + 14 + 18 = m$

J $13 \times 12 \times 14 \times 18 = m$

GO ON

21 Which figure is an acute triangle?

A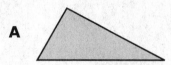

B

C

D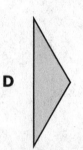

---

22 The table shows the prices of various items at a book fair.

Item	Price
History book	$15.65
Math book	$13.55
Science book	$16.05
Poetry book	$16.85
Art book	$13.75

Camila bought two items. She gave the cashier $40 and received $10.60 in change. Which two items did Camila buy?

F Poetry book and art book

G Math book and poetry book

H History book and art book

J Math book and science book

GO ON

23 Emilio has 1.45 pounds of meat to make hamburgers. He buys 1.7 more pounds of meat. How many pounds of meat does Emilio have in all?

   A 1.62

   B 3.15

   C 3.85

   D 2.52

---

24 Martina walked $\frac{7}{12}$ mile to her friend's house. Which distance is shorter than $\frac{7}{12}$ mile?

   F $\frac{6}{10}$ mile

   G $\frac{11}{20}$ mile

   H $\frac{5}{8}$ mile

   J $\frac{6}{9}$ mile

GO ON

25 Which statement does **NOT** describe the figure?

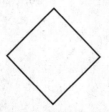

A   The figure is a square.

B   The figure has two pairs of parallel sides.

C   The figure has no right angles.

D   The figure is a parallelogram.

26 A decimal is written in the place-value chart.

Ones	.	Tenths	Hundredths
0	.	6	2

Which shows the decimal written as a fraction?

F $\frac{62}{100}$

G $\frac{62}{10}$

H $\frac{26}{10}$

J $\frac{26}{100}$

GO ON

27 Six classes are going to a museum. Each class has 23 students. At the museum, guides will take groups of 8 students each on tours. How many tour guides are needed?

A 29

B 18

C 17

D 15

---

28 Use a protractor.

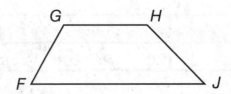

Which angle measures 45°?

F ∠F

G ∠G

H ∠H

J ∠J

GO ON

29 Courtney has 500 photos saved on her digital camera. She deletes 36 of them. Then she arranges the remaining photos in 4 folders on her computer. Each folder has the same number of photos. Which equation could be used to find the number of photos, p, that Courtney puts in each folder?

A $500 - (36 \div 4) = p$

B $(500 - 36) \div 4 = p$

C $500 + (36 \div 4) = p$

D $(500 + 36) \div 4 = p$

---

30 The model is shaded to show $\frac{3}{12}$.

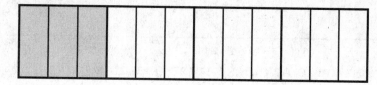

Which fraction is equivalent to $\frac{3}{12}$?

F $\frac{1}{3}$, because 1 square is shaded, and 3 squares are not shaded

G $\frac{3}{4}$, because 3 small rectangles are shaded, and there are 4 squares in all

H $\frac{3}{9}$, because 3 small rectangles are shaded, and 9 small rectangles are not

J $\frac{1}{4}$, because 1 square is shaded, and there are 4 squares in all

31 Parker has 3 hours to do his homework in 4 subjects. He spends an equal amount of time on each subject. How many minutes does he spend on each subject?

Record your answer and fill in the bubbles. Be sure to use the correct place value.

			.		
⓪	⓪	⓪		⓪	⓪
①	①	①		①	①
②	②	②		②	②
③	③	③		③	③
④	④	④		④	④
⑤	⑤	⑤		⑤	⑤
⑥	⑥	⑥		⑥	⑥
⑦	⑦	⑦		⑦	⑦
⑧	⑧	⑧		⑧	⑧
⑨	⑨	⑨		⑨	⑨

32 Use the number line to help answer the question.

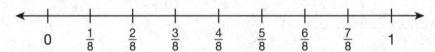

$$0 \quad \frac{1}{8} \quad \frac{2}{8} \quad \frac{3}{8} \quad \frac{4}{8} \quad \frac{5}{8} \quad \frac{6}{8} \quad \frac{7}{8} \quad 1$$

Which expression has a value of $\frac{5}{8}$?

F $\frac{7}{8} - \frac{2}{8}$

G $\frac{1}{8} + \frac{3}{8}$

H $\frac{2}{8} + \frac{5}{8}$

J $\frac{6}{8} - \frac{3}{8}$

GO ON ▶

33 Which lines appear to be perpendicular?

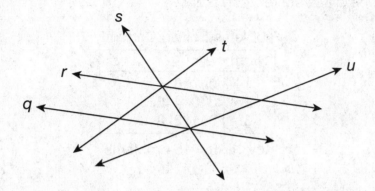

A Lines q and r

B Lines s and t

C Lines r and t

D Lines q and u

34 Mr. Jenkins flew 10,786 miles last month. This month, he flew 12,956 miles. What is the total number of miles Mr. Jenkins flew in these two months?

F 22,632 miles

G 23,732 miles

H 22,742 miles

J 23,742 miles

35 The stem-and-leaf plot shows the number of math problems that the students in one class solved correctly.

Problems Solved Correctly

Stem	Leaf
1	5 7 8
2	0 0 4 5 5 7 9
3	0 1 2 2 3 5

Key: 1 | 5 = 15 problems

Which statement is true?

A Five students solved more than 30 problems correctly.

B There are 19 data items displayed in the stem-and-leaf plot.

C Three students did not solve any problems correctly.

D The most problems solved correctly by a student is 29.

---

36 A lawn is in the shape of a rectangle. It is 15 feet wide. The length is 8 feet longer than the width. What is the area of the lawn?

F 120 square feet

G 105 square feet

H 76 square feet

J 345 square feet

GO ON

37 Determine the amount represented by the money shown as a decimal.

What digit is in the tenths place?

A 2

B 1

C 6

D 8

---

38 Michael drew a figure with the following characteristics.

- The figure has four sides.
- The figure has only one pair of parallel sides.
- All four sides do not have the same length.
- The figure has two right angles.

Which figure could Michael have drawn?

F Square

G Rhombus

H Trapezoid

J Rectangle

39 The tallest tree in Raj's yard is 30 meters tall. How many millimeters tall is the tree?

  A 300 millimeters

  B 3,000 millimeters

  C 30,000 millimeters

  D 300,000 millimeters

---

40 Carla draws this area model to help her find the product of two numbers.

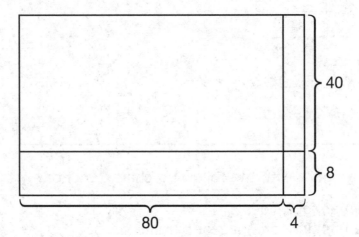

Which equation does her area model represent?

  F 84 × 48 = 3,232

  G 88 × 44 = 3,232

  H 84 × 48 = 4,032

  J 80 × 40 = 3,200

GO ON

41 Use a protractor.

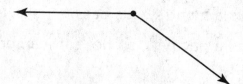

What is the measure of the angle?

A 35°

B 45°

C 135°

D 145°

---

42 The price of a DVD movie collection is $36.15. Which expression has the same value as 36.15?

F $3 \times 100 + 6 \times 1 + 1 \times \frac{1}{10} + 5 \times \frac{1}{100}$

G $3 \times 10 + 6 \times 1 + 5 \times \frac{1}{100}$

H $3 \times 100 + 6 \times 10 + 1 \times \frac{1}{10} + 5 \times \frac{1}{100}$

J $3 \times 10 + 6 \times 1 + 1 \times \frac{1}{10} + 5 \times \frac{1}{100}$

GO ON

43 Which of the following describes a variable expense?

    A Mr. Fernandez buys a monthly bus pass.

    B Ms. Johnson makes a payment on her car loan on the 16th of each month.

    C Mrs. Scott buys groceries every Friday.

    D Mr. Yamada pays his car insurance every three months.

---

44 How many lines of symmetry does the figure have?

    F 1

    G 3

    H 5

    J 10

GO ON

45 The length of a rectangle is 9 inches. The area of the rectangle is 72 inches. What is the width in inches?

Record your answer and fill in the bubbles. Be sure to use the correct place value.

			.		
⓪	⓪	⓪		⓪	⓪
①	①	①		①	①
②	②	②		②	②
③	③	③		③	③
④	④	④		④	④
⑤	⑤	⑤		⑤	⑤
⑥	⑥	⑥		⑥	⑥
⑦	⑦	⑦		⑦	⑦
⑧	⑧	⑧		⑧	⑧
⑨	⑨	⑨		⑨	⑨

---

46 Felicia records the amount each of her plants grew over the past week. She shows the data in the dot plot.

Plant Growth (inches)

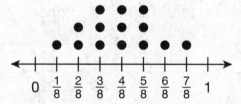

How many plants grew more than $\frac{4}{8}$ inch?

F 3, because there are 3 dots over $\frac{4}{8}$

G 5, because $3 + 1 + 1 = 5$

H 6, because $1 + 2 + 3 = 6$

J 8, because $3 + 3 + 1 + 1 = 8$

GO ON

47 The model below represents a fraction.

$$\frac{1}{8}\ \frac{1}{8}\ \frac{1}{8}\ \frac{1}{8}\ \frac{1}{8}\ \vdots\ \frac{1}{8}\ \vdots\ \frac{1}{8}\ \vdots\ \frac{1}{8}$$

Which is **NOT** a way to decompose this fraction?

A $\frac{1}{8} + \frac{1}{8} + \frac{1}{8} + \frac{2}{8}$

B $\frac{2}{8} + \frac{3}{8}$

C $\frac{1}{8} + \frac{1}{8} + \frac{1}{8} + \frac{1}{8} + \frac{1}{8} + \frac{1}{8}$

D $\frac{2}{8} + \frac{2}{8} + \frac{1}{8}$

---

48 The table shows the number of batteries in different numbers of boxes.

Number of Boxes	Number of Batteries
1	48
2	96
3	144
4	192
5	

If the pattern continues, how many batteries are in 5 boxes?

F 384

G 144

H 240

J 960

STOP

Practice Test 2

Name: _____

DIRECTIONS

Read each question carefully. For a multiple-choice question, determine the best answer to the question from the four answer choices provided. For a griddable question, determine the best answer to the question. Then fill in the answer.

1 Use a protractor.

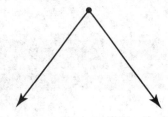

What is the measure of the angle shown?

A 75°

B 85°

C 105°

D 15°

---

2 Which fraction has the same value as the decimal shown in the place-value chart?

Ones	.	Tenths	Hundredths
0	.	3	9

F $\frac{93}{10}$

G $\frac{93}{100}$

H $\frac{39}{10}$

J $\frac{39}{100}$

GO ON

3 Emma buys 5.35 pounds of pizza dough. She uses 2.78 pounds of dough for dinner and freezes the rest. Which model represents the amount of pizza dough that she freezes?

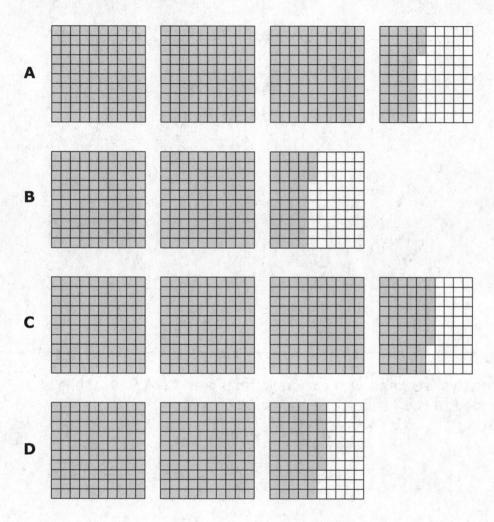

4   A school buys 22 calculators. Each calculator costs $78. Which expression gives the best estimate of the total cost?

F   80 × 30   H   100 × 20

G   100 × 25   J   80 × 20

---

5   The total sales this weekend at a car dealership was $344,989. What is 344,989 rounded to the nearest ten thousand?

A   340,000   C   345,000

B   344,000   D   350,000

GO ON

6 The model represents a rectangular room.

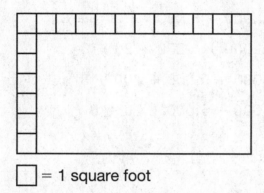

☐ = 1 square foot

Which of the following could be used to find the area of the room?

F Multiply 12 by 6.

G Multiply 12 by 7.

H Multiply 13 by 6.

J Multiply 13 by 7.

GO ON

7   Which expression has the same value as 8,506,028?

    A   8,000,000 + 500,000 + 60,000 + 200 + 80

    B   8,000,000 + 500,000 + 6,000 + 20 + 8

    C   8,000,000 + 50,000 + 6,000 + 200 + 8

    D   8,000,000 + 50,000 + 6,000 + 20 + 8

---

8   The table shows the numbers of markers in given numbers of packages.

Number of Packages	Number of Markers
1	36
2	72
3	108
4	144

How many markers are in 12 packages?

    F   48   **H**   180

    G   432   **J**   362

GO ON

9 Use the place-value chart to help answer the question.

Thousands Period				Ones Period		
Hundreds	Tens	Ones	,	Hundreds	Tens	Ones

A warehouse received 528 boxes of crayons. Each box has 100 crayons. How many crayons did the warehouse receive?

A 528,000

B 52,800

C 5,280

D 528

---

10 Billy ran the 50-yard dash twice. His first time was 8.74 seconds and his second time was 9.17 seconds. What was his combined running time, in seconds?

Record your answer and fill in the bubbles. Be sure to use the correct place value.

GO ON

11 Sharon models the difference $\frac{5}{9} - \frac{2}{9}$ with fraction strips. Which model represents the difference?

A | $\frac{1}{9}$ | $\frac{1}{9}$ | $\frac{1}{9}$ | $\frac{1}{9}$ | $\frac{1}{9}$ | $\frac{1}{9}$ | $\frac{1}{9}$ | $\frac{1}{9}$ | $\frac{1}{9}$ |

B | $\frac{1}{9}$ | $\frac{1}{9}$ | $\frac{1}{9}$ | $\frac{1}{9}$ | $\frac{1}{9}$ | $\frac{1}{9}$ | $\frac{1}{9}$ | $\frac{1}{9}$ | $\frac{1}{9}$ |

C | $\frac{1}{9}$ | $\frac{1}{9}$ | $\frac{1}{9}$ | $\frac{1}{9}$ | $\frac{1}{9}$ | $\frac{1}{9}$ | $\frac{1}{9}$ | $\frac{1}{9}$ | $\frac{1}{9}$ |

D | $\frac{1}{9}$ | $\frac{1}{9}$ | $\frac{1}{9}$ | $\frac{1}{9}$ | $\frac{1}{9}$ | $\frac{1}{9}$ | $\frac{1}{9}$ | $\frac{1}{9}$ | $\frac{1}{9}$ |

---

12 A pool is in the shape of a rectangle. It is 8 feet wide. The length is 9 feet longer than the width. What is the perimeter of the pool?

F 34 feet

G 50 feet

H 72 feet

J 136 feet

GO ON

13 Katrina makes necklaces. She sells them for $30 each. The table shows the costs for parts that Katrina needs to make a necklace.

Part	Cost
Chain	$5.50
Locket	$6.80
Jewels	$3.45

What is Katrina's profit for selling one necklace?

A $14.25

B $14.75

C $15.25

D $15.75

---

14 The weight of Mark's chicken salad is 28.16 ounces. Which expression has the same value as 28.16?

F $2 \times 100 + 8 \times 1 + 1 \times \frac{1}{10} + 6 \times \frac{1}{100}$

G $2 \times 10 + 8 \times 1 + 1 \times \frac{1}{10} + 6 \times \frac{1}{100}$

H $2 \times 100 + 8 \times 10 + 1 \times \frac{1}{10} + 6 \times \frac{1}{100}$

J $2 \times 10 + 8 \times 1 + 6 \times \frac{1}{100}$

GO ON

15 Kent draws a diagram to model a math problem.

312

n	162

x	*x*	*x*	*x*	*x*	*x*

Which problem could Kent have modeled?

A Martha had 312 bottle caps in her collection. She gives each of her 6 friends an equal number of bottle caps. She has 162 bottle caps left. How many bottle caps did each friend get?

B Martha had 312 bottle caps in her collection. She receives 162 more caps from her 6 friends. Each friend gives her an equal number of caps. How many caps did each friend give?

C Martha had 162 bottle caps in her collection. She receives 312 more caps from her 6 friends. Each friend gives her an equal number of caps. How many caps did each friend give her?

D Martha had 312 bottle caps in her collection. She gives 162 bottle caps to her 6 friends. Each friend receives an equal number of bottle caps. How many bottle caps did each friend get?

---

16 Casey bought 24 boxes of crackers for a party. Each box has 42 crackers. How many crackers does she have in all?

F 1,008   **H** 1,440

G 144   **D** 800

GO ON ➤

17 Alejandro walks $\frac{7}{10}$ mile to school. Which distance is greater than $\frac{7}{10}$ mile?

A $\frac{4}{6}$ mile   **C** $\frac{3}{5}$ mile

B $\frac{6}{8}$ mile   **D** $\frac{6}{9}$ mile

---

18 Nathan recorded the amounts of time that students in his class spent on math homework the day before.

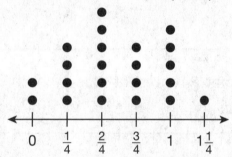

Math Homework Time (hours)

How many students spent less than $\frac{3}{4}$ hour on math homework?

F 22 students

G 21 students

H 16 students

J 12 students

GO ON

19 Yolanda drew a figure with the following characteristics.

- The figure has four sides.
- The figure has two pairs of parallel sides.
- All four sides have the same length.
- The figure has no right angles.

Which figure did Yolanda draw?

A Square

C Trapezoid

B Rhombus

D Rectangle

---

20 Which decimal does point *P* represent?

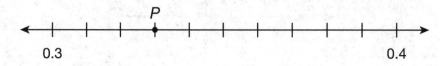

F 0.03

H 0.33

G 0.3

J 0.43

GO ON

21 Jocelyn bakes 7 batches of cookies. Each batch has 12 cookies. She puts them in bags with 8 cookies each. How many full bags does she have?

A 12

C 10

B 7

D 4

---

22 Stanley drew a 135° angle. Which could be the angle that Stanley drew?

F

G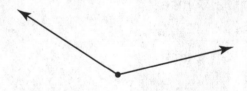

H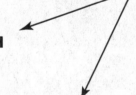

J

GO ON

23 A rectangle has a perimeter of 96 centimeters. The width of the rectangle is 16 centimeters. What is the length of the rectangle?

A 3 centimeters

C 6 centimeters

B 32 centimeters

D 64 centimeters

---

24 Franklin recorded the amount each of his classmates grew over summer vacation. He put the data in the dot plot shown below.

Classmate Growth Over Summer Vacation (inches)

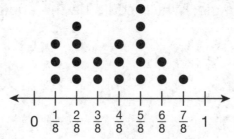

What was the difference between the greatest growth and the least growth?

F $\frac{6}{8}$ inch

G $\frac{8}{8}$ inch

H $\frac{5}{8}$ inch

J $\frac{1}{8}$ inch

GO ON

25 Curtis has 600 music files saved on his computer. He downloads 36 more files. Then he arranges them in 6 folders. Each folder has the same number of files. How many files does he put into each folder?

Record your answer and fill in the bubbles. Be sure to use the correct place value.

			.		
⓪	⓪	⓪		⓪	⓪
①	①	①		①	①
②	②	②		②	②
③	③	③		③	③
④	④	④		④	④
⑤	⑤	⑤		⑤	⑤
⑥	⑥	⑥		⑥	⑥
⑦	⑦	⑦		⑦	⑦
⑧	⑧	⑧		⑧	⑧
⑨	⑨	⑨		⑨	⑨

---

26 Use the models to help answer the question.

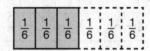

There are two small, identical cakes. Adrienne ate $\frac{3}{6}$ of one cake. Pat ate $\frac{4}{6}$ of the other cake. How much cake did they eat in all?

F 1

H $1\frac{3}{6}$

G $1\frac{1}{6}$

J $1\frac{4}{6}$

GO ON

27 Francisco lives 0.86 mile from school. What fraction is equivalent to 0.86?

A $\frac{86}{100}$

C $\frac{0.86}{100}$

B $\frac{8.6}{100}$

D $\frac{86}{10}$

---

28 The table shows the prices of some video games.

Video Game	Price
Boat Battle	$14.85
Sand Blaster	$14.55
Lightning Blitz	$15.35
Cube Twist	$13.85
Zombie Time	$15.65

Nigel bought two games. He gave the cashier $40 and received $10.60 in change. Which two video games did he buy?

F Boat Battle and Sand Blaster

G Cube Twist and Lightning Blitz

H Sand Blaster and Zombie Time

J Boat Battle and Cube Twist

GO ON

29 Marietta bought 3 liters of lemonade for a picnic. How many milliliters of lemonade did Marietta buy?

A 30,000 mL

C 300 mL

B 3,000 mL

D 30 mL

---

30 The models below are shaded to represent two different fractions.

Which statement correctly compares the fractions?

F $\frac{8}{12} > \frac{5}{7}$

H $\frac{8}{12} < \frac{5}{7}$

G $\frac{2}{7} < \frac{4}{12}$

J $\frac{2}{7} = \frac{4}{12}$

GO ON

31 The writing assignment scores for some students are shown below.

31, 37, 44, 28, 28, 45, 41, 40, 29, 35, 43, 38, 35, 36, 29, 45, 39, 41

Which stem-and-leaf plot represents the data?

A

Scores

Stem	Leaf
2	8 8 9
3	1 3 5 6 7 8 8 9
4	0 1 1 3 4 5 5

Key: 3 | 6 = 36 points

C

Scores

Stem	Leaf
2	8 8 9 9
3	1 5 5 5 6 7 8
4	0 1 1 3 4 5

Key: 3 | 6 = 36 points

B

Scores

Stem	Leaf
2	8 8 9 9
3	5 5 6 7 8 9
4	0 1 1 1 3 4 5 5

Key: 3 | 6 = 36 points

D

Scores

Stem	Leaf
2	8 8 9 9
3	1 5 5 6 7 8 9
4	0 1 1 3 4 5 5

Key: 3 | 6 = 36 points

---

32 Arturo measures the length of his teddy bear. Which is the most reasonable measurement for the length of Arturo's teddy bear?

F 30 centimeters

H 30 meters

G 30 kilometers

J 30 millimeters

GO ON

33 The rule for the input-output table below is "Subtract 4 from each input."

Input	Output
8	4
11	7
13	9
20	16
?	26

Which of the following could be used to find the missing input in the table?

A Subtract 4 from 26.

B Subtract 4 from 20.

C Add 4 to 26.

D Add 4 to 20.

---

34 Ms. Tolliver flew 8,486 miles in January. In February, she flew 10,254 miles. How many more miles did she fly in February than in January?

F 1,772 miles

G 2,232 miles

H 2,768 miles

J 1,768 miles

GO ON

35 Margot has 3 yards of fabric. She divides it into 9 equal pieces. How many inches long is each piece of fabric?

A 4 inches   **C** 12 inches

B 8 inches   **D** 16 inches

---

36 Use the number line to help answer the question.

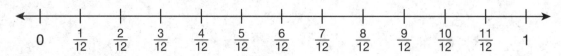

Which expression is equivalent to $\frac{7}{12}$?

F $\frac{4}{12} + \frac{5}{12}$ **H** $\frac{11}{12} - \frac{4}{12}$

G $\frac{2}{12} + \frac{6}{12}$ **J** $\frac{10}{12} - \frac{5}{12}$

GO ON

37 Look at the figure below.

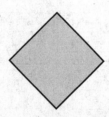

Which term could **NOT** be used to describe the figure?

A Rhombus

B Square

C Trapezoid

D Rectangle

---

38 Nomar is saving money to buy a bicycle. The bicycle costs $248. He saves $16 each week. How much more money does he need after 13 weeks?

F $19

G $20

H $40

J $50

GO ON

39 Each model below represents a decimal number.

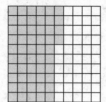 

Which statement correctly compares these decimals?

A 0.54 = 0.47   **C** 0.54 < 0.47

B 0.54 > 0.47   **D** 0.47 > 0.54

---

40 Dana is a baker. She filled 12 boxes of assorted cookies. The table shows the number of each type of cookie in a box.

Box of Assorted Cookies

Cookie	Number in a Box
Chocolate chip	20
Oatmeal	16
Peanut butter	12

How many cookies did Dana use to fill the 12 boxes?

F 288   **H** 480

G 576   **J** 600

GO ON